Data Management: a gentle introduction

Other publications by Van Haren Publishing

Van Haren Publishing (VHP) specializes in titles on Best Practices, methods and standards within four domains:

- IT and IT Management
- Architecture (Enterprise and IT)
- Business Management and
- Project Management

Van Haren Publishing is also publishing on behalf of leading organizations and companies: ASLBiSL Foundation, BRMI, CA, Centre Henri Tudor, CM Partners, Gaming Works, IACCM, IAOP, IFDC, Innovation Value Institute, IPMA-NL, ITSqc, NAF, KNVI, PMI-NL, PON, The Open Group, The SOX Institute.

Topics are (per domain):

IT and IT Management
ABC of ICT
ASL®
CMMI®
COBIT®
e-CF
ISO/IEC 20000
ISO/IEC 27001/27002
ISPL
IT4IT®
IT-CMF™
IT Service CMM
ITIL®
MOF
MSF
SABSA
SAF
SIAM™
TRIM
VeriSM™

Enterprise Architecture
ArchiMate®
GEA®
Novius Architectuur Methode
TOGAF®

Business Management
BABOK® Guide
BiSL® and BiSL® Next
BRMBOK™
BTF
CATS CM®
EFQM
eSCM
IACCM
ISA-95
ISO 9000/9001
OPBOK
SixSigma
SOX
SqEME®

Project Management
A4-Projectmanagement
DSDM/Atern
ICB / NCB
ISO 21500
MINCE®
M_o_R®
MSP®
P3O®
PMBOK® Guide
Praxis®
PRINCE2®

For the latest information on VHP publications, visit our website: www.vanharen.net.

Data Management: a gentle introduction

Balancing theory and practice

Bas van Gils

This book is dedicated to my two children:
Koen van Gils and Stijn van Gils.
You are my rock stars.

Van Haren PUBLISHING

Colophon

Title:	Data Management: a gentle introduction
Subtitle:	Balancing theory and practice
Author:	Bas van Gils, managing partner @ Strategy Alliance
Illustrations:	Andy Lo Tam Loi
Reviewers:	Mirjam Visscher and Tanja Glisin
Text editor:	Lisa Gaudette and Steve Newton (Galatea)
Publisher:	Van Haren Publishing, 's-Hertogenbosch
ISBN hard copy:	978 94 018 0550 6
ISBN eBook (pdf):	978 94 018 0552 0
ISBN ePUB:	978 94 018 0555 1
Edition:	First edition, first impression, February 2020
Lay out and DTP	Coco Bookmedia, Amersfoort – NL
Copyright:	© 2020 Van Haren Publishing

Foreword by Tony Shaw

I wonder if Bas van Gils had in mind the quote by Albert Einstein, that "Everything should be made as simple as possible, but not simpler", because in this book you are about to read, he has created a "gentle introduction" which truly serves the purpose of explaining data and data management. Personally, when I first got into the world of data 20+ years ago, and coming from a background in marketing and business development, I had to learn about data management through the gradual osmosis of interacting with data professionals. While this is useful in understanding the "what" of real-world practice, it doesn't fill in the theoretical foundations of "how" and "why" which are necessary to understand why that real-world practice works the way it does. I know I would have come up to speed a whole lot faster, if I'd had access to this book.

One of the big themes in corporate data today is dataliteracy, and as organizations strive to become more data-driven, then it's a theme that will only grow in relevance. Data is not a trend that's going to flame out in a few years, so just like financial literacy and human capital management, it is now obvious that data literacy is going to be a critical knowledge requirement for all managers and executives in the future. As such, we should be thinking about data education in the same way we think about financial and HR education, building the foundations in schools and universities, then continuing to apply those foundations to practical experience through employee onboarding programs, and broader corporate training.

This book serves these objectives well. All the important enterprise-level data management topics are included. It serves as a valuable curriculum for someone just starting out in a professional data career, or indeed for someone who like me, who picked up bits and pieces without much structure to my learning. Bas's explanations are clear, and build upon each other systematically. I personally appreciate the research that has gone into identifying the clearest definitions available, even when that means quoting other sources. Bas has effectively curated the "best of" from existing industry literature, and tied everything together into a consistent whole, through his own lucid insight, analysis and explanations.

I wish you, the reader, well whether this is the start of your data management journey, or like me, you are finding structure for your fragmented knowledge. You have found an excellent resource to help you fulfill your objectives.

Tony Shaw, CEO & Founder of Dataversity
October 2019

Foreword by Hans Weigand

"Language (die Sprache) is always a mediator", the famous Von Humboldt wrote 200 years ago. "It is between the finite and the infinite", he continues, "and at the same time between one individual and the other". In traditional philosophical categories: as a subject-object relator and a subject-subject relator. That Von Humboldt spoke using the terms finite and infinite says something about his view of the human subject (its finiteness, in several respects). It is important to note that when Von Humboldt calls language a mediator, he explicitly wants to say that the two things that get mediated do not exist independently of each other, but that in a way they come into existence through the mediation. The mediator is more than a formal relationship. That is why for him language is not a coding system where an (arbitrary) sign is determined for something that already exists for us. Such a coding system does not *make* language, it *presupposes* language.

To some extent, the characterization of Von Humboldt for language can also be applied to data, the subject of this book. Yes, the formal data structures in a computer have been designed, so as such they are not language in the Von Humboldt sense. Still, they draw on language, and so take over some of its characteristics. Data also mediates between subjects. This is one reason why data needs to be protected, as identified in chapters 17 and 21 of this book, and why "shared understanding" is a fundamental goal. It is also mediating with an infinite world around us. To use a phrase of Bas, "data codifies what we know about the world". At another place, data is defined as the combination of fact and meaning. If this is true (and who am I am to question Bas?), it means that managing data has two rather different faces. Because managing facts, as stored in files on a disk, is quite different from managing such an intangible thing as "meaning". I don't want to push this point too much, but I think here is one reason why data management is not simple and not comparable to the management of physical assets such as vehicles or library books, in spite of some similarities.

When data is a mediator, it also runs the risks of the fate of the mediator: always to fall in between. So that neither the IT department nor the business unit cares for it; that there is no budget for it. That it is seen as instrumental only, and so is not a genuine concern in its own right. In the short history of IT so far we have learned that this would a big mistake. Data needs to be recognized as an asset, and needs to be managed. Not as a goal in its own of course – a point that is stressed by Bas several times in this book. It remains a mediator, but still, it needs to be managed properly. Therefore I am glad with this book that takes data management seriously. A book that tries to integrate insights on data management from theory and practice. A book that can not only serve practitioners and companies that struggle with data management but that can also be a good reference text for academic courses in the field of Information Management or Data Science. I wish it all the best!

Dr. Hans Weigand, Associate Professor Information Systems, Tilburg University
October 2019

Preface

When I started my studies at Tilburg University in 1998, one of the first things that I learned was an appreciation for the 'golden triangle' of processes, data, and systems. Only through careful alignment of these three can organizations function well. It was interesting to see that so many people – academics and professionals alike – worried mostly about either *systems* or *processes*, while *data* appeared to take the back seat.

After my studies, I started working on my dissertation at Nijmegen University. The focus of my research was *Web information retrieval*. The main idea behind my research was based on economic principles: if you have *demand* and *supply* of data, then all you have to do is "match" the two. How hard can that be? After all, the topic of information retrieval had been studied for decades. Let's just say that I learned a lot in those days, not just about the *information needs* of people surfing the Internet, but also about semantics, data modeling, data structures, etc.

Since then, I have worked in many different roles, from IT professional to strategy consultant and pretty much every role in between. Over the years, I noticed that *data* was becoming an increasingly important topic. People started to recognize that mishandling data was costing the organization in missed opportunities, rework, reputational damage, etc. and that products and services could be greatly enhanced when enriched with data. Around this time, people started talking about data as "the new oil" and recognized it for the valuable asset that it really was. This was further strengthened by the apparent rise of topics such as *artificial intelligence*, *data science*, and *big data*.

I started studying *data management* in earnest around 2008. A few years later, Tanja Glisin suggested I study the DAMA DMBOK [MBEH09] which really opened my eyes to the depth and breadth of the field. I found that the DMBOK was *the* reference within our field at the time, especially when complemented with other – more in-depth – publications. The second version of the DMBOK was published in

2017 and showed the significant improvement of our knowledge of the field [Hen17]. I have used both versions of the DMBOK over the years, both as a reference during consultancy assignments and teaching.

The DMBOK is a great reference, but may practitioners find it too theoretical to be of practical use. A more *pragmatic* book that combines theory with practical recommendations is missing. After much debate and discussions with friends, many of whom I have interviewed for this book, I decided to attempt to fill this gap.

The decision to actually move forward with the writing project was made in March of 2019, while visiting the Enterprise Data World conference in Boston, Massachusetts. I wrote the first version of the book during the summer months of 2019 and am forever grateful for all the support and help I received. There are so many people to thank and I sincerely hope I am not forgetting anyone. First of all, I would like to thank my colleagues at Strategy Alliance for their patience and help in preparing the manuscript. I would also like to thank Maurits van der Plas, Ivo van Haren, and Bart Verbrugge of Van Haren Publishing: I know that I have strong opinions on how/ what I want with the book - and I have probably tried your patience over and over. Then, of course, there are the people who graciously granted me interviews to use in this book – you are all heroes:

- *Marco van der Winden is manager of the corporate data management office at PGGM, a Dutch pension provider.*
- *Marc van den Berg is managing director of* IT *and Innovation at* PGGM, *a Dutch pension provider.*
- *Frank Harmsen is managing director at* PNA *and professor at Maastricht University.*
- *Lisa Gaudette is director in the Office of Sponsored Programs and Research of Clark University.*
- *Jan Robat is head of data quality management at* ABN AMRO.
- *Fanny Vuillemin is senior data manager at* AXA.
- *Céline Lescop is lead data architect at* AXA.
- *Piethein Strengholt is principle data architect at* ABN AMRO.
- *Eric D. Schabell is global technology evangelist and portfolio architect director at Red Hat.*
- *Tanja Glisin is an experienced data management professional and frequent collaborator of the author of this book.*
- *Norbert van de Ven is data governance consultant at Hot ITem.*
- *Stijn Hoppenbrouwers is professor of Data & Knowledge Engineering at* HAN *University of Applied Sciences, Arnhem and assistant professor at Radboud University Nijmegen.*
- *Jeroen Cloo is partner at Novius Adviesgroep.*
- *Kiean Bitaraf is data management consultant at Deloitte.*
- *Raymond Slot is managing partner at Strategy Alliance.*

- *Paul Heisen is senior enterprise architect at De Lage Landen (DLL).*
- *Robin Vuyk is head of business architecture and design at PGGM, a Dutch pension provider.*
- *Daan Riepma is a smart data consultant at Axians.*
- *Ronald Damhof, "just a data-guy", self-employed, often in the role of enterprise (data) architect in large (mostly public) organizations.*

The book wouldn't have been nearly as good without the help of Lisa Gaudette. Thank you so much for your patience, hard work, and grammar/ punctuation lessons. Whenever I thought we had cleaned up a piece of text, you always found more ways to make it better. I would also like to thank Mirjam Visser for her extensive review of the manuscript as well as the pleasant discussions we had on data management. Last but not least, I would like to thank my family for their support. I know I have been hiding behind my computer to finish the manuscript and wouldn't have been able to make so much progress without your flexibility and support.

As a last remark, I would like to point out that a lot of time and effort went into checking the material. Any errors that remain are my own. I hope you find the book interesting and useful. Enjoy the read!

Bas van Gils
October 2019

Contents

PART I: THEORY

PART II: PRACTICE

List of figures

1 Introduction

It is often said that "data is the new oil". It is hard to figure out with any certainty who wrote about this metaphor first. A cursory search on Google suggests it was used originally in an article by The Economist [Par17] with many authors following suit by describing why, for all practical reasons, data is *not* the new oil (e.g. [Mar18]). Whatever the practical implications, the metaphor at least illustrates that data is an important business asset that deserves to be managed as such. This is the field of data management (or DM for short). See also sidebar 1.

> **Sidebar 1. Interview with Marco van der Winden (Summer 2019)**
>
> My experience is that the importance of data is underestimated in the way that there was/ is no primary focus on it. Living in the low countries where there is an abundance of water, data is mostly seen as something that can be easily be obtained, just like water. To continue the comparison, the Dutch are very good with containing the water streams and keeping the seawater outside with dikes. But with data we are less experienced. We let data sometimes uncontrollably flow though our fields without knowing where it goes or even why we are doing it.
>
> We are not in the Middle Ages (when we became increasingly proficient at water management) and it should be clear that data must be governed in a way that we are more in control and that we can profit more from it. By the way, I think that a comparison with oil is not a smart one. Sooner or later there will be a shortage of oil. Above that, there are also some environmental disadvantages with oil. Data is more like water. It's the source of all living things. You can't live without it and there will always be water.
>
> *Marco van der Winden is manager of the corporate data management office at PGGM, a Dutch pension provider.*

A key question that needs answering is: what does that entail? In other words: what is data management (DM) and how do you make it work? These are hard questions. Data is often seen as an abstract "thing" that sits in the realm of the IT department.

This isn't helped by the fact that a lot of technology is so closely related to data that it is easy to confuse one for the other. Worse, data management professionals are prone to using complicated terminology such as *metadata, master data, lineage* and so on, which makes it hard for outsiders to truly understand what is going on. This is not a good thing: DM is an important capability that organizations must master[1].

To illustrate this point, I will borrow a slightly altered example from [Soa11] in example 1.

Example 1. Data management benefits
Assume you are working for a large global company with approximately 10 million customers. On average each customer purchases 1.2 products every year. Your strategy is to attempt to get more revenue from the existing customer base, rather than try to capture a bigger market share. To that end, a global *customer 360* initiative is considered. The data management team and marketing have worked together to compile a business case.

First, it is expected that a better overview of each customer will increase the number of purchases from 1.2 to 1.4, which is expected to raise an extra 8 million dollars in revenues over three years. Furthermore, it is estimated that the direct cost of wading through duplicated/ inconsistent data about customers by customer service representatives adds up to about half a million dollars over three years. The direct cost of the IT department around data integration issues is expected to be reduced by another half a million dollars over three years. This adds up to nine million dollars in benefits. Would that justify a significant investment in data management?

1.1 GOALS FOR THIS BOOK

One of the best ways to make progress in our field is to put knowledge in the public domain such that everyone can benefit from it. There are many ways to do this: scientific studies provide academic rigor but tend to be low on practical relevance. Handbooks such as the DMBOK[2] are the inverse: there is a lot of practical value but they tend to be low on the academic rigor [Hen17]. Balancing rigor and relevance is tricky to say the least. This book leans towards the practical relevance side and provides academic rigor whenever possible. The unique selling point of this book will lie in the fact that it offers (1) an up-to-date overview of the field, (2) with practical guidance in the form of a capability-based framework, and (3) is supported by real-world evidence through mini case studies.

1 Throughout this book, I will use the term *capability* to signify an ability/ discipline that an organization may have. The simple formula capability = capacity × ability further signifies that the organization not only has to master the ability, but also have sufficient resources with the right abilities available in order to be successful.

2 The DMBOK is the Data Management Body of Knowledge. It is a reference book by DAMA, the Data Management Association. The DMBOK compiles data management principles and best practices.

The overall objective is to show that data management (DM) is an exciting and valuable capability that is worth time and effort. More specifically, I hope to achieve the following goals. First, I hope to give a "gentle" introduction to the field of DM by explaining and illustrating its core concepts. In doing so, I will demystify terminology as much as possible. To this end, I will use a mix of theory, practical frameworks such as TOGAF, ArchiMate, and DMBOK, as well as results from real-world assignments [The11, The16a, Hen17].

Second, I will offer guidance on how to build an effective DM capability for your organization. I will do so by considering various *use cases*, linked to the previously mentioned theoretical exploration as well as the stories of practitioners in the field.

1.2 INTENDED AUDIENCE

The book aims at a broad audience: busy professionals who "are actively involved with managing data". This might be a bit too broad because it is hard to imagine a book that would successfully address the needs of strategic decision makers all the way down to analysts and database administrators. The book is also aimed at (Bachelor's/ Master's) students with an interest in data management. A more specific characterization of the (professional) audience is:

- In the strategic/ tactical/ operational continuum, I will go for the middle ground. This means: stay away from executives and top management. It also means: stay away from true day-to-day business operations.
- In the business/ technology continuum, again, I will aim for the middle ground. It is increasingly true that there is no real difference between business and IT but for the sake of the argument: I am aiming at business people with a sense of IT, IT people with a sense of business and those who straddle both worlds.
- Industry-wise, the book should be agnostic and should be applicable in different industries such as government, finance, telecommunications etc.

Typical roles that come to mind are: data governance office/ council, data owners, data stewards, people involved with data governance (data governance board), enterprise architects, data architects, process managers, business analysts and IT analysts.

1.3 APPROACH

In this book, I will combine elements from theory and from practice. The former comes in the shape of citations to books, articles and web resources. I will attempt to link to original sources whenever possible, but also make an attempt to give the book a look-and-feel that is not too academic. The same goes for the practical part: I will combine my own experience of 15+ years as a consultant and teacher with stories from other professionals. I will provide the names of organizations and people whenever possible. In some places, stories have been anonymized to ensure privacy, or to comply with non-disclosure agreements. The theory part of the book will give a broad overview of the field of data management. The practical part will cover specific topics and use cases in more depth. More detailed coverage of specific topics can be found by following the citations or reaching out to listed practitioners.

The book is mainly aimed at busy professionals - while I also take into account that students and perhaps even scholars will find the book useful. Because of this, I have made two decisions with respect to the book structure. First of all, I have chosen to split the book into three main parts: theory, practice, and closing remarks. Furthermore, I have chosen to keep the chapters as short and to the point as possible and also make a clear distinction between the main text and the examples. Because of this choice, the book will have many short chapters. If you are already familiar with the topic of a chapter, you can easily skip it and move on to the next.

2 Data as an asset

Synopsis *- In this chapter, I will give an overview of why data is one of the key assets of an organization. To achieve this, I will first define the notions of data and asset. Then I will show what it means for data to be an asset. I will do this by stressing the relationship between processes (the "engine" of the organization), and data (the "fuel") which are both needed to create value. I will illustrate the value of data through two short examples.*

2.1 DATA

So far, I have been using the word "data" colloquially without really defining it. Experience shows that people use the word differently so I will explore this concept first. On any such venture, the first step is to check a dictionary. The lemma for *data* from the Merriam-Webster Dictionary has three definitions:

1. Factual information (such as measurements or statistics) used as a basis for reasoning, discussion, or calculation.
2. Information in digital form that can be transmitted or processed.
3. Information output by a sensing device or organ that includes both useful and irrelevant or redundant information and must be processed to be meaningful.

These definitions are very similar to the way of thinking in the *Design & Engineering Methodology for Organizations* (DEMO) approach where a distinction is made between three levels of abstraction: *forma* - being all about documenting/ expressing facts and data; *informa* - being all about thought and reasoning; and finally *performa* - being all about using facts and data in the real-world, for example to decide on a course of action [RD99, Die06].

Citing earlier work from the mid 1980s by Appleton, Peter Aiken - one of the eminent writers about DM - positions the term *data* in relation to other concepts such as facts and information [App86, AG13]. Figure 2.1 summarizes this way of thinking. One of the things that can be learned from this diagram is that data is said to consist of facts which have a meaning. Another important aspect is that data can be used, which shows intelligence. Comparing this approach to the previously cited definition, the question arises whether it is possible, or even useful, to *clearly* and *unambiguously* distinguish between the concepts of *data* and *information*: the Merriam-Webster Dictionary definition for *data* heavily relies on the notion of information and vice versa.

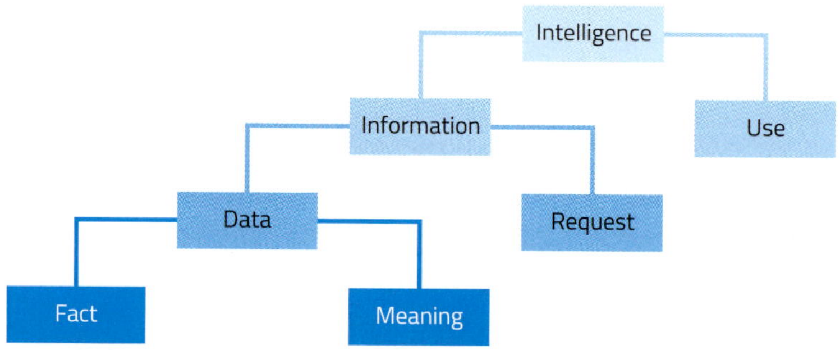

1. Each FACT combines with one or more MEANINGS.
2. Each specific FACT and MEANING combination is referred to as a DATUM.
3. An INFORMATION is one or more DATA that are returned in response to a specific REQUEST.
4. INFORMATION REUSE is enabled when one FACT is combined with more than one MEANING.
5. INTELLIGENCE is INFORMATION associated with its USES.

Figure 2.1 Fact, data, information and intelligence

For purposes of this book, I will not make a hard distinction between the two concepts. I will use the term *data* as an umbrella term, meaning all three definitions from the Merriam-Webster Dictionary. Even more, I intend to use it both as the "raw ingredient" (data codified in systems) and how it is used in business processes (sometimes called "information" by other authors). I will expand on this discussion further in chapter 6. Example 2 clarifies this way of thinking further.

Example 2. Data management benefits

Suppose you are an avid runner, like me. Your coach has explained that your heart rate provides a good indicator of how your body is doing and that it should be used to guide your bi-weekly training sessions. After purchasing a heart rate monitor, you go out for your first run.

During your run, you can check your new gadget. It will measure how you are doing and individual data points are shown as you go along. Presumably, the gadget will also store this data, so that it can later be transferred to some online application for further processing. Together with your coach, you can use this data to analyze your fitness and training schedule for weeks to come.

2.2 ASSET

As stated in the opening paragraph of chapter 1: it is often said that "data is an asset". For example, the DMBOK states [Hen17]:

> *Data and information are not just assets in the sense that organizations invest in them in order to derive future value. Data and information are also vital to the day-to-day operations of most organizations. They have been called the "currency", the "life blood" and even the "new oil" of the information economy. Whether or not an organization gets value from its analytics, it cannot even transact business without data.*

The question that needs to be answered is: what is an asset? Relying once more on the dictionary, an asset can be defined as "an item of value that is owned or possessed". Let's explore that further through the cases listed in example 3.

Example 3. Examples of assets

Assume the asset is a *car*. It has different types of value to me: it gets me from A to B, but it also has monetary value. Now assume that the asset is *money*. Its value is in the security that I have some buying power to take care of myself. Finally assume that the asset is *customer data*. Its value is that I know who my customers are, where they live and what they have purchased in the past so that I can help them well in the future.

The examples show that assets can be tangible or intangible. They also show that assets have value. The latter point deserves further exploration. In previous research, I have shown that value is both *personal* (one person may see it differently than another person) and *situational* (in one situation it may be worth more than another) [Gil06]. Again, two small examples illustrate the point:

Example 4. Value of assets

The first example pertains to art. Let's take a famous painting such as *White on White*[1] by Kazimir Malevich. Some will claim it priceless, whereas others will claim it to be something so simple that a five-year-old can create it. Both observers, of course, are correct. This shows the *personal* nature of the valuation of assets.

The second example pertains to the value of water when compared to money. In most cases, I would value $10 over a small bottle of water. When standing in the middle of the desert, though, I may think differently. This shows the *situational* nature of valuation of assets.

1 https://en.wikipedia.org/wiki/White_on_White, last checked 2 June 2019.

The implications for *data as an asset* are clear: when we say that we consider data to be an important asset then we mean that we believe that the data in our systems has much value, either intrinsic (we have data that is worth money, for example if we sell it) or indirectly (which means we can use it in our processes to create value). This, finally, brings us to the relationship between *data* and *business processes*.

Before we dive into this relationship, there is one point that should be made. There is a big distinction between *data assets* and *tangible assets*: there is only one copy of a tangible asset but this doesn't have to be the case for (intangible) data assets. To put it differently: you can make as many copies of data assets as you like without affecting the original. If this were the case for physical assets then we would all be as rich as Croesus for sure. This property of data is important in chapters to come when we talk about storing, using, transferring, and managing data.

2.3 DATA AND PROCESS

This brings me to the final part of this chapter: the relationship between *data* and *process*. It is safe to say that data does not magically spring into existence. On the contrary: creating data takes effort by business professionals, for example by adding data into computer systems or by manipulating existing data to create new data.

The fact that we are not so (consciously) aware of this is not surprising. Years ago – before the computer era – a lot of our data sat in paper files and records. Creating data meant getting in there and updating the files. More data meant more paper. More paper meant more space required to store the data. This, eventually, lead to bigger and bigger libraries[1]. In the computer-age this is different: most data is now stored digitally and adding more bits and bytes requires very little extra physical space.

Producing data in business processes is useful in itself. Things become more interesting when we consider where else that data can be used/ where else data can be put to good use to create value. Example 5 illustrates this point.

Example 5. Data and processes
Suppose you work at a company that leases expensive medical equipment to hospitals. Each time the company closes a new deal with a hospital, its records are updated (new data is added to their systems). The value of this data is that it proves that the transaction took place and that the company is owed a certain fee each time.

1 An interesting overview of the history of libraries can be found in [Mur09].

The data is likely to be used in other parts of the company as well. For example, sales and marketing representatives are interested in the data to investigate whether they can cross-sell insurance products with the newly leased equipment, whilst management will be interested in monthly sales reports to see how well the company is doing.

This example illustrates a point that I cannot make enough: there is a strong relationship between business processes and data (see e.g. [BRS19] for a recent discussion of this topic, bridging the gap between research and practice). Data without use in processes has no value. Processes without data cannot happen: if processes are the value creation engine of the organization, then data is its fuel. As a corollary of this discussion, this book will also have much say about processes and not just about data.

Data can only be used if it is of the right quality and can be found. The former point is easily understood: just like poor materials will likely lead to the construction of a poor physical asset, so does poor data lead to poor process performance. The latter point requires a bit more explanation. The general thinking seems to be: our data is stored in our systems and we know which systems we have – so how hard can it be to find out data? Example 6 shows that in practice this may not be as easy as it seems.

Example 6. Finding data
Let's go back to the library case that was mentioned previously. Libraries are structured in such a way that, by and large, it should be straightforward to find the books and articles that you need. In the old days this was done through extensive cataloguing, classification, and index systems. These days all of this is automated[1]. It is true that in most organizations all data is stored electronically in systems. In theory it should be easy to find. However, do you have any idea how many systems your organization has for storing data about customers or products? Chances are there are dozens! Finding the right information for use is one of the key challenges for many organizations.

1 If you want to know more about information retrieval, consider reading e.g. [Pai99] - which also has a good historical overview.

The point that this example tries to make is that data is often dispersed across many systems which makes it harder to locate the right data for the right person doing his/ her job at the right time. This, in turn, shows that the value of data depends on more than it being a correct representation of the real-world: being able to use it in processes in a timely manner might be just as important. If your data is "correct" but it can't be found in time to be used in a process then, in fact, its value is very low, or even zero.

2.4 VISUAL SUMMARY

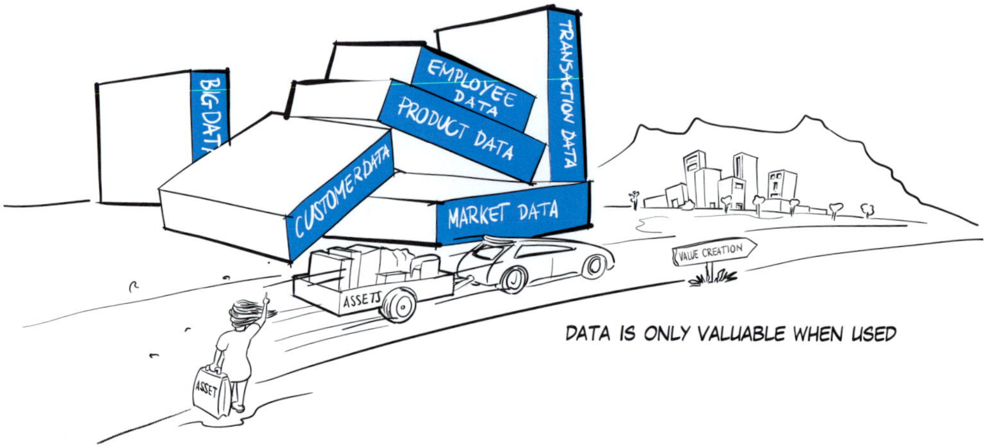

3 Data management: why bother?

***Synopsis** - This chapter picks up where the previous chapter left off: if data is an important asset, then it should be managed as such. In this chapter, I will briefly introduce the Data Management Body of Knowledge (DMBOK) reference work on data management upon which part I of this book is based. I will use this as a backdrop to discuss some of its key challenges for data management. The challenges are illustrated with small examples.*

3.1 A DEFINITION OF DATA MANAGEMENT

In the previous chapter, I have discussed the concept of *data as an asset* to signify the importance of data for an organization. We pick up the discussion with a claim: if data is such an important asset to the organization, then it should be managed as such. This is the realm of data management.

Simply put, DM is the capability that is concerned with managing data as an asset. This definition is still somewhat vague and requires further clarification. In [AB13], Peter Aiken points out that "any holistic examination of the information technology field will reveal that it is largely about *technology* – not about *information*". We begin by stating that data management is largely about putting the "I" back in "IT". This observation shows that DM is not solely an IT capability.

Sidebar 2. Interview with Marc van den Berg (summer 2019)

Many organizations are currently experiencing challenges with data due to past decisions and are paying the price because of the investment they have to make to fix their data after the fact. At the same time, these organizations want to make a quantum leap forward and reap the benefits from new technologies such as big data and artificial intelligence. This will not work, as first you must have your house in order. In my view this means: make sure you have shared goals about what you want to achieve with data, and subsequently align business and IT to attain those goals.

Marc van den Berg is managing director of IT and Innovation at PGGM, a Dutch pension provider.

It appears that in most organizations there is no longer a real, meaningful difference between "the business side of the organization" and "the IT side of the organization", at least not in the classic sense of business/ IT alignment literature from the 1980s and 1990s [PB89, HV93]. With the rise of process automation, digital/ digitalization we see that the two perspectives are now intertwined to such a degree that the distinction is fading rapidly (see e.g. [RBM19, Gue12] in which a distinction is made between digitalization of existing processes, or by a more radical departure and creating digital, information-enriched value propositions). In this context, it feels safe to say that DM is an important capability for the organization, regardless of whether it leans towards business, IT, or both.

The DMBOK definition of DM is as follows [Hen17]:

> *Data management is the development, execution, and supervision of plans, policies, programs, and practices that deliver, control, protect, and enhance the value of data and information assets throughout their lifecycle.*

The interesting aspect that can be learned from this definition is that data management encompasses many activities that together enable the organization to use data effectively. For now, this exploration of the definition of DM will have to suffice. A more detailed discussion will follow in chapter 7.

The DMBOK also states that these activities are likely to be cross-functional and that "the primary driver for data management is to enable organizations to get value from their data assets, just as effective management of financial and physical assets enables organizations to get value from those assets". The value of DM is discussed further in the next section.

3.2 VALUE OF DM

The key point of DM is to manage data as an asset which helps the organization to derive value from its data assets. As such, it has no direct business value. Its value is more indirect; it enables the organization to achieve goals through data. This means that organizations should think carefully about which goals they want to achieve through the use of data and what would be required to realize these goals.

In a recent article about *data strategy*, this was compared to the world of sports [DD17] such as soccer or ice hockey. In these sports, you'll never win the game if you only do defense: it will be hard for the opponent to score goals, but you'll never get to score goals yourself either. The inverse is also true: you'll never win the game if you only do offense: you'll probably score a few goals, but it will be super easy for the opponent to score goals since there is no one to defend your own goal.

The trick to being successful is to balance between offense and defense and to make sure that the two stay connected. Example 7 illustrates this point.

Example 7. Balancing data management offense and defense
This example stems from the early 2000s when I did a consultancy assignment with a large Dutch governmental organization. Roughly speaking, the organization had several units which served citizens as well as businesses. The organization was structured along the lines of a classic front-office, mid-office, and back-office pattern. At the front-office level the units operated independently. At the mid-office and back-office level, this organization was attempting to standardize several processes and systems. This included the launch of a data delivery platform which served both analytics and reporting functions.

From a business perspective it was very clear what the value of data was and how it could be used to fuel their business processes (data management offense). From an IT perspective it was – after some searching – clear what data was available in which system and how it should be transported to the data delivery platform in a timely manner while retaining high levels of data quality (data management defense).

Unfortunately, communication between the two groups was less than optimal – to say the least. The effect was that it took *years* before their supply of data on this platform was well suited to meet the demands of business stakeholders, and a lot of the data that had been loaded on the platform early on was never actually used. This endeavor was not only costly, it also gave data/ DM a bad reputation at this organization.

The same line of thinking also applies to DM. Here, defense pertains to "grip on data", meaning the activities through which the organization knows what data assets they have, where and when they were created, what their quality is, etc. This is what traditionally was seen as DM. In this context, offense pertains to generating value through the use of data, meaning the activities related to using data in business processes. This can be in various shapes and forms such as selling the data itself, handling business transactions, using big data analyses to detect fraud patterns or to use traditional business intelligence reports to manage some business unit.

3.3 KEY CHALLENGES FOR DM

The final topic for this chapter deals with two questions: what are the key challenges that DM attempts to solve and what are key challenge to overcome when getting started with DM?

The first challenge you have to tackle is for the organization (or at least key stakeholders in the organization) to recognize that DM is really a "thing" they should worry about. As stated previously, many people seem to think along these lines: data is stored in our systems, we know which systems we have, so what's the big deal? The thinking has to change to: processes are the value creation engine of the organization and we change systems all the time so we should really take good care of our data to help us to be successful. This transition is usually the biggest challenge. Sidebar 3 illustrates this point.

Sidebar 3. Interview with Marco van der Winden (Summer 2019)

We are now realizing that data is the link between business(-operations) and systems. It is the universal language between business and IT. We have to understand that it will make our lives easier instead of more complex by focusing on data and not on systems or our own operation. My experience is that people only think that focusing on data is about more rules, more work, and being more accountable. I think (and hope) that we'll understand we have to spend less time on acquiring data and changing our operations in favor of the more exciting things we can do with our data.

Marco van der Winden is manager of the corporate data management office at PGGM, a Dutch pension provider.

It is often the case that discussions about DM lead to the question of a *business case*, possibly with the exception of situations where regulators simply demand that an organization has a strong DM capability. Making a business case is the second challenge and it is a topic that we will address in greater detail in chapter 23. This challenge ties in with the previous one: if people confuse data for systems, then it is hard to argue that the organization should invest in managing its data. One aspect that I would like to mention is this: rather than boiling the ocean[1] it often makes more sense to identify a small area that needs improvement, solve it, and use the "win" as a catalyst to set up the next improvement iteration.

The third challenge is related to building a DM capability that is "just right" for the needs of the organization. In many cases we see that this capability is over-engineered or

1 The phrase "boil the ocean" is a colloquialism that refers to taking on an overly large and potentially impossible task given the reality of your resource.

too focused on implementing tools that will act like a silver bullet and make all the problems go away. The purpose of part II of this book is to show how specific topics in this category can be solved by building the DM capability one step at a time.

3.4 VISUAL SUMMARY

SUCCESSFUL DATA MANAGEMENT REQUIRES OFFENSE AND DEFENSE

4 Positioning data management

__Synopsis__ - This book is about data management, so I will position data management as the center of the universe, at least as far as this book is concerned. In this chapter, I will clarify the role of data management, by relating it to other (management) capabilities such as business process management (BPM), enterprise architecture, and IT management. I will also briefly discuss the philosophical considerations related to the challenge of building an effective data management capability. I will base this discussion on the Cynefin framework and the concept of antifragility [SB07, Tal12].

4.1 THE CENTER OF THE UNIVERSE

In the introduction of chapter 2, I presented an analogy between processes as the value creation engine of the organization, and data as the fuel for this engine. The point of this analogy is that it is hard to meaningfully separate the two, as "data" and "process" are so intertwined. Yet, this book is about data management (DM) so this topic will be front and center in most of this book. More specifically, in part I, I will discuss DM and its functional areas from a theoretical perspective. I will attempt to do so in an *objective* manner[1]. In part II, I will offer *good practices* for building an effective data management capability.

While DM is important, it can hardly be discussed without considering its context. For understanding DM from a theoretical perspective, as well as for designing a program to build or improve a DM capability, it is recommended to take a *systems perspective of the organization*, meaning that (1) we should consider the

---

1 It is often argued that it is impossible to be fully objective when observing or researching a domain. For example, [McG83] claims that the only things humans can do objectively is *counting*, and even that is open to debate. The point that I am trying to make is that I will attempt to give an overview of what the theory says about each of the functional fields without going into practical recommendations.

organization as a system that operates in a specific context, (2) we should consider all relevant perspectives on this system as determined by key stakeholders, and (3) we should consider both structural properties of the system (i.e. how is it organized? Which "parts" can we distinguish?) as well as how it behaves (i.e. what happens in the organization? How does it behave in relation to its environment?).

With this in mind, I will position DM in relation to other (management) capabilities in the upcoming sections, keeping in mind the "golden triangle" in our field: data (DM), processes (business process management -BPM), and systems (IT management). I will also discuss two topics that are closely related to, or even part of, data management, but that did not get chapters of their own: information/data analysis, and database management. The section on *enterprise architecture management* will tie these three perspectives together. Figure 4.1 clarifies this further. I will also offer a philosophical consideration on the complexity of building or improving a DM capability as a backdrop for the chapters in part II of this book.

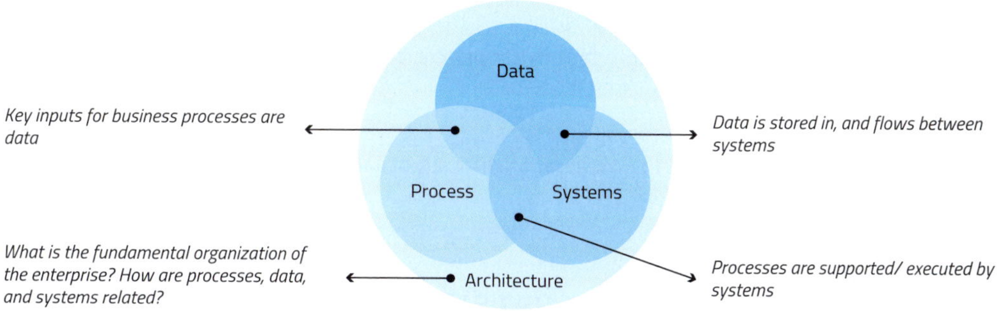

Figure 4.1 Positioning data management

4.2 DM AND BUSINESS PROCESS MANAGEMENT

Business processes form the value creation engine of the organization. Many definitions have been proposed in literature and common characteristics of these definitions are: (1) processes consist of a series of steps, (2) processes are executed by (human/ computer/ machine) actors, (3) processes are executed to achieve a goal, (4) processes may or may not be *designed* (i.e., some processes are ad-hoc, others are executed along the lines of a pre-design "script"), and (5) processes may or may not be described in a process model. Business process management originated in and became popular in the 1980s and 1990s and encompasses techniques such as Lean and Six Sigma. An abundance of literature is available on (successful) business process management (e.g. [Wes07, SqE08, Kir09]).

The premise behind business process management (BPM) is that the activities of the organization should be coordinated in such a way that strategic outcomes are achieved and that resources (people, time, money, materials) are used as effectively as possible in achieving those outcomes. Processes transform inputs (e.g. a frame, wheels, saddle, etc.) to outputs (e.g. a bike). Increasingly these inputs and outputs are also "informational": data about which parts are used, who did the assembly of a (physical) product and when, are common examples. For many organizations the inputs are solely informational in nature: for example, banks and insurance companies do not have a physical/ tangible product that is created. Instead, they offer services to their customers, and data (about customers, products, financial positions, market conditions, etc.) are the "fuel" for the processes.

This is also where the worlds of DM and BPM meet. From a BPM perspective you could argue that the inputs and outputs of processes are data, and since these are key to the successful execution of these processes, they should be managed accordingly. This means that we want to know *what* data is used where, *which systems* we can find it in, *what the quality is*, etc. Turning this argument around, you could also say that data is the key asset of the organization (chapter 2). Processes manipulate the data, and should be managed as such. This means that we want to know which processes manipulate the data, what the intended use of data is, who is responsible for these processes, etc.

It is safe to conclude that, in practice, both capabilities are important and tightly linked.

4.3 DM AND IT MANAGEMENT

It appears that the distinction between *data* and *system* is difficult to grasp for many stakeholders. The stakeholders in example 8 conflated data and systems and had formed the mental image that "data cannot be to blame": any error in the data must be caused by poor systems design, so that is where the problem must lie. There is something to be said for this line of reasoning. It makes sense from a systems perspective but not so much from a DM perspective.

Example 8. Data and systems

In the early days of a recent project, I ran into the following situation. We were trying to get an answer to the question "do our business stakeholders believe there is a data quality management problem in the organization?"

We held a series of interviews with groups of stakeholders to explore this topic. In one of the meetings, a stakeholder commented as follows: "Data quality problems? No, I don't think we have those. We do have a lot of system problems though. People fill in all kinds of nonsensical data, data from different systems is hard to integrate, and our management reports are always late. So, perhaps we should stop talking about data management and start fixing these problems?"

IT management is, like business process management, an important capability that has received much attention over the last few decades, both in academic and business discourse. Loosely defined, IT management is about managing IT resources (applications, infrastructure) according to an organization's priorities and needs. There are several major frameworks in this area, including ITIL and COBIT [Per16, ISA12].

Taking a slightly broader perspective, it can be argued that software/ system development and its associated methodologies should also be considered. This would also put frameworks such as Scrum in scope of this discussion [Rub12], as would system development philosophies such as *domain driven design* [Eva04] or architecture approaches such as *micro services* [New15].

The point that I am trying to make is that IT management is a broad capability which includes a number of aspects, many of which have a link to data and data management. Simply put: data is *stored* in systems and *flows* between systems. When done well, the DM and IT management can reinforce/ strengthen each other. Let me offer two examples to illustrate:

- One of the key processes in IT management is *incident management*. Through this process, organizations attempt to ensure that IT services are restored as soon as possible after an incident. This process is very similar to data quality issue management (see chapter 16). Given how closely related *data* and *systems* are, it may make sense to align these two processes.
- One of the key considerations in systems development is *user interface design*. This discipline is traditionally largely focused on making sure user interfaces are *easy to use* and the interaction between user and system to ensure work can be performed effectively. From a data management perspective, this would include such aspects as consistent use of language, intuitive use/ ergonomics, and ensuring that there are "guard rails" in place that will prevent users from entering an incorrect input that the system will not be able to process correctly.

Here, too, it is safe to conclude that, in practice, both disciplines are important and tightly linked.

4.4 INFORMATION/DATA ANALYSIS

The terms *information analysis*, *data analysis*, and *information management* are closely related and – as with so many terms – are defined differently depending on the context and author. For example, in the Netherlands, the term *information management* currently has very little to do with the management of information. Instead, it tends to mean the capability to understand and manage IT requirements and the associated portfolio of required projects to implement them. The more general definition of this term is the organizational capability to manage the lifecycle of data, which is quite close to how DM is defined.

In my view, information/ data analysis is a capability that operates on a completely different level of abstraction. The purpose of this type of analysis is, in the context of the information needs of a stakeholder or group of stakeholders, to analyze the interplay between process, information/ data, and systems and document a functional/ technical design that can be used to implement these requirements through the development or adaptation of IT systems.

Many of the techniques that I will discuss in chapter 11 are also used for information/ data analysis. Classic approaches that fall into this category – developed in the 1990s and still highly relevant today – are *structured analysis and design* [You89] and *information engineering* [Mar89, Mar90a, Mar90b].

4.5 DATABASE MANAGEMENT

Database management is the capability that is concerned with designing, implementing, and running databases that help to make data available to the right person, at the right time. This is a fairly technical discipline and for this reason I have chosen not to give it a chapter of its own in this book.

Databases come in many shapes and forms. The *relational* model, developed by Codd in the 1970s, is still by far the most popular approach for structuring and storing data [Cod70, Cod79]. This model is based on the notion of mathematical relations. A relation can be seen as a *table*[2] with a heading that lists the attributes of the relation (i.e. a *Person* relation may have *First name, Last name, Birth date* as attributes) and a body consisting of tuples/ rows with values that represent the population of the table (i.e. {'Bas', 'van Gils', '06-dec-1976'}).

One of the key points of the relational model is that data structures are designed a priori in such a way that they can be queried in many different ways to answer any question that people may have about the data. In other words, the "cost" of time spent in designing the data structures is balanced by the" "value" of flexible querying. Data structures are rigorously designed and tend to be fairly static. Adjusting them tends to have a major impact on IT systems. A more recent development is to work with database systems where the line of reasoning is the inverse: get data in the system and do not worry too much about structuring the data a priori. Instead,

2 In [Dat12], C. J. Date explains that tables are not the *same* as mathematical relations but people have come to think of them like this. If you are interested in database design, I highly recommend this book.

the structure of the data in the database is analyzed when the system is queried. In this case, the benefit of "ease of getting data into the system" is balanced by the cost of "querying becomes a little harder". Several types of databases fall into this category of NoSQL-systems (see e.g. [RW12] for a good overview as well as advantages/ disadvantages of each).

On an (even) more technical level, database management concerns decisions about how to set up the infrastructure to host databases, whether systems should have a failover option (i.e. if one system is unavailable, then the other will take over), or what the implications are of hosting the data "in the cloud."

4.6 DM AND ENTERPRISE ARCHITECTURE MANAGEMENT

Enterprise architecture (EA) is a capability that considers organizations from a "big picture view". The capability evolved from both the business/ IT alignment literature [PB89, HV93] and IT engineering/ architecture [Zac87, ISO11, The11, The16a, GD14, GD15, RWR06, RBM19].

It appears that each architecture approach uses its own definition of architecture. Most of these approaches at least relate to the definition that is presented in the ISO/ IEC/IEEE 42010 standard about *Systems and software engineering – Architecture description* which states that the architecture of a system[3] is about two things (1) the fundamental organization of that system and (2) the principles guiding the design and evolution of that system [ISO11]. A more elaborate discussion is presented in chapter 12.

The "big picture view of the enterprise" relates to the first aspect, and gives a clear overview of the relationship between key elements in the organization. Typically, this is about the "golden triangle": business process, data, and systems. Architecture modeling languages (e.g. ArchiMate) are capable of visualizing this big picture view. One discussion that crops up frequently is: "where does 'architecture' stop and where do more detailed analyses (of processes, systems, and data) begin?" There is no simple answer to this question: the word "fundamental" from the definition of architecture is a subjective term. What might be fundamental for one stakeholder may be a (potentially irrelevant) detail for another. Figure 4.2 illustrates how architecture (models) are linked to more detailed designs.

3 An "enterprise" or "organization" is seen as a system.

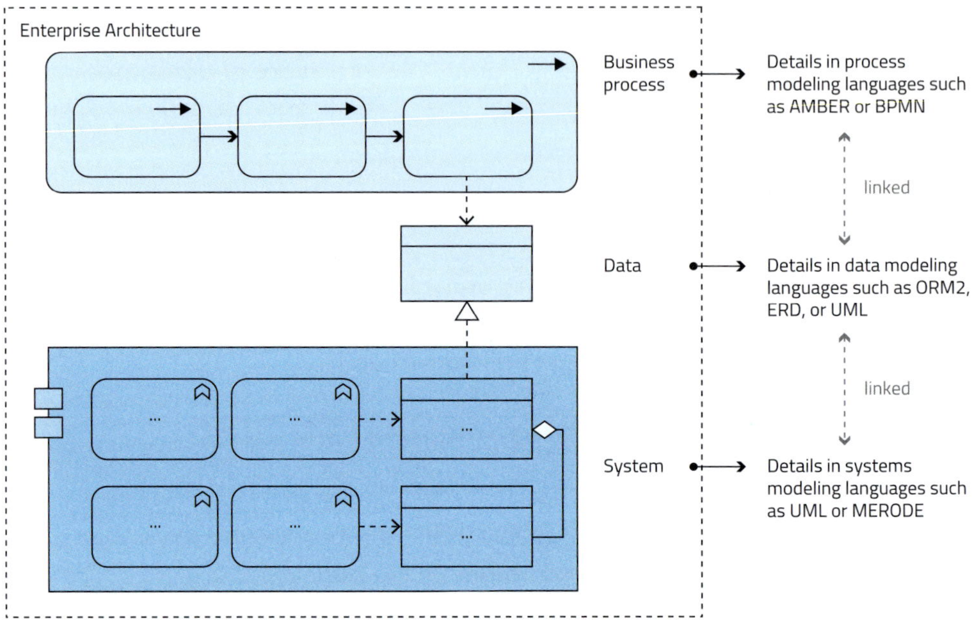

Figure 4.2 From architecture to a more "detailed design"

From the perspective of enterprise architecture, data (architecture) is but one of the aspects that is to be considered. To put it differently, *data architecture* is considered to be a part of *enterprise architecture*. Switching perspectives, one could argue that *data architecture* (chapter 12) is but one aspect of *data management*.

In my view, both perspectives are equally true and valuable. Here, too, it is safe to conclude that, in practice, both capabilities are important and tightly linked. As a side note, I would argue that the relationship between enterprise architecture and business process management, as well as the relationship between enterprise architecture and IT management are very similar to the relationship between enterprise architecture and data management (see figure 4.1).

4.7 PHILOSOPHICAL CONSIDERATIONS

As you will see in part I of this book, the field of DM covers many subjects, called *functional areas*. Because of this, people tend to call DM a *complex* field. In this section, I will discuss whether this claim is justified. I will use the Cynefin framework[4] as a theoretical foundation [SB07]. In this framework, five "problem solving modes", or "problem types" are distinguished, as shown in figure 4.3.

4 Cynefin is a conceptual framework for sense-making and decision-making, developed in the 1990s.

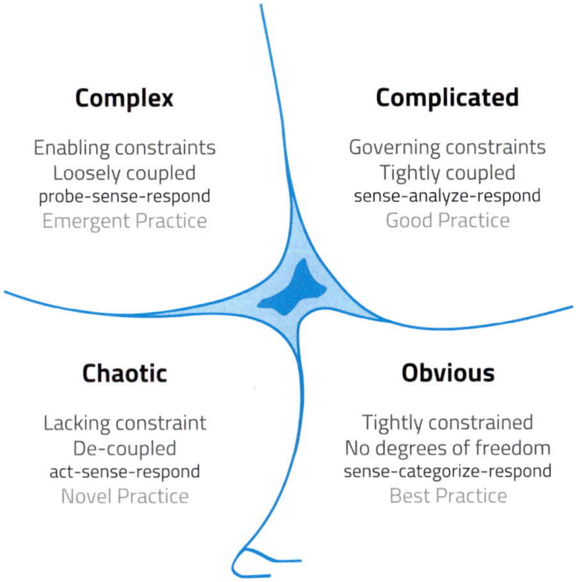

Figure 4.3 The Cynefin framework, based on [SB07]

- **Obvious -** For problems in this domain, a best practice is immediately clear. In this domain, as soon as you recognize the problem ("it is one of those"), then you'll know what to do. Here, the relationship between cause and effect is evident. A good example is the situation where you want to ensure that data is available for review later: you store it and make sure that there is a backup available.
- **Complicated -** In this domain, there is no immediate apparent solution to the problem at hand. How- ever, it is possible to discover *the* solution through careful analysis. More formally, the relationship between cause and effect can be found through analysis by someone with the required expertise, thus uncovering a good practice. A good example is building/ debugging a software system. There are many interlinked parts in a software system but you know that, given enough time for analysis, you will eventually discover how to fix the system and make it do what it is supposed to do.
- **Complex -** This domain is characterized by the fact that the relationship between cause and effect can only be discovered in hindsight. In other words, no matter how strong your analysis capability is, the very nature of problems in this domain is such that no best/ good practice can be determined a priori. In this mode, you develop a hypothesis of what *could* work and only by trying out this hypothesis can you discover what works. In this domain, we speak of *emergent practices*. A good example is a merger of two organizations: no matter how careful you plan, you cannot predict the final outcome. All you can do is hope that the interventions that you designed (hypothesis) work out for the best.

- **Chaotic** - This domain, is characterized by chaos and panic. There is so much going on and at such a high pace, that time for analysis and rational planning is lacking. What is required is decisive leadership and *action* to return to a more stable (simple/ complicated/ complex) state. In this domain we speak of *novel practices*. A good example is the situation where the systems of a company are breached, customer data has been leaked at a massive scale and, as a consequence, investors are dumping their stock – threatening the future of the organization. This is bound to lead to a panic. One of the first things that is needed here is decisive leadership to help "cool off" the situation. Only then can more rational, analysis-based methods kick into place.
- **Disorder** - This domain represents situations where it is unclear which of the other four domains are relevant. Usually this is because the decision maker/ analyst is still trying to get a sense for a specific situation and needs more evidence to come to a meaningful conclusion.

This framework can be used to analyze the *implementation* of DM in practice. In other words, it can be used in the context of part II where I present *use cases* around building or improving a DM capability. In my view, the *obvious* domain is not relevant for this discussion: aspects which are so simple that the solution is immediately obvious have no place in this book. Similarly, the *chaotic* domain also has no place in this book: when the existence of the organization is at stake, then DM practices are unlikely to save the day. This means that only the *complicated* and *complex* domains are relevant for this discussion.

Many tasks in the DM realm fall into the *complicated* domain. For example, documenting which data is in which system, or how data is combined to form new data might be much work, but with careful analysis and enough time and resources, it can be done. Key to success for these tasks is to have enough skilled professionals with the right tools and an incentive to "make it work".

A large part of the work, however, is in the *complex* domain. As soon as people, their work, and their behavior are involved, you enter the *complex* domain. Human behavior, especially when considered in the social context of an organization, can't be analyzed to the extent that *the* ultimate solution to a problem can be found. Borrowing from the work of Morgan, I would argue that a *machine* or *engineering* perspective of the organization is likely to lead to disastrous results when used to implement the DM capability [MGR97].

A more "human" perspective (the organization as a social system or the organization as an organism) – is likely to yield far better results. These perspectives do more justice to the fact that DM tools and techniques should be fitted to what is already present in the organization and should take the culture, beliefs, concerns, and social setting of the organization into account.

Considered as a whole, I believe that building/ improving the DM capability in an organization is definitely in the complex domain and that the only way to succeed is to adopt a people-first approach to this task. This will be a major theme in part II of this book.

The ultimate goal is to build an *effective* DM capability. In my view, *effective* means that it is both *fit for purpose* in the current situation but also in the future. This is closely related to the notion of *antifragility* as introduced by Taleb in [Tal12]:

> *Some things benefit from shocks; they thrive and grow when exposed to volatility, random- ness, disorder, and stressors and love adventure, risk, and uncertainty. Yet, in spite of the ubiquity of the phenomenon, there is no word for the exact opposite of fragile. Let us call it antifragile. Antifragility is beyond resilience or robustness. The resilient resists shocks and stays the same; the antifragile gets better.*

Antifragility is not an easy-to-understand concept and is easily confused with *robustness*. A characteristic of *robustness* is that it is capable of handling a certain level of stress. Or, more aptly formulated, it is designed and built to handle a certain level of stress. An antifragile system, by contrast, only gets better when more stress is experienced, as illustrated by example 9.

Example 9. Antifragility
A first example of antifragility comes from children at play. Children will very quickly learn how to deal with unfairness, uncertainty and failure. For many children, experiencing these things a few times will help them build coping mechanisms, which makes them better prepared for the future.

Similarly, in business as in other situations, professionals who experience *failure* (defined as: not reaching a predefined goal in the allotted time with the allotted resources) repeatedly will build resilience and character, and this will give them the experience to do better next time.

When building/ improving a data management capability, I believe that *antifragility* is a good quality to strive for. In my mind it captures the essence of what you want to achieve: a DM capability that gets better and better as a result of it being "used" and "tested" in practice. This is a guiding principle for the good practices in part II of this book.

■ 4.8 VISUAL SUMMARY

PART I

Theory

5 Introduction

In the upcoming chapters, I will discuss the theory of data management by giving an overview of the relevant terminology and a discussion of key data management topics. Each chapter discusses a single data management capability. The chapters are based on theory (the DMBOK and other sources), as well as my experiences in the field. Throughout these chapters, I have included many examples to illustrate key points, as well as brief interviews with people from the field. In this way, you will get a good overview of the field.

I have used the following principles for structuring part I of this book:

- Each chapter is kept as short and to the point as possible, as I am trying to convey the main points rather that give a complete coverage of a specific topic.
- There is no single best way to implement data management in an organization. Each organization is different. This implies that processes, roles, and responsibilities will be different in each organization. Therefore, I focus on the key concepts and shy away from guidance/ definitive statements on "who does what". This is partially covered in chapter 33 in part II of this book.
- Data management is not an "isolated capability", meaning that its processes, roles, responsibilities, and tools are highly connected to others. I have included brief discussions to key topics related to data management in several chapters. For example, the chapter on data governance has a link to IT governance. These discussions are kept deliberately short in order not to over-emphasize their importance.

Before diving in, I would like to stress that these chapters are very much connected and equally important. I have strived to give each topic equal attention. The discussion is deliberately neutral and avoids implementation recommendations. These are left for part II of this book.

6 Terminology

Synopsis *- Professionals in the field of DM/ IT use a specific lingo. Unfortunately, the terminology is not as standardized as I would like. In this chapter, I will give an overview of the most important terms as they are used in this book.*

6.1 INTRODUCTION

Professionals in the DM/ IT field have a reputation for being precise and consistent. Since this is the case, you would expect that terminology used would also be highly standardized and precisely defined. A careful study of several International Organization for Standardization (ISO)/ International Electrotechnical Commission (IEC) standards such as [ISO07, ISO12, ISO15] and comparison with the DMBOK and TOGAF [Hen17, The11] shows that this is far from the truth: the terminology is *vaguely the same but precisely different.*

In my view, this is a bad thing: how can we successfully engage people who are not so data-literate when we cannot agree on basic terminology? At the same time, I am very much aware that changing how people use language is far from easy. The purpose of this chapter is to introduce the terminology that is used in this book. The guiding principle is to align as much as possible with the aforementioned standards.

A small warning: defining terminology is both an art and a science. The text that follows is a little more academic in nature than in the rest of this book.

6.2 DATA CODIFIES WHAT WE KNOW ABOUT THE WORLD

In chapter 2, I briefly discussed the data/ information dichotomy and claimed that, at least for purposes of this book, there is little difference between these two terms.

In my view, data *codifies* what we know about the world in the form of text, numbers, graphs, images and so on[1]. In more technical terms, this means that data can be either structured (which typically means it is in tabular form), unstructured (such as a random piece of text), or semi-structured (such as an e-mail, which consists of a header and main body).

Linguistically, the term *data* is the plural form of the term *datum*, which at least suggests that there is something such as a "basic building block for data". I'll call this a *data point*. I'll use the term *record* to signify a (semi) structured group of data points that belong together, similar to paper records in physical catalogs used prior to today's digital data storage. Note that records typically consist of several standardized *fields* that are filled in with actual data points. The easiest way to understand what a field is, is to think of a record as a form with predefined fields that can be filled in. Last but not least, a group of records together forms a *data set*. Example 10 illustrates these definitions.

Example 10. Data, data point, record, field and data set

The diagram shows data that is stored in a system (outer box). The small inner boxes signify the records in this system. Each record has three fields: the *name*, *birthday* and *birth city* of a *per- son*. In this example there are six records in total, each having three data points matching the three fields that make up a typical record. The top row is grouped (dashed box): this signifies the data set with records about people that were born in Tilburg. Another potential data set would be: the group of all records for people born before 1960.

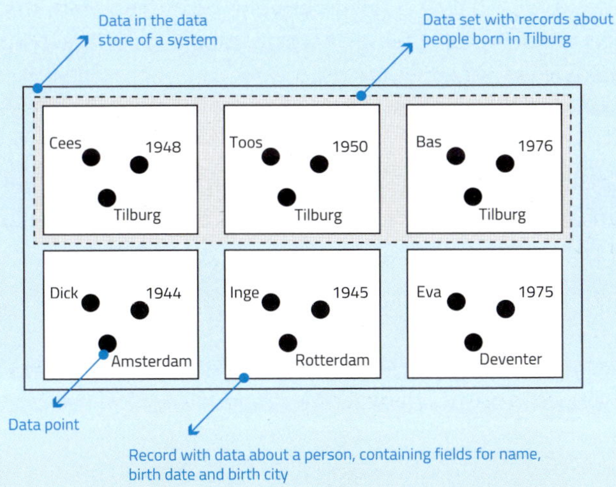

1 The classic works on information theory such as [Sha48] provide more insight in the use of the word *codifies*.

6.3 STORING DATA IN SYSTEMS

In the example, I use the word *system*. In this context, I use the term to signify a (digital) information system. In this section, I will introduce the terminology that is related to how data is stored in systems[2]. Systems typically have one or more *data stores*: parts of the system that are concerned with storing data. Defining different areas for storing data can be useful for different reasons such as privacy and security (a data store with privacy-sensitive data requires more security measures)[3] or performance (data stores that are critical to the performance of a process may have extra computing power assigned to them).

Data is stored in systems in various ways. By far the most common way to structure data in systems is through *tables* such that each *row* of the table maps to a *record* (see also section 4.5). More precisely put: the *column headings* of the table match the names of the *fields* in the record, and the intersection of rows and columns (the "cells" of the table) contain the individual *data points*. Example 11 builds on the previous example and illustrates these definitions.

The diagram uses a model fragment to show how tables in a data store are defined. Modeling is an important part of DM. Data models – as well as other types of models – are explained in more detail in chapter 11.

Example 11. Storing data in tables
The lower part of the diagram is taken from the previous example and shows three person-records. However, this time each record also has a unique ID. The top part of the diagram shows the definition of what a typical record looks like. It shows that each record has four fields and also shows the data type. Last but not least, it shows whether a field is automatically generated or not.

The example has two tables that are related through a dependency. These links between tables make it possible to answer questions such as "show me all orders where the customer was born before 1960".

2 For the tech-savvy readers: in this chapter, I will mainly focus on data that is stored in *relational databases*. The terminology mostly fits with other structures (e.g. NoSQL [RW12]) as well.

3 A more extensive discussion of data security can be found in chapter 17.

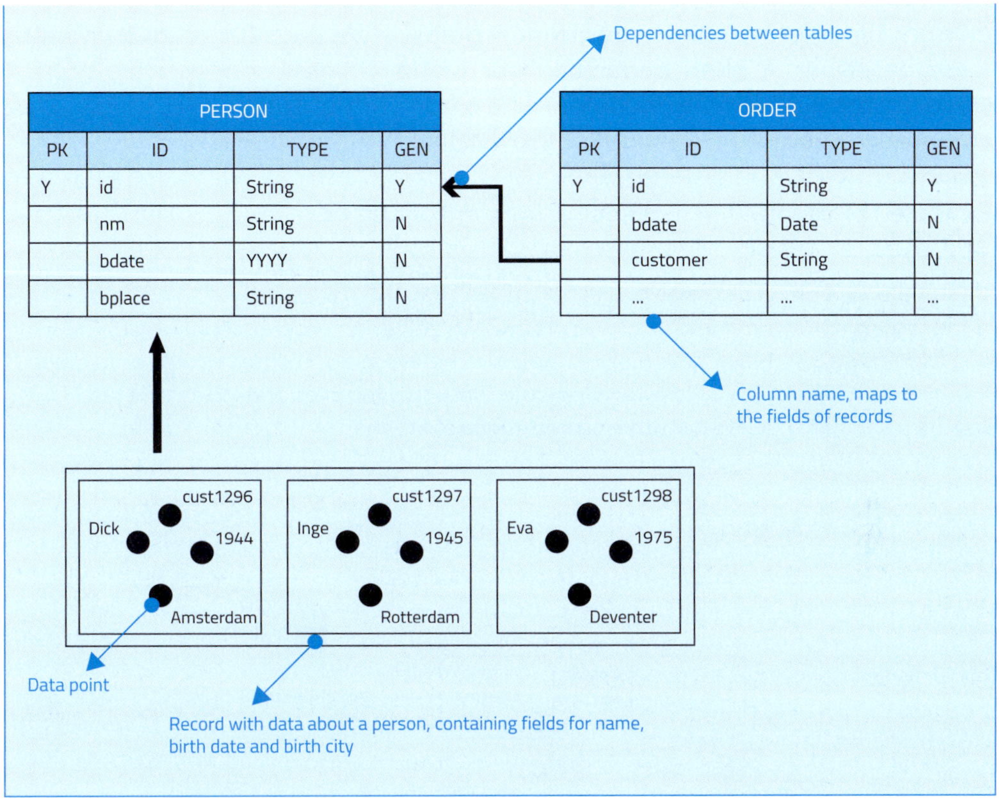

6.4 DATA IN PROCESSES

The previous section discussed data from an IT perspective. In this section, I will switch gears and discuss data from a business (process) perspective. This is a major shift to another level of abstraction: rather than considering exactly how data is structured and stored in systems, this perspective is all about understanding which *type* of data is required to make processes run.

Every process has inputs and outputs which may be data or something physical. These inputs and outputs can be described using *business concepts*[4]. Business concepts are defined as "the things that business stakeholders talk about". When talking about business concepts, you completely ignore how data is structured and stored in systems.

One of the things that is key for good data management is that these business concepts are clearly defined. This often leads to the creating of a (business)

4 Many good words are being used in literature, such as "business term", "business object" and "business concept". I went with the latter because this makes it easy to align with the notion of *conceptual data models* that is introduced in chapter 11.

glossary. The glossary is discussed in further details in chapters 10 and 28. By studying these definitions, it often becomes clear which business concepts are related. These relationships can be documented in a conceptual data model, which will be discussed in chapter 11 (see also section 4.4 on information/ data analysis).

Example 12 illustrates the main points from this discussion.

Example 12. Data in processes

The diagram shows a single invoicing process which has an order as input and an invoice as output. These business concepts are related to each other, as well as to other business concepts. The solid arrows indicate these relationships. The labels on these relationships give an indication of how to interpret them.

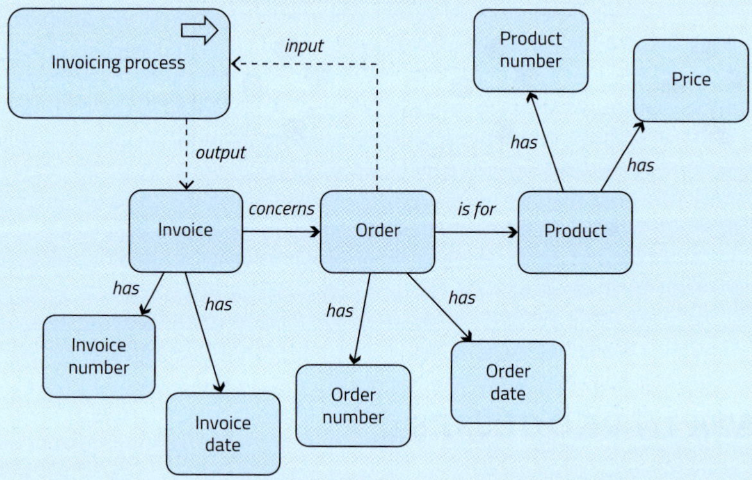

6.5 CONNECTING THE BUSINESS AND IT PERSPECTIVE

The questions that remain are: how are *business concepts* stored in systems? How are the business and IT perspectives connected? When *database systems* became popular in the 1970s, a technique was developed to analyze and "normalize" data structures in an effective manner: the relational model [Cod70, Cod79, Dat12] (see also section 4.5). Around the same time, various modeling approaches were developed to visualize what these data structures should look like. Chief among them was the *Entity Relationship Model* [Che76]. The main idea behind this type of modeling approach is to analyze how business concepts should be structured in such a way that they can efficiently be stored in database systems. This level of analysis straddles the business and IT perspectives. Models at this level of abstraction are often called *logical data models*, something which will be discussed in more detail in chapter 11.

What is relevant for purposes of this chapter is that business concepts and their relationships are transformed into a logical structure of *data elements*, which can be either *entities* or *attributes* of these entities. As with business concepts, entities can also be connected through relationships (hence the name Entity Relationship Diagram (ERD) that is frequently used). Example 13 explains this further.

Example 13. Data elements

The diagram shows four entities, each with several attributes. Even more, the entities are related and there is a verbalization attached to each relationship. Compare this diagram, which lists *data elements* to the diagram in example 12, which lists business concepts. The diagram with business concepts lists the things that business talks about. Apparently, *order line* is not something business stakeholders talk about, or else it would have shown up as a business concept. However, in order to store data in the system in an effective manner, the *order line* is needed as it stores the combination of *products* and required *quantity* for a specific *order*.

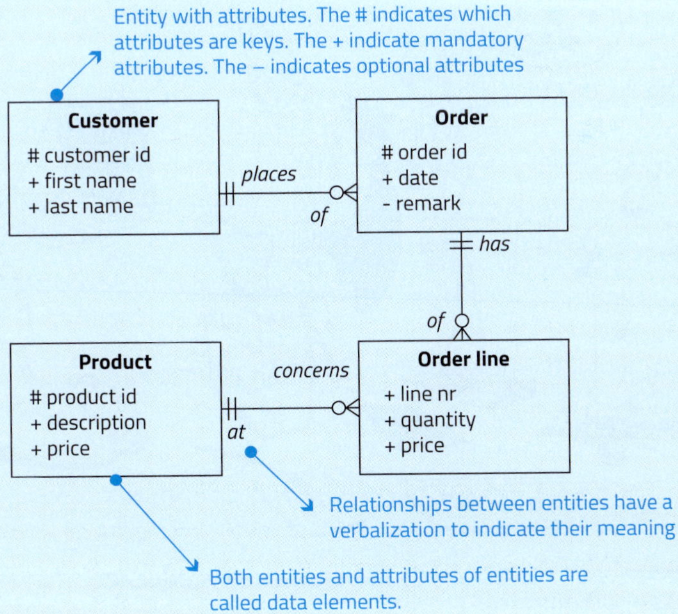

This small example, of course, doesn't show all the intricacies of going from the level of business concepts to the level of data elements. The purpose of the example is only to show that the relationship between business concepts and data elements is complicated at best[5]. Mapping business concepts to data elements is only one part of the analysis, though. The second part consists of mapping the data elements to tables and columns. This is a far more straightforward process: typically, entities map on tables and attributes map on columns[6].

6.6 OUTLOOK

The goal of this chapter was to discuss base terminology in the field of data management. Important terms are *business concept, data element, entity, attribute, table, column, field,* and *record*. In addition to introducing important terminology, this chapter expanded on definitions with examples and created links to other chapters. By doing so, this chapter provides a basis for a consistent and complete framework for data management that can be used in practice.

6.7 VISUAL SUMMARY

DATA MANAGEMENT PROFESSIONALS USE SPECIALIZED VOCABULARY

5 If you are interested in this process, look up a good reference work on normalization in database systems such as [Dat04].

6 There are exceptions to the rule and the underlying database technology should be taken into account. This is, however, beyond the scope of this discussion.

7 Data management: a definition

***Synopsis** - This book is about data management (DM). Roughly defined, DM is about managing data. In this chapter, I will introduce a definition of data management which is based on the standard reference for DM, the Data Management Body of Knowledge (DMBOK) [Hen17]: it is the capability that organizations have in order to manage data as an asset. In this chapter, I will also discuss the topics (sub capabilities) that are part of the field of DM.*

7.1 INTRODUCTION

In chapter 2, I discussed how many organizations see *data* as one of their most important *assets*. A loose definition of DM therefore is: the capability that the organizations have in order to manage data as an asset. While this gives a good idea of the *purpose* of DM, it doesn't say much about what it entails to *do* DM. The definition from the DMBOK gives a bit more insight [Hen17]:

> *Data management is the development, execution, and supervision of plans, policies, pro- grams and practices that deliver, control, protect and enhance the value of data and information throughout their lifecycles.*

In a recent article about *data strategy*, already mentioned in section 3.2, this was compared to the world of sports such as soccer or ice hockey [DD17]. The purpose of DM is twofold:

- **Grip on data** - This is what the first part of the DMBOK definition talks about. This part of the definition gives an overview of the types of activities that are involved in DM: the idea is to determine what we want to do with data (plans) and set up policies and practices (guard rails) to steer the organization in the right direction. This direction entails, on the one hand, the delivery of data to turn it into value but also how the controlling, protection, and enhancement of data assets can make that happen. A big task indeed.

- **Value creation through the use of data** - The latter part of the DMBOK definition suggests that the purpose of DM is to turn data into value throughout its lifecycle. After its creation it can be used and reused in processes until eventually the data gets archived or destroyed.

The analogy from example 14 clarifies these two perspectives further.

Example 14. The data river

In this example, I will compare water that flows through a river to data that flows through an organization. The example is illustrated below:

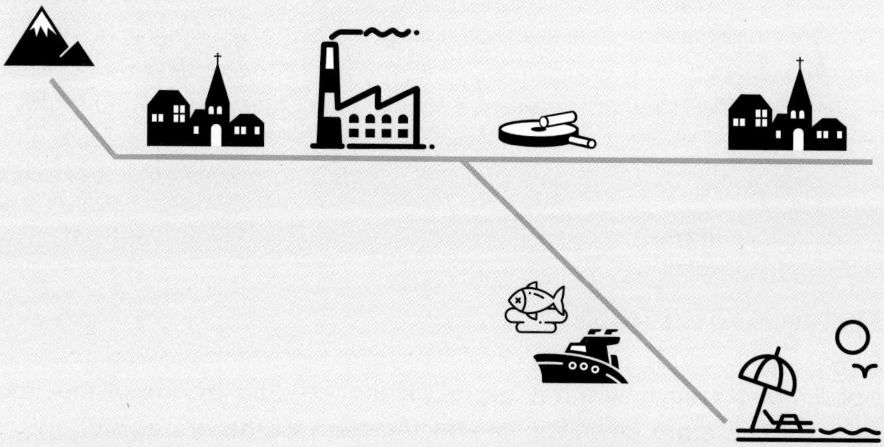

Consider a river that starts in the mountains. Assuming that high up the mountains there is little or no pollution, the water is expected to be clean. This is the equivalent of data that gets created in a process and stored in a system. As a rule, data tends to be correct/ or high quality here too.

When the water starts flowing down the mountain it passes a few villages where people use it for various purposes: drinking water, shower, and perhaps it is used by a local factory in its production process, polluting the water somewhat. As long as the factories are downstream, most of the upstream citizens won't mind too much. This is the equivalent of data that "moves" through the organization, from system to system, to be used in various processes. There is a high risk of introducing "pollution" in the form of problems with the data quality. Here too, if you are upstream then the problems with data quality from downstream won't affect you too much.

The water keeps flowing and a bit downstream there is a big dam and power plant. Here the speed of the flow of water is controlled and it is used to generate power for local towns. After the dam, the river forks. One of the streams flows into a water cleaning facility after which it continues on to the next village. The other end flows to what used to be a cool beach but is now deserted because of the polluted water. This is called *data movement* and techniques related to it stem from an area called *data integration*. The equivalent of the dam/ power plant is a system that controls the flow of data. After that comes the fork in the data river. In one data stream there is a data quality solution that cleanses the data making it usable for local users. In the other stream there is no such solution.

Last but not least, police boats have started patrolling the river to make sure no other illegal dumps of waste take place. The equivalent of the police boat is a governance structure where data management professionals check for misuse of data or prevent the introduction of errors into the data.

Note how, in both cases, the emphasis is on *flow*. Note also, that a local solution (e.g. cleaning water/ data) helps in one point but not in the other – it may be a better idea to fix issues upstream. Note also that in both cases, governance structures are in place to make sure things run smoothly. In both cases, the point is to make sure that certain things are in place ("grip") such that value can be derived from the asset, be it water or data. The comparison can probably be extended further but this gives a fair indication of how water and data are similar.

The analogy of the data river was invented by Luuk Spronk-van Lieshout and Emine Ozturk, two data stewards at PGGM – a Dutch pension provider.

In this book, I will take the point of view that DM is an organizational *capability*. The capability of the organization depends on certain resources (people, systems) being in place. These resources together make sure that there is enough grip on data and enable the organization to use data and get value from its data assets.

7.2 MANAGING THE LIFECYCLE OF DATA

Considering that DM is about balancing between "grip" and "value creation", a notion that needs careful exploration is the *data lifecycle*, which is the process of creation – use – archive/ destruction of data. Example 14 briefly hinted at it already: data is created somewhere (presumably in a process, leading to an update of systems) and is subsequently used in many places in the organization. The one point that is missing from this exploration is that data should eventually be archived/ destroyed. In many industries, there are regulations in place that stipulate when and how data should be archived/ destroyed.

What makes it hard to manage data along its lifecycle is that it never gets used up: you can make as many copies as you like without impacting the "original". These copies may float around the organization and there is no telling what they will be used for if you are not careful. In order to successfully manage data across its lifecycle, organizations should at least keep careful track of where data goes but also should have governance structures in place to make this happen.

7.3 DECONSTRUCTING DM

Balancing between the two goals of DM is a big task and many things have to be in place to make that happen. One of the strong points of the DMBOK that I have mentioned several times so far lies in the fact that it has broken down the field of DM into smaller pieces called *functional areas*. For my purposes, it makes more sense to call them *(sub) capabilities*, signifying that together they contribute to the overall DM capability. Figure 7.1 shows what this partitioning looks like. This visual is often called "the DMBOK wheel."

What the DMBOK does is take each of these areas and attempt to give a broad overview of what its objectives are, which activities are part of it, which inputs/outputs can be expected, and what type of tooling are required for support. It also describes good practices. The book is written by many authors, each taking care of a particular area. Unfortunately, this means that not all chapters are equally well aligned and that there are several small inconsistencies in the book. All in all, it is an impressive work which offers a great introduction to, and guidance for the field of DM.

Looking at the wheel, note how some areas appear to consist of two topics. For example at the bottom it says there is an area that covers *reference data management* and *master data management*. In this book, I will take a slightly different approach and make sure that – in the chapters to come – each chapter covers a single topic. I have taken a slightly different perspective that is mostly in line with the wheel. I have deliberately left out certain topics such as *database operations management* (which is, in my view, mostly an IT capability dealing with how data technology should be run and operated) and *document & content management* (which deals with unstructured data: whilst this is important, it is not the focus of this book). I will cover the topics listed in table 7.1. Example 15 illustrates that in practical settings, many of the DM capabilities are required *together* to achieve success.

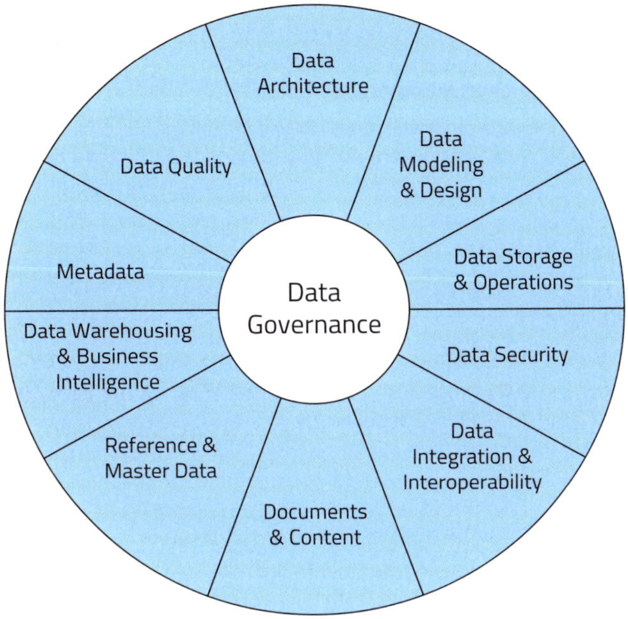

Figure 7.1 The DMBOK wheel

Example 15. Data management example
This example is based on a real-world case at a Dutch governmental agency in the mid-1990s. One of the challenges this organization faced was a large backlog of reports that had to be completed from a regulatory perspective (business intelligence, reporting). Creating these was far from easy because data was dispersed over many systems across the organization, and there was no standard environment (e.g. a data warehouse) to bring it together (integration). To make matters worse, different departments and professionals were in disagreement about key aspects such as data definitions, ownership of data, and quality of the data (governance, quality).

Ultimately this was, of course, resolved. It took years of debate and several reorganizations to solve these problems. One of the key success factors in the end was that the organization leveraged processes, systems, policies, and procedures that were already in place and extended them one step at a time.

Table 7.1 DM topics

Chapter	Topic	Short introduction
9	Data governance	Data governance is the enterprise discipline concerned with starting, managing, and sustaining the DM program. Key topics are accountability, decision-making, and supporting the program.
10	Metadata	Metadata is, loosely defined, data about data. Anything you know about your data is metadata. This is a foundational thing for all the other capabilities: it is crucial to know definition, location, etc. of your data.
11	Modeling	Modeling is all about "making sense of data through boxes and arrows". I have already shown some examples in chapter 6. This area is closely related to Architecture, and focuses on (data) modeling techniques.
12	Architecture	Architecture is about "fundamental properties of a system, and the principles guiding design and evolution" [ISO11]. The key challenge relates to getting to grips with the data landscape, in light of the overall architecture of the enterprise.
13	Integration	Integration deals with the movement of data from process to process, from system to system. The main contribution is a set of techniques and approaches to ensure that data flows through the organization so that it can be used where needed.
14	Reference data	Reference data is about "understanding data through data". This is the realm of code lists and hierarchies of codes. An example would be codes for geographical areas where the company does business, or codes that define the types of products the company offers.
15	Master data	Master data is concerned with creating a "golden copy" of data about key business concepts for the organization, by creating a single version of the truth. There are many ways to achieve this. This area ties in closely with Integration.
16	Quality	Data quality is about data that is fit for purpose. It is about setting requirements (a *norm)* and taking corrective action when data doesn't meet them. This may entail different quality attributes, such as correctness and completeness.
17	Security	Security is about a risk-based approach to protecting data assets. It is concerned with defining a data security policy, data classification (confidentiality, integrity, availability) and implementing measures to keep data safe according to this policy.
18	Business intelligence	Business intelligence (BI) is concerned with *reporting* what happened in the past and with data-driven predictions about the future (*analytics*).
19	Big data	Big data is still a major trend. It is about data sets with many data points (volume) that change rapidly (velocity) and often of various types (variability) [ZEDR+11]. Dealing with this type of data is completely different from traditional (little) data from a technical perspective, and opens the door to a whole range of new insights from a business perspective.
20	Technology	This area is not listed in the DMBOK wheel. I've included a chapter on this topic to give a focused, high-level overview of relevant developments in the area of data/ DM technology.

7.4 VISUAL SUMMARY

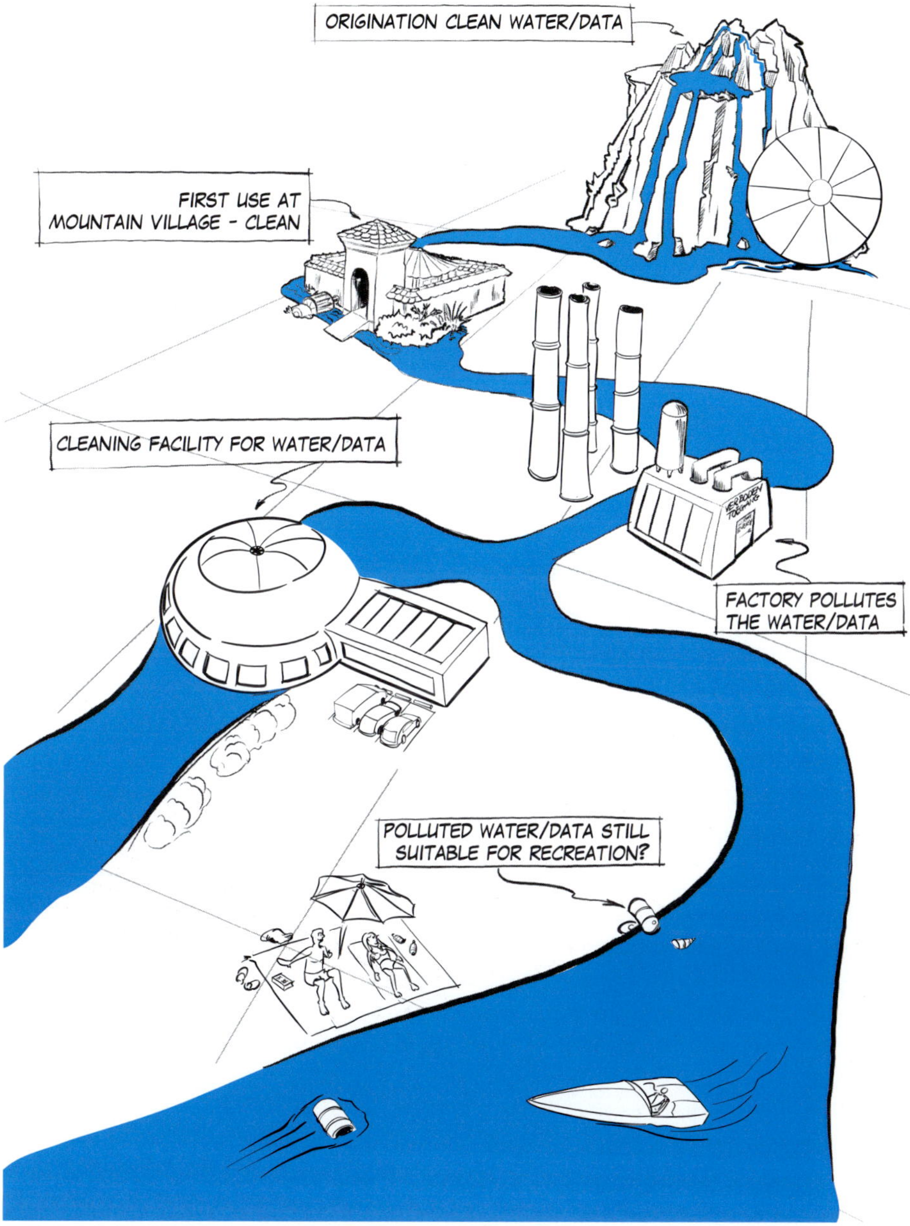

8 Types of data

Synopsis - In this chapter, I will give a high-level overview of the distinction between five different types of data: transaction data, master data, business intelligence data, reference data, and metadata. For each, I will also provide links to other chapters.

8.1 CLASSIFYING DATA

Most organizations have large amounts of data. This is a well-known fact and one of the reasons why DM is such an important topic. What's more, they typically also have many different *types* of data. Classifying data can be useful for different purposes. For example, it may help to decide on the approach to DM, or to decide what type of media it should be stored on. Many different classification schemes have been proposed. This is illustrated in example 16.

Example 16. Data classification

Data can be classified to indicate the type of use: descriptive data (describe a state of affairs in the real-world), diagnostic data (show how well something – e.g. a process – is functioning), predictive data (make predictions about a future state of affairs), or prescriptive data (define parameters to ensure that a certain process or system performs as desired).

Another way to classify data is to consider what it describes: i.e. geographic data (what a specific area looks like), weather data (past/ present/ future weather for a specific area), and people data (such as names, addresses, and relationships to other people).

While useful, these types of classifications are not the main topic of this chapter. Instead, I will look a level deeper and consider five related types of data. I already hinted at these in table 7.1 where I gave an overview of the DM topics that I will discuss in this book.

8.2 FIVE FUNDAMENTALLY DIFFERENT TYPES OF DATA

In this section, I will give a high-level overview of five fundamentally different data types and indicate in which chapter I will discuss these further. The point is not so much to give an extensive discussion here but to make the reader aware that there are different types of data before launching into detailed discussions about governance, architecture, etc. in future chapters. Figure 8.1 outlines the five types of data.

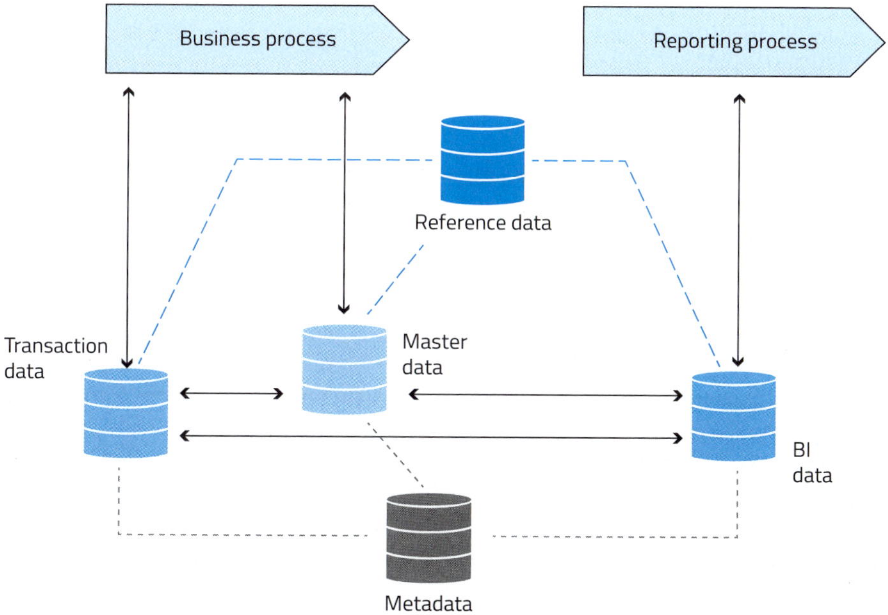

Figure 8.1 Five types of data

8.3 TRANSACTION DATA

The first type of data is *transaction data*. This type of data usually provides a description of some event that took place in the real-world, such as a purchase, a payment of an invoice. Assuming business goes well, you will typically have *many* records of this type that are created every day: every time someone makes a purchase or payment, for example. Also note that these records tend to be highly structured and you want to keep track of all of them so that you can later analyze how business is really going.

8.4 MASTER DATA

The second type of data is *master data*. To understand what this is about, consider a situation where you have half a dozen systems where you store data about your customers. One of your customers calls with a complaint. In which system are you going to look to find out what is going on? Even more, how are you going to deal with the situation where systems are in disagreement (one system says this customer has his office in Amsterdam, whereas the other claims it is in Rotterdam)?

To tackle challenges of this type, organizations typically want to organize a "golden record" or "single version of the truth" which *must* show what the organization believes to be true. There are many ways to implement this as we will see in chapter 15. This is both complex and costly and organizations typically only do this for their most important business concepts, such as *Party / Customer*, and *Product*. Typically, this type of data does not change all that often (ask yourself this: how often do people move or change their name? How often do you introduce new/ retire old products?). Example 17 shows that transaction data may also contain (references to) master data objects.

Example 17. Master data & transaction data
Suppose that you have just sold a product called *Cool8* to a customer whose name is *John Doe*. The record of this transaction will show such things as a time stamp, the actual store where the purchase was made, which employee was involved and so on.

From a master data perspective, two business concepts are of interest: the *customer* and the *product*. This customer may have made previous purchases at this store, or perhaps at other stores. If this customer purchases a lot of our *Cool8* product then this may be useful to know. If this customer used to purchase *Cool7* and has now switched to *Cool8* then it may also be useful to find out why and what that implies for future sales.

Now, suppose that John Doe *did*, in fact, make purchases at various stores but under different names (John Doe, John H. Doe, John Howard Doe). Can we reconcile this? Can we figure out with any degree of certainty who is who and which products were purchased when Mr. Doe calls with a complaint?

8.5 BUSINESS INTELLIGENCE DATA

Most transaction systems only hold the last version of data. This means that when a customer moves from A to B, then the fact that he used to live at A is often lost. Transaction systems typically also store data at the finest level of granularity. For (historic) reporting and (predictive) analytics this may not always be the best solution. This is where the category of *business intelligence* (BI) *data* comes into play. The idea is to create data sets of transaction data and master data. This data set contains historic data for timeline analysis. The data set is structured in such a way that data can be easily aggregated and summarized for reporting and analysis purposes. Chapter 18 will discuss BI in more detail. Example 18 illustrates this point.

Example 18. BI data

Suppose your company has a number of product lines: the *CoolX* line of products as well as several others. Even more, the company also offers various services to customers. Separate systems keep track of all purchases, services requests, payments and so on.

From a reporting perspective, management may be interested in questions such as: how many products of a certain type did we sell per store and how does that deviate from previous quarters? Do we retain our customers when they move? A similar line of reasoning applies to analytics questions such as: what would be a good service to cross-sell with our *CoolX* product to a specific group of customers? To be able to answer these questions, data must be consolidated. Often this means looking at the data from a historic perspective. Even more, individual records are less important in this situation than the patterns that are present in the data.

Whether this type of data is updated frequently depends on the architecture of your information systems landscape. In some cases, updates in data from transaction systems and master data systems are pushed to the BI environment once or twice a day. In other situations, this is done in (near) real-time.

8.6 REFERENCE DATA

The fourth type of data is *reference data* which is perhaps the most elusive of all. Reference data is used to make sense of other data, often through *codes* or *hierarchies of codes*. The idea is that by using a code, you give a very precise meaning to something that is potentially very complex. Example 19 gives two simple examples.

Example 19. Reference data
The simplest examples are look-up lists such as zip codes in the US, or a list of all valid country names. By comparing the zip code/ country that a customer tells us, we can immediately assess whether the data he provides is at least valid[a].

As a more complex example, consider the use of industry classification codes to label organizations you do business with. For example, code 440000 is all retail traders, 445000 is a child of 440000 and is the code for food and beverage stores. Code 445200 is a child of 445000 and signifies specialty food stores such as 445210 (meat markets), 445220 (fish and sea food markets), and 445290 (other specialty stores). Using such codes consistently allows us to easily find all *specialty food stores* by looking for all stores that are labelled 445000 or one of its sub-codes.

a The issue of data quality dimensions such as validity (is a value allowed according to some criteria) versus correctness (is it a true representation of the real world) is part of the discussion in chapter 16.

Reference data may seem like a really simple and straightforward concept yet in practice this is hardly the case. In chapter 14, I will discuss the relevant theory in more detail. Also note that reference data tends to be static. Using reference data in real-world situations will be discussed in more detail in the examples in part II in this book.

8.7 METADATA

The fifth and last type of data that I will discuss is *metadata*. Loosely defined, metadata is "data about data". Anything you can know about your data is metadata. Through metadata you can answer questions such as: what is the definition of "customer"? In which processes do we create customer data? How does customer data flow through our information systems? The list goes on and on. As an organization you can (and perhaps should) collect metadata about all other types of data. Having a good set of metadata available is foundational for managing and governing your data. Metadata is discussed in more detail in chapter 10.

8.8 VISUAL SUMMARY

9 Data governance

Synopsis *- In this chapter, I introduce the topic of data governance. Data governance is the capability that deals with accountability for data. I will first position data governance in relation to (other) data management (activities). Then I will provide an overview of key data governance themes based on the Data Management Body of Knowledge (DMBOK) [Hen17]. Last but not least, I will give an overview of a modern approach to data governance based on three key roles: data owners, data users, and data stewards.*

9.1 INTRODUCTION

The word *governance*, or its associated verb *to govern*, has many definitions and interpretations, depending on the context in which it is used. Many people seem to associate this word with (the use of) power; with laying down and enforcing the law. This view is indeed close to the Merriam-Webster Dictionary definition which uses phrases such as "to exercise continuous sovereign authority over" and "to control, direct, or strongly influence the actions and conduct of". The DMBOK defines data governance as follows [Hen17]:

> *Data governance is defined as the exercise of authority and control (planning, monitoring, and enforcement) over the management of data assets.*

This definition screams a command-and-control, top-down approach to governance: make plans, define rules, implement, enforce, and punish when the rules are not followed. This isn't the only way to implement data governance, though. In this chapter, I will first show how to position data governance in relation to data management. I will then follow-up with a discussion of the data governance activities as listed in the DMBOK and a discussion of a modern approach to data governance through *data stewards*, *data owners*, and *data users*. I will end the chapter with a brief discussion of the relationship between data governance and other governance processes that may be followed in the organization.

9.2 DATA GOVERNANCE AND DATA MANAGEMENT

Looking closely at the definition of data governance from the DMBOK, it becomes clear that there is a relationship between *data governance* (DG) and *data management* (DM). This relationship – also pointed out by John Ladley in [Lad12] – is highlighted in figure 9.1 which was taken from the DMBOK. The idea is straightforward and not unlike the *separation of powers* in modern day (western) politics[1]: separate decision-making and oversight (DG) from the actual execution of DM activities. In my view, this has several implications.

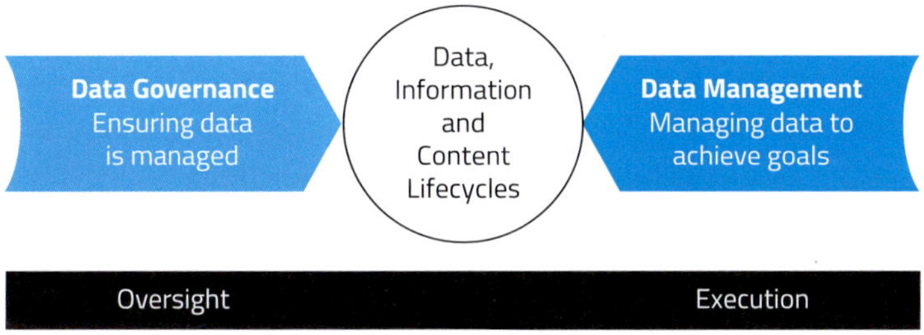

Figure 9.1 Data Governance & Data Management (Taken from [Hen17])

First of all, DG is not so much about governing *data* (which are innate) but more about governing the *people* who handle data. In other words, it is about deciding what people can and can't do with data, as well as ensuring that there are guard rails in place to make that happen. Whether this happens in a top-down fashion (define the policy, analyze implications, implement the policy) or in a bottom-up fashion (capture good practices from across the organization in a policy and arrange for sign-off) is a whole different matter.

A second implication deals with the type of decisions to be made: strategic, tactical, and operational. Example 20 illustrates different types of DG decisions that organizations deal with.

Example 20. Data governance decisions

Strategic decisions

Setting up a data strategy is a prime example of a strategic decision. This entails questions such as: how and where do we want to create value with data? How does our business model evolve when we leverage data as a key asset? Are we going to let business units control their own data, or are we trying to achieve synergies between

1 https://en.wikipedia.org/wiki/Separation_of_powers, last checked; 12 June 2019.

business units? Another example is the development of a data management strategy to complement the data strategy. Relevant questions here are: how good should our data management capability be? Are we going to centralize or decentralize certain data management functions?

Tactical decisions
Setting up governance structures, appointing people in DM/ DG roles, and approving policies are good examples of tactical decisions. These types of decisions bridge the gap between the strategic and operational levels.

Operational decisions
Approval of definitions of business concepts, dealing with conflicting definitions or data quality requirements, and sign-off on data quality improvement initiatives are good examples of operational decisions. The focus here is on decision-making about the operational data management activities.

Let's examine these examples from the perspective of the DMBOK wheel as shown in figure 7.1. There is a reason that DG is in the center of the wheel: decision-making is something that is required for all capabilities in the wheel.

9.3 DATA GOVERNANCE ACTIVITIES IN DMBOK

If DG is all about decision-making then the question is: what do we make decisions *about*? The previous example gave some suggestions. To give a more formal answer I will briefly discuss several governance topics that are listed by the DMBOK. This is by no means a complete summary of the DMBOK, nor is it intended to be. Instead, I am trying to give a broad enough overview to provide you with an understanding of what DG is all about.

One of the key topics is to define the *organizational structure* for DG in the form of steering committees, boards, and different roles in the organization. This is closely related to the *operating model type*, which helps to decide which activities are carried out and where. The main models that are listed are: centralized DG, replicating the DG structure across business units with little central coordination, and a federated approach to DG where there is a distribution of decision-making between business units on the one hand, and a central body on the other.

The DMBOK also advocates an approach to governance that uses *data stewardship* as a cornerstone. Data stewardship is defined as "a label to describe accountability and responsibility for data and processes that ensure effective control of data assets". This definition is abstract. A more informal definition would be: data stewards are those people who (hands-on) take care of data assets across the enterprise and therefore are assigned accountability and responsibility for those data assets.

The last topic that is mentioned is *policy-making*. Policies codify general principles and rules with respect to the use of data assets. Typically, this includes such things as formal roles and responsibilities[2], procedures for handling data quality issues, and rules for data classification.

Data governance is a big topic that requires many roles across the organization to collaborate. The DMBOK lists several roles that contribute to effective DG, including business executives, data owners/ stewards, architects, compliance teams, other governance bodies, and data professionals. How to set this up properly is discussed in several chapters in part II of this book.

9.4 A MODERN APPROACH TO DATA GOVERNANCE

The modern approach to data governance is based on three roles and is illustrated in figure 9.2. These roles are as follows:

- **Data owner** - The data owner is the person who is ultimately accountable for a data set. The data owner ensures that data is fit for the purpose of the people who want to use it. As a rule of thumb, data ownership lies where data is created, as this is the only place where its correctness can be verified. This is illustrated in example 21.
- **Data user** - The data user is the person who wants to use/ uses data. Typically, the data user negotiates with the data owner about data access. Common topics are: what (types of) data does the user wish to use? What are data definitions? What are data quality requirements?
- **Data steward** - The data steward is the person with hands-on responsibility for managing the data. Data stewards tend to have a mixed business/ IT background[3]. Both the data owner and the data user tend to have management positions. Therefore, people in these roles tend to be supported by data stewards, as shown in figure 9.2.

2 Typically in the form of a RACI matrix. See e.g. https://en.wikipedia.org/wiki/Responsibility_assignment_matrix. Last checked: 12 June 2019.

3 It is hard to find people with this dual background. As an alternative, many organizations work with stewardship duos: a business data steward paired to an IT data steward.

> **Example 21. Assigning data ownership**
> Suppose we are looking for the data owner for the "product" business concept in a company that produces electronics. New products tend to be defined by the Product Development Department. The decision to actually move forward in launching new products together with the opinion of other departments (e.g. Marketing) are of course considered, but ultimately the accountability for new products lies with this department. Therefore, someone in this department should also be designated the data owner role for the "product" business concept.

Note that this approach to data governance addresses only one piece of the puzzle: it deals with the accountability of data assets but does not address the overarching issues such as policymaking and alignment. As such, this approach should always be complemented by other approaches to achieve a sufficient level of data governance maturity.

Figure 9.2 illustrates this way of thinking. The top of the diagram is all about coordination between different organizational roles. This is where the actual governance activities happen: data owners and data users, supported by data stewards, negotiate the use of data. The bottom part of the diagram signifies the storage and flow of data in such a way that the agreement is met.

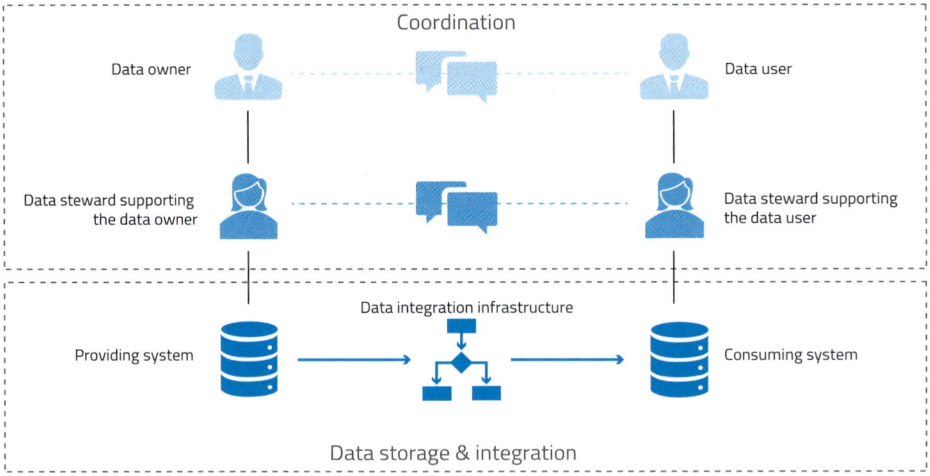

Figure 9.2 Data governance model

Several questions remain, such as: how do you find good data owners and data stewards? How do they perform their role effectively? The theme here is *non-invasive data governance* which will be explained in more detail in part II – in chapter 25 – of this book.

9.5 POSITION OF DATA GOVERNANCE

I will close this chapter with a brief discussion of the position of data governance in the organization, especially in relation to other governance processes in the organization. I often hear arguments along the lines of "Data resides in our systems, so data must be an IT thing. As a consequence, data governance should fall under the jurisdiction of IT governance". There is some merit to this position but only if you believe that data/ data management is an IT topic. I tend to disagree.

As explained in this book, I believe *data* to be a topic of its own and one that should not be positioned as yet another IT topic. Consider once more figure 9.2. The top layer of this diagram shows governance activities from a data perspective, using the ownership/ stewardship model. This is intended to govern the data *in* the systems, not the systems themselves. This would be the realm of IT governance which has its own models and frameworks for governance, most notably COBIT (see e.g. [ISA12]). As processes, data, and systems are all important, so are their governance activities and I believe that they should co-exist. Governance activities should complement each other and should therefore be coordinated. The way this works best really depends on the local setting and culture of the organization: there is no single optimum answer to that problem.

9.6 VISUAL SUMMARY

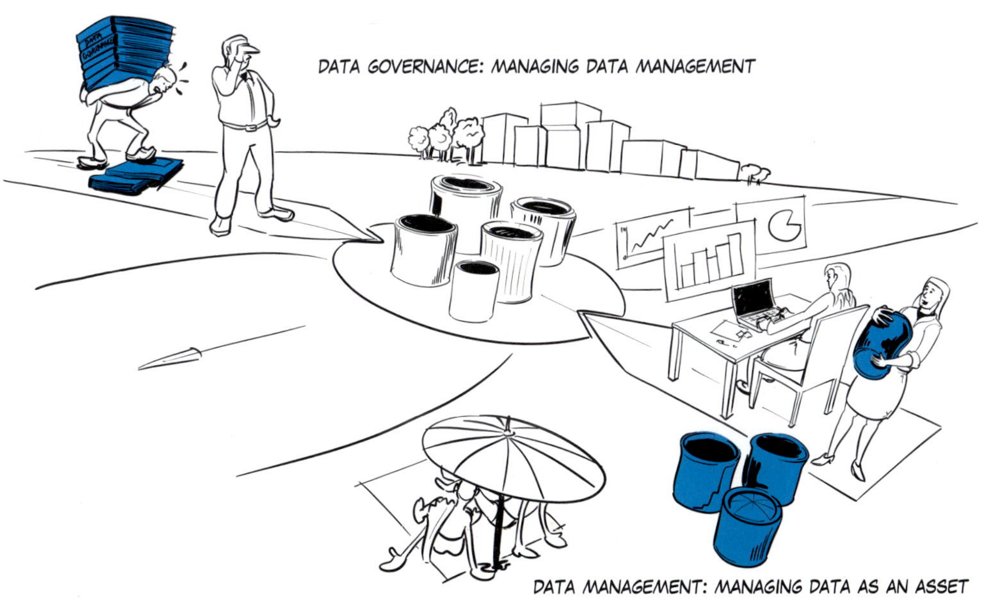

10 Metadata

***Synopsis** - Metadata is defined as "data about data". In this chapter, I will discuss three types of metadata: business, technical, and operational metadata. I will also show that metadata is foundational for all data management/ data governance activities. Last but not least, I will offer some theoretical considerations on how to set up a metadata repository.*

Managing and governing data requires that you have a good understanding of your data. It helps to know *what* data you are working with, what it means, where to find it and so on. This is the realm of *metadata*. Collecting metadata is not a goal in and of itself. It is, however, foundational for most other data management activities [Pom15, Hen17]. In this chapter, I will discuss the different types of metadata first. I will then, mainly through short examples, make the link with data governance and other data management activities. I will finish with a short discussion about using metadata repositories.

10.1 TYPES OF METADATA

There are many things you can or should want to know about your data. How you divide your metadata in logical groups doesn't really matter in practice. Grouping metadata in categories makes it easier to talk about it and helps to set up effective *metadata repositories*. I will follow the same structure as the DMBOK.

10.1.1 Business metadata

The first group of metadata is *business metadata*. The DMBOK states that "Business metadata focuses largely on the content and condition of the data and includes details related to data governance". In my view, this includes everything you want to know about data from a business perspective. Typically, this type of metadata is described at the level of business concepts (See section 6.4).

Names are important. The *names* of a business concept give us a good idea of what data is about in a general sense. It may seem really straightforward and easy but you would be surprised how much debate there can be about names of business concepts (see example 22).

Example 22. Names of business concepts
A few years ago, I did an assignment at a car lease company. Simplifying the example slightly, the lease was paid for by companies (e.g. consultancy firms) and the employees of these companies (e.g. consultants) drove the vehicles. We had to deal with a large data set about the companies that paid the bills. One department demanded that the name of the business concept was *customer*, whereas the other stated that the person driving the car was the customer, so a better name would be the *counter party*. A good discussion about definitions and how to distinguish between different business concepts resolved the conflict between these two departments.

Closely related to names are *business definitions*. Business definitions are pieces of natural language that business stakeholders can understand, intended to give a precise and unambiguous meaning to a business concept. In the assignment from example 22, good definitions helped to disambiguate between different business concepts and, as a consequence, to manage data sets effectively.

Closely related to business definitions are *business rules*. Business rules describe, in a way that business stakeholders can understand, what is or isn't allowed with business concepts, such as illustrated in example 23.

Example 23. Business rule
Building on the definitions of business concepts that were discussed in example 22, the lease company could issue a rule that said, *"No counter party may lease more than 25 vehicles without approval from the head of sales"*.

Typically, these business rules translate to technical measures in information systems to automatically ensure that rules are followed.

The last type of business metadata discussed here is closely related to data governance: *ownership and stewardship* are important things to know about your data. As an owner/ steward you are probably aware of your responsibilities but it would be good for your colleagues to also find out about that fact. This will help to quickly locate the right people in case of, for example, issues with data quality.

10.1.2 Technical metadata

The second group of metadata is *technical metadata*. The DMBOK states that "Technical metadata provides information about the technical details of data, the systems that store data, and the processes that move it within and between systems". While business metadata is about the business context of data, this group of metadata focuses on how it is stored in and flows between systems. Typically, this addresses another group of stakeholders, such as system operators, architects and system analysts. Technical metadata often relates to *data elements* (See section 6.4).

At this level too, names are important. This time the naming discussion pertains to the *database tables* and *column names* (See example 11). These names are often cryptic and short, such as *PRSN* for a data element *Person*, or *LOC* for *Location*. These cryptic and, above all, short names stem from the time that *storage* of data was expensive in which case shortening names – even at the expense of readability – had value. This is no longer a real issue but the habit stuck with database designers.

Data rarely stays within one system. As discussed in example 14, it behaves more like a river and flows from process to process, from system to system. The way this is implemented is also technical metadata. Leaving the technical details until chapter 13, good examples of technical metadata are ETL[1] job details and source-to-target mappings[2] which illustrate how data is transformed from source systems to target systems in a data flow. The name that is commonly used is *lineage*, which signifies how data moves through an information systems landscape. This is illustrated in example 24.

10.1.3 Operational metadata

The last group of metadata is *operational metadata* which, according to the DMBOK "describes the details of the processing and accessing of data". This type of metadata pertains to what actually happened to individual records and data points.

Consider again the flow of data. Let's say that this happens in batches (twice per day). When a batch job completes, details about the execution are typically stored in *log files* which provide important clues to what happened to the data. Along the same lines, *processing errors* are also logged which are useful for fixing data quality problems. The list of examples is nearly endless. This is largely a technical discipline

1 ETL stands for Extract, Transform, and Load. It is a technique that is used to move data from one system to another. More details will follow in chapter 13.

2 A source-to-target mapping shows how data structures in a *source system* map on data structures in a *target system*, such that data can be slotted in the right place when it is transported from source to target.

and very closely related to the field of IT operations. If you are interested in a good overview, see [Los13, chapter 9].

Example 24. Lineage

This example revolves around the business concept *Debt Service Coverage Ratio* which is a financial term that gives an indication of how well a company can fulfill its financial obligations. This ratio is calculated by dividing *Net Operating Income* by *Total Debt Service* (note: this would be a good business definition, which is business metadata). This *Total Debt Service* consists of a *Principal Payment* component and an *Interest Payment* component. The diagram shows where data associated with each business concept is stored. The diagram shows that *S5* needs data from all the other systems. In data management terminology, this would mean that all the flows originating at the other systems combined form the lineage of *Debt Service Coverage Ratio*.

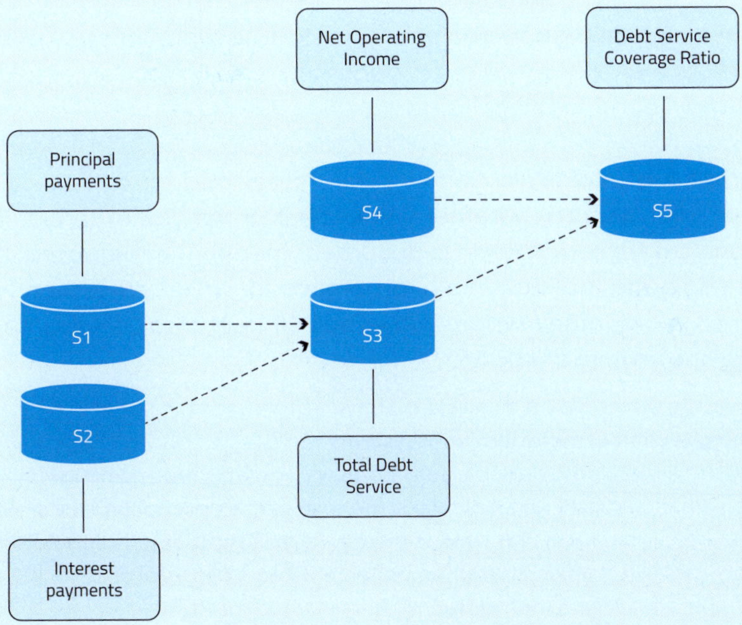

10.2 METADATA IS THE FOUNDATION

In my view, metadata is *foundational* for all data management and data governance activities. You need to know "things" about the asset you are managing or governing. To see why, consider the following questions:

- How do you want to manage customer data if you have no shared and approved definition of the *Customer* business concept?

- How do you want to reconcile two data sets about *Customer* when there is no shared definition about this business concept, nor do we know in which systems these data sets reside?
- If data moves from system to system to system before it is used on a report, how can you address data quality challenges with this report if you don't know anything about the *lineage* of associated data?

Metadata is required to solve all these problems. Whether this metadata should be collected, stored, and managed in a central repository, however, is a whole different question.

10.3 METADATA REPOSITORIES

In this final section, I will switch gears and discuss metadata repositories: where and how do you store your metadata. I will avoid discussing specific vendors or solutions and focus on the main considerations instead.

So far, I have shown that metadata comes in all shapes and forms. You already have metadata at your disposal, whether you know it or not. For example, if you have a list of definitions tucked away in a document then that is metadata. If you have an internal wiki page that lists who is responsible for which data, then that is metadata too. Even more, many systems have built-in (technical) metadata that you can access as shown in example 25.

Example 25. Getting technical metadata from systems
This example uses the MySQL database platform[3]. The first line asks the system to DESCRIBE a table with the name Party. Below this line follows the description which says that there is a field called pid (party id) which uniquely identifies parties, that there are various mandatory (not NULL) fields, and some optional (NULL is allowed) fields. This description of a table is technical metadata.

```
mysql> DESCRIBE Party;
+---------+-------------+------+-----+---------+---------------+
| Field   | Type        | Null | Key | Default | Extra         |
+---------+-------------+------+-----+---------+---------------+
| pid     | int         | NO   | YES |         | AUTOINCREMENT |
| fname   | varchar(20) | NO   |     | NULL    |               |
| lname   | varchar(20) | NO   |     | NULL    |               |
| seks    | char(1)     | YES  |     | NULL    |               |
| bdate   | date        | YES  |     | NULL    |               |
+---------+-------------+------+-----+---------+---------------+
```

3 http://www.mysql.com

The metadata is there, whether you know it or not. This means that, from a DM perspective, you have to answer the question: what type of metadata do I want to collect and manage in a central repository? To answer that question, you have to dig deeper and look into more detailed questions pertaining to how data is used across the enterprise such as: do we want to standardize the names of business concepts across the enterprise? If so, then it makes sense to build a centralized business glossary which lists terms and definitions. If not, then perhaps a decentralized or federated approach makes more sense.

A second consideration concerns the degree of autonomy that IT teams have. The question is similar as above: do all of our IT teams have full autonomy, or do they have to use the same platforms and comply with the same standards? If there is a high degree of standardization, then you could argue the case for building a central repository for your technical metadata. If not, then the investment may simply be too big.

Of course, legislation may also be a factor to consider. Data is becoming a more and more important asset for organizations. In some cases, poor ethical choices, or poor data handling has had a less than desirable impact on society. A breach of the systems of a company may lead to private data about customers being exposed. Using data that had been collected for one purpose could be used for completely different purposes which may put customers in a tight spot. Insurance companies buying access to health related data (How often do you work out? What did you eat? How much alcohol do you typically consume?) to determine your insurance rates are a good example. These concerns have caused lawmakers to create new legislation which is intended to protect the general public from mishandling data.

Quite often, legislation comes with the necessity to collect specific metadata, enabling governing bodies to verify compliance. As an example, SolvencyII-legislation[4] requires that companies can quickly produce an overview of lineage of data. Having to comply with this type of legislation may be a determining factor in deciding how you will collect and manage your metadata and what type of tools you will want to choose.

To finish this discussion about metadata and associated tooling, I will give a short overview of different *types* of metadata tools in table 10.1, as well as a small warning. The warning is this: a fool with a tool is still a fool but makes disaster faster. The point being: selecting a great tool doesn't solve your problems. Using it well does!

4 See e.g. https://en.wikipedia.org/wiki/Solvency_II_Directive_2009, last checked: 15 June 2019.

Table 10.1 Metadata repository examples

Tool type	Description
Business glossary	Gives an overview of business concepts and their definitions. Most tools in this category also list other aspects such as ownership and stewardship metadata.
Data dictionary	Similar to a business glossary but lists data elements rather than business concepts. Data dictionaries tend to also include more technical details about data.
Data catalog	Lists business concepts and/or data elements as well as their definitions but also provides access to the underlying data sets.
Database systems	Gives an overview of the structure of data as stored in the system. Example 25 illustrates this type of metadata.
Reference data repository	Reference data explains how certain data should be interpreted (see section 8.6 and chapter 14). As such it is often seen as a form of metadata too.
Data quality dashboards	An indication of the quality of a data set says something about the data under consideration. This too is sometimes seen as a form of metadata.

■ 10.4 VISUAL SUMMARY

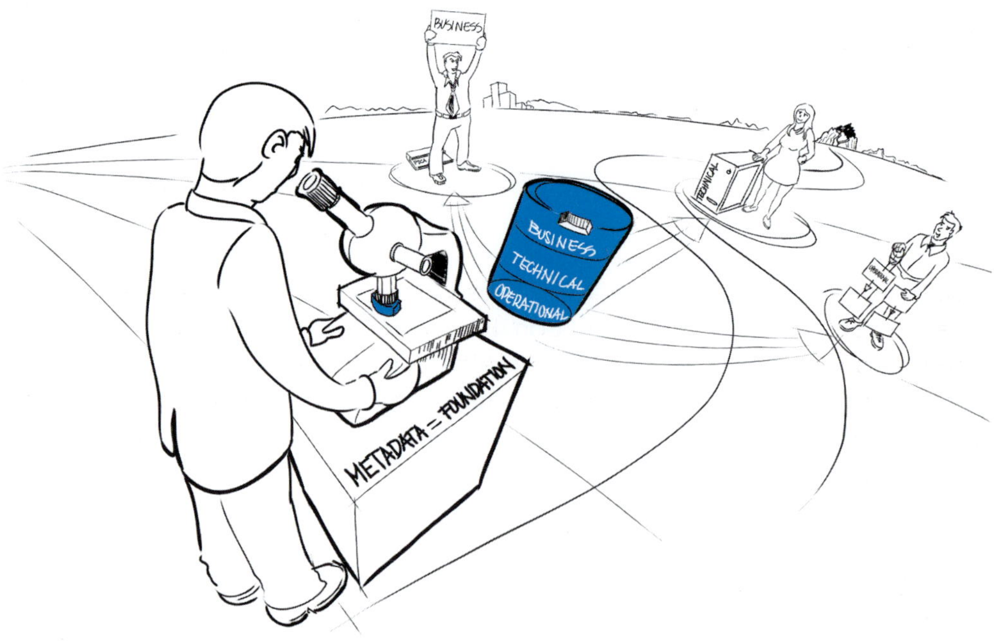

11 Modeling

Synopsis *- Modeling is a an important aspect of data management (DM). It is the practice (and, in my opinion, the science and art) of making sense of the world through "boxes and arrows". This can be done at different levels of abstraction, and using different modeling languages. The purpose of this chapter is to give a high-level overview of the field of data modeling and is not intended as a tutorial. Chapter 12 will use some of the insights presented in this chapter.*

I will start this exploration with important research that was done in the 1990s and ultimately led to the publication of the FRISCO report [FHL+98]. Ignoring some of the finer points of this report, the main idea is that *actors* (potentially with different *concerns*) all observe some *domain* (sometimes called: Universe of Discourse or UoD for short). These actors all have a (mental) model of what is going on in this UoD. In order to get a *shared* understanding of this UoD, they use *model representations*, often in the form of "boxes and arrows".

While the distinction between *model* and *model representation* is important from a theoretical perspective, I will use the two interchangeably in this book. I will first discuss the scope and different abstraction levels for models. Then I will give a short overview of different modeling languages. I will finish this chapter with a discussion of data modeling in relation to other DM capabilities such as metadata management and data governance.

11.1 SCOPE

When starting to create a model, the first question that needs to be answered is: what is the *scope* of the modeling effort? There are three dimensions to scope: (1) which part of the organization are we going to model? For example, do we focus on everything that has to do with the Marketing department? (2) What is the time scope? For example, do we create a model of the current situation, or some desired future situation? (3) Are we focusing on data only, or are we also considering other aspects such as process, departments, and systems?

The choice of scope typically depends on the type of problem that you are trying to solve. The last aspect largely determines which type of modeling language you are going to use (section 11.3). In the upcoming section on abstraction levels, the focus is on models that only cover the data aspect.

11.2 ABSTRACTION LEVELS

Different abstraction levels are used for data modeling. I have briefly touched upon this discussion already in chapter 6. I will mainly follow the DMBOK [Hen17]:

- **Conceptual level** - This level of abstraction focuses purely on understanding a specific UoD. In technical terms, the conceptual level is "implementation independent". Typically, organizations create (1) a *subject area model* and (2) each subject area is fleshed out in more detail in a *conceptual data model*, consisting of business concepts and their relationships.
- **Logical level** - This level deals with the question of how data is to be structured so that it becomes suitable for storage in information systems, or for flowing between information systems. The process typically follows the lines of *normalization*[1]. Models at this level are typically created either (a) for the entire enterprise, trying to get a sound understanding what the ideal-world structure of data should be, or (b) for specific information systems, trying to understand how data is structured in a specific system. The two need not be the same.
- **Physical level** - This level goes beyond structuring data and considers how data is going to be stored or transmitted between systems. This takes the technology to be used under consideration. At this level you typically consider which data types to use, where optimizations through the use of indexes are used etc.

This way of thinking is illustrated in example 26. The modeling languages/ notations are explained in section 11.3.

1 See e.g. [Dat04] or https://en.wikipedia.org/wiki/Database_normalization (last checked: 16 June 2019) for more details about normalization

Example 26. Abstraction levels

The diagrams below show, in order, a conceptual, enterprise logical, system logical, and physical data model. The top model shows four business concepts and relationships between them. The label on the relationship is added to help the reader understand its meaning.

The second diagram is an enterprise logical data model and shows how we believe that data should be structured. It shows that *Employee*, *Organization*, and *Department* are data elements with several attributes attached and that *Employee* is specialized into two subtypes: *Contractor* and *Internal staff.*

The third diagram is the system logical data model and shows how the data will actually be stored in an information system. Note that in this case, the two subtypes are gone. Instead there has been a choice to add an *Employee type*. This adds flexibility to the model because we can add types when we have to.

The last diagram is the physical data model. Here we've indicated primary keys, foreign keys, data types and all sorts of other technical details required to build the data model in a database system.

Conceptual data model

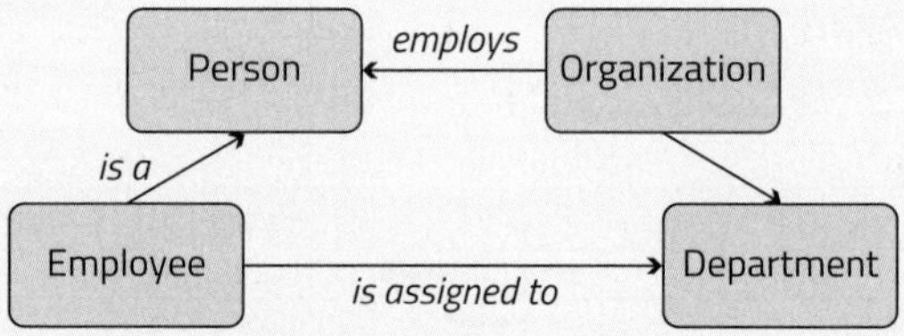

Enterprise logical data model

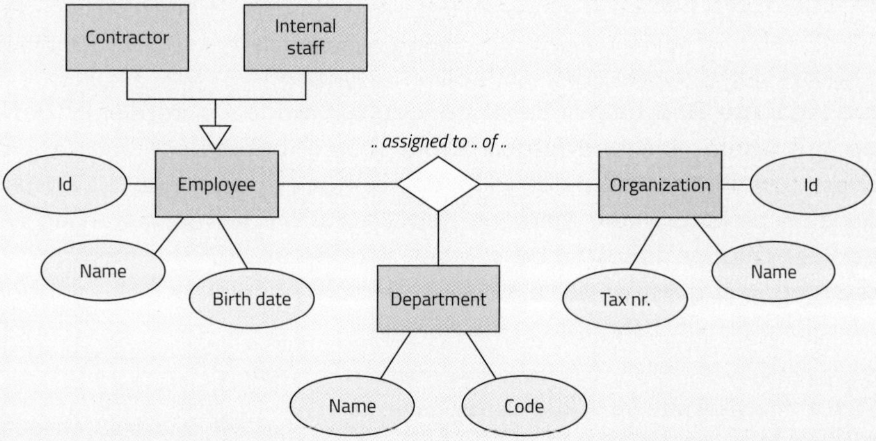

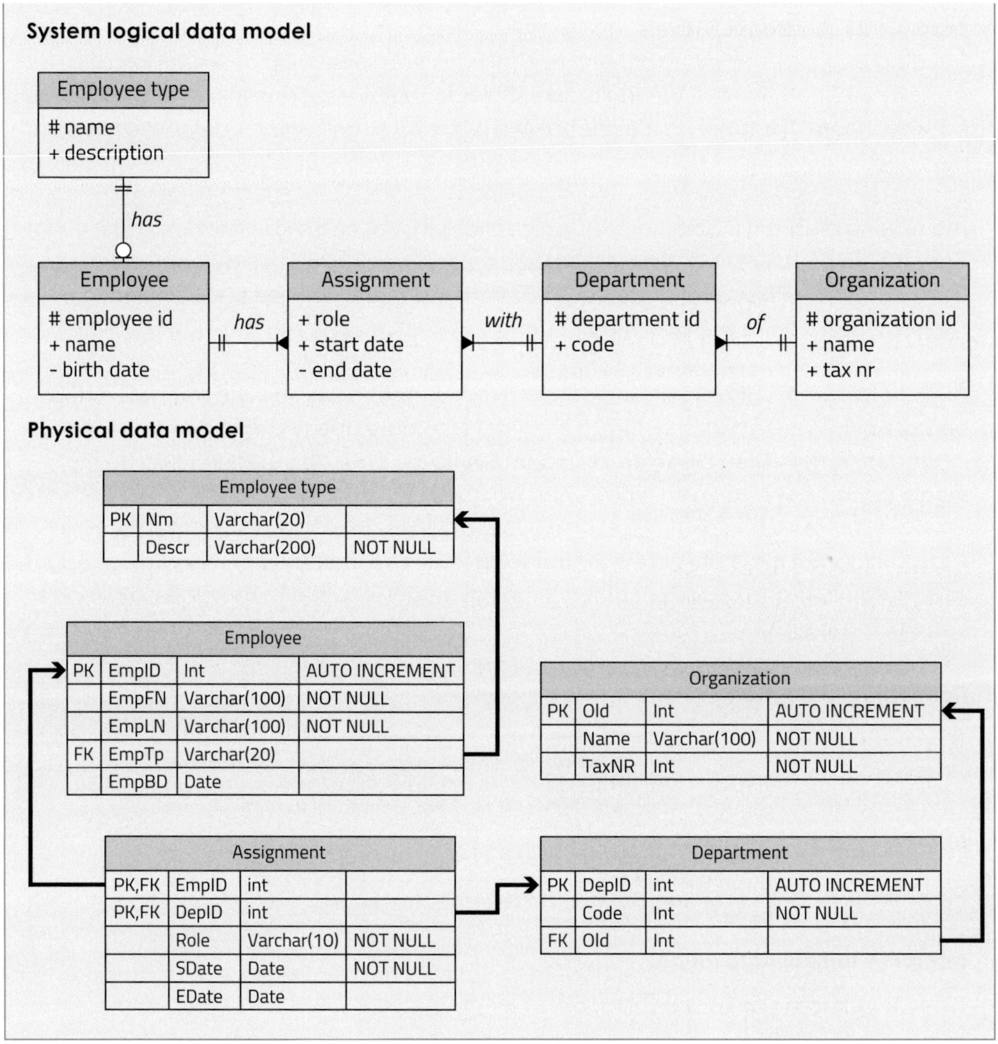

The practical use and relevance of conceptual models is frequently debated. In situations where time and resources are scarce, people ask questions about usefulness, contribution to project goals, and overall added value. This is especially true for agile projects where there is a heavy focus on delivering working systems (and documentation tends to be scarce). It appears that the more technical-focused models (e.g. the *physical* models) are more popular. See also sidebar 4 for considerations about (conceptual) modeling.

Sidebar 4. Interview with Frank Harmsen (summer 2019)

The recognition of the importance and relevance of conceptual models is a cyclic phenomenon; every now and then, larger organizations invest in conceptual modeling, stress the importance of it, and then, gradually, let it slip or even forget why it is relevant in the first place (the well- known "corporate amnesia"). In our view [at PNA], a model is not a model when the concepts are not defined. We use examples from real life to develop and test definitions and semantics. The downside of this is, that it is often time consuming. From a theoretical perspective it is well known that the time spent on conceptual modeling in the early stages of a project is a splendid investment but the awareness of this is, at least in practice, not universal.

In the early days of agile software development, for instance, many teams just started to code, which might work in very small projects but fails in the more serious stuff. In the larger organizations where I work, conceptual modeling therefore definitely has a position, and yes, sometimes attempts are made to erode this position due to all kinds of reasons (ignorance and time pressure probably being the most important ones). Obviously, conceptual models have big advantages to make projects more controllable, project results more "testable", get more involvement and commitment from users and other non-technical staff, avoid misunderstandings, and so forth. An example where conceptual modeling really made the difference was a project in health care with an exceptionally high amount of stakeholders, each having a different perception of the main concepts of the "universe of discourse". An agile project, with a "quick and dirty" approach with some technical models failed dramatically, because each stakeholder group was actually quite dissatisfied with the various releases of the prototypes. The project started all over again and this time with the development of some simple but solid conceptual models; they induced a lot of discussion among the stakeholders but the costs of this discussion were way less than the benefits of the proper modeling approach: a project that was delivered on time and within budget, with a product that was accepted by everyone.

Frank Harmsen is managing director at PNA *and professor at Maastricht University.*

11.3 MODELING LANGUAGES

There have been many debates about what type of modeling language works best for (data) modeling. One might go as far as to say that data professionals have fought "holy wars" about this topic. We all have our preferences, I suppose. Here, I have chosen to include three types of modeling approaches that I come across regularly: fact-based modeling with *Object Role Modeling* (ORM2), entity relationship modeling (ERD), and architecture modeling with *ArchiMate*[2].

11.3.1 Fact-based modeling

Fact-based modeling is an approach to (data) modeling where observations about some UoD are seen as *facts*. By careful analysis of these facts, the modeler

2 I have deliberately not included the Unified Modeling Language (UML) in this overview [RJB04]. UML is mostly used for designing software systems. Its *class diagrams* can be used for data modeling, yet this is far from common. A good overview of how to use these diagrams for data modeling is presented in [Hay11].

distinguishes between *fact types* in which *object types* play a role. These object types are drawn as "boxes" and represent *business concepts* in the model. There are many fact-based modeling approaches but *Object Role Modeling* (ORM2) is probably the most well-known language [Hal07, HM10].

Fact-based modeling approaches focus on the *conceptual* level of abstraction. The conceptual models that we've seen so far (in example 26) have used a very informal notation with simple "boxes and arrows". By contrast, ORM2 is a formal modeling language built on mathematical set theory. This means that it has a very precise notation.

Example 27. ORM2: graphical and textual notation

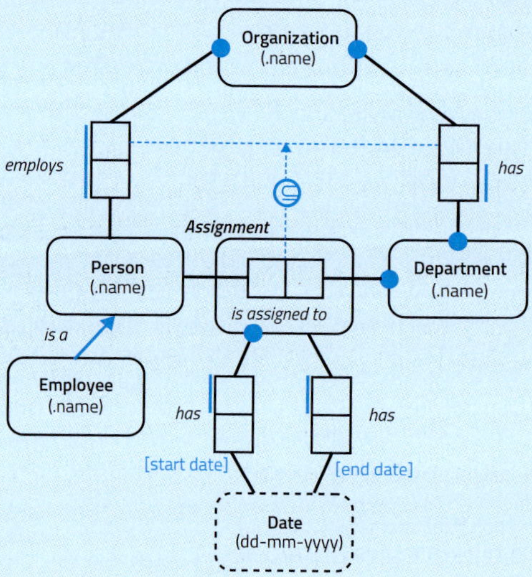

Object types + reference scheme:
- Organization (.name)
- Person (.name)
- Department (.name)
- Employee (.name)
- Assignment (of Person to Department)

Value types + format:
- Date (dd-mm-yyyy)

Fact types
- Person *is assigned* to Department
- Organization *employs* Person
- Organization *has* Department
- Assignment *has* Start date
- Assignment *has* End date

Subtype defining rules
- Employee *is a* Person *employed by an* Organization

Constraints
- an Organization must employ at least one Person
- an Organization must have at least one Department
- a Department must belong to exactly one Organization
- a Department must have at least one Person
- the Assignment (*of a* Person *to a* Department) must have exactly one start date
- each Person *assigned to a* Department must *be a* Person *employed by the* Organization *having* that Department

Example 27 illustrates this by showing an ORM2 model in both its graphical (left side) and textual (right side) notation. I will end this discussion by illustrating how (part of) the analysis works to arrive at this model. The analysis starts with observations that "*Bas works for Strategy Alliance*". This observation is translated to a qualified sentence: "*the Person with name 'Bas' works for the Organization with name 'Strategy Alliance'*". We can now distinguish between the two object types *Person* and *Organization* (which represent business concepts), their identification with names, and the relationship between them, verbalized as *works for*. Note that the precision of this model comes at the expense of the readability of the graphical diagram: not many business stakeholders will know how to interpret such a diagram.

11.3.2 Entity relationship modeling

The second language that I will discuss is in fact a group of modeling languages called *Entity Relationship Diagrams* (ERD). The idea is to model *entities* – which represent the "things we talk about", their *attributes* – representing characteristics of these "things", and the *relationships between entities*[3]. The first ERD notation was developed in the 1970s and many versions have been proposed and used since then [Che76, Mar89, Mar90a, Hay13]. These versions are all based on the same premise (entity type with attribute types being interrelated) and vary mainly in their graphical notation.

I've included several examples of ERD models already in this book. Most notably, example 26 has an enterprise logical data model using one notation, and a system logical data model using another. It is also possible to use ERDs at the conceptual level of abstraction.

11.3.3 Architecture modeling with ArchiMate

The modeling languages so far have focused on modeling within the realm of data. There are also cases where you're interested in the interplay between business (e.g. processes), data (e.g. business concepts, data elements) and systems (e.g. applications, infrastructure). This requires a different type of modeling language. ArchiMate is such a language. It was developed in the Netherlands and is currently an open standard[4] that is adopted and maintained by The Open Group [Wie14, GD15, The16a, Lan17].

This language is elaborate and covers many different aspects. A short overview:

- In ArchiMate we distinguish between a *core* and *extensions*.
- ArchiMate has a formal grammar, which means that the relationships (lines) between concepts (boxes) are very precisely defined.
- The core consists of five layers: strategy (with concepts such as capabilities and resources), business (with concepts such as process, business object, actor), application (with concepts such as applications and data objects), infrastructure (with concepts such as nodes and system software), and physical (with concepts such as equipment and facility).
- In each layer within the core, we model *active structure elements* (things that are capable of showing behavior), *passive structure elements* (inputs and outputs of behavior) and *behavior* itself.
- Extensions include a motivation extension (stakeholders and their concerns), and an *implementation and migration extension* (plateaus, work packages).

3 The name is actually a misnomer as it models entity *types* (e.g. *Person*) rather than actual entities (e.g. 'Bas').
4 'Open', in this context, means that the standard is freely available online and that practitioners help to improve the standard through a community process.

The language is extensive and aligns well with architecture approaches such as TOGAF [The11, GD14]. I believe it is also ideal for data management initiatives where the interplay between processes, data, and systems is key. This is illustrated in example 28.

Example 28. ArchiMate modeling

The diagram below shows part of an ArchiMate model. The yellow boxes represent model elements at the business layer, whereas blue boxes represent the application layer, and the green boxes represent the infrastructure layer. The diagram shows a *hiring process*. One of the steps is *register a new employee*. This step can only be performed by someone in the role of *HR manager*. The output of this step is an *employee record*, which is a (business concept). This record is stored in the *HR System* as the *Person* data element. It also shows that this process uses automated functionality (*Registration service*) that is offered by this system. Further, the system has four main functions, which manipulate its internal data elements. Last but not least, the diagram includes a data flow from the *HR system* to a *Party Management System*.

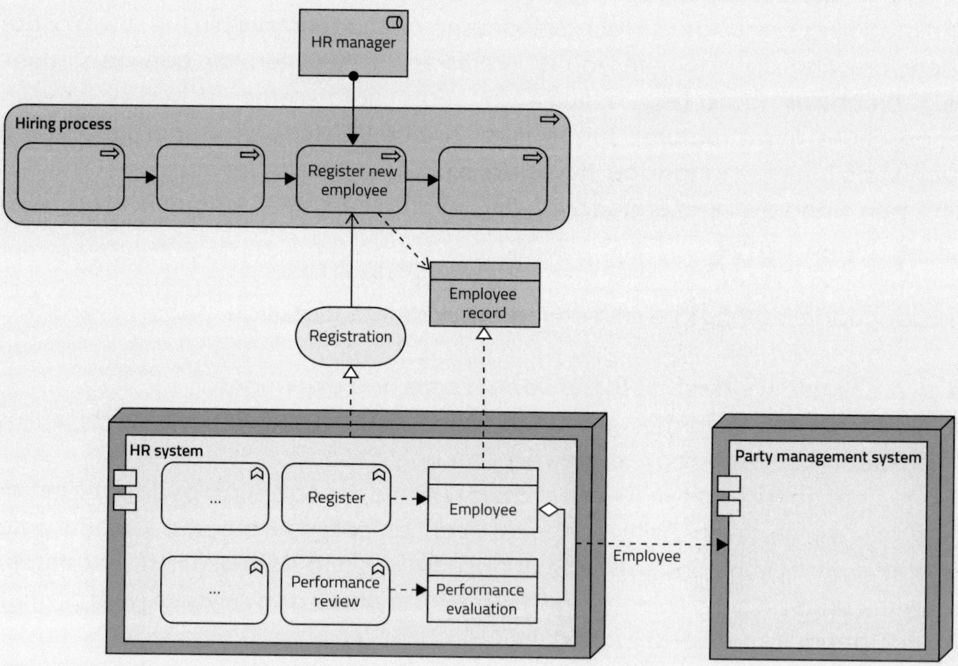

11.4 RELATIONSHIP TO OTHER DM CAPABILITIES

By now you might be thinking: why should I care so much about the many different ways to draw boxes and arrows? In my view, models are a means to an end. They give insight and overview in how things are interrelated, either within the realm of data (using e.g. ORM2, or one of the ERD models) or across domains (using e.g.

ArchiMate). This communication-aspect of models and modeling should not be underestimated. Many think of models as *designs* that capture the output of an analysis and design process. This is not incorrect. The point, however, is to capture this knowledge in a way that makes it possible for different stakeholders to see and use the same concise representation for their own purposes. This works best when the models are tightly linked to a common vocabulary/ business glossary.

These insights can be important for several other DM capabilities. The most obvious benefit of using data models is to understand the design of data structures in information systems. Also, from a *governance* perspective, models help to understand the context in which data is used and thus facilitate decision-making. Models help to visualize key aspects of metadata: a long list of definitions of business concepts is useful but showing how business concepts are related provides extra insights which are useful for decision-making. The same goes for technology considerations as will be discussed in chapter 13: it helps to see how technology supports business applications and business processes.

11.5 VISUAL SUMMARY

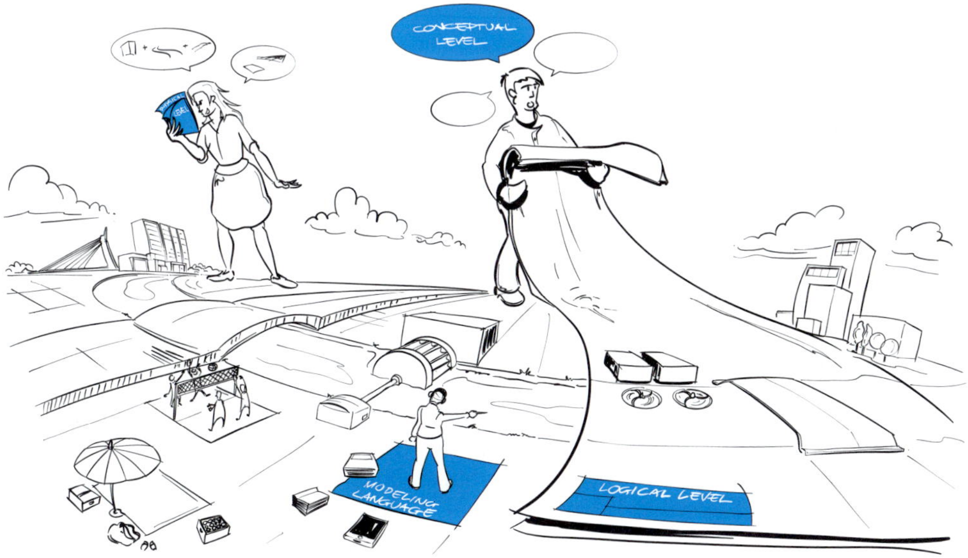

12 Architecture

Synopsis *- In this chapter, I will introduce the field of data architecture. In chapter 2, I explored the relationship between data and information, and stated that I will not make a sharp distinction between these two terms in this book. This also goes for this chapter: I will not distinguish between data architecture and information architecture. In my view, data architecture is a capability that sits between data management and enterprise architecture. I will start with a brief exploration of what architecture means. I will use this together with the DMBOK definition to show what data architecture is all about. This includes an exploration of what architects do, and how their work products contribute to successful data management in organizations. I will end the chapter with a brief exploration of the relationship between data architecture and other data management capabilities.*

12.1 ARCHITECTURE

This chapter is about *data architecture*. What *is* data architecture? The simple answer is "data architecture is the architecture of data" but that still doesn't tell us much. I will first have to define the concept of *architecture* itself. A myriad of definitions have been proposed and most – including TOGAF and ArchiMate [The11, GD14, The16a] – are built on the definition that was developed by the International Standards Organization (ISO), the International Electrotechnical Commission (IEC), and the Institute of Electrical and Electronics Engineers (IEEE) [ISO11]. This standard distinguishes between three related aspects:

- **Architecture -** Fundamental concepts or properties of a system in its environment embodied in its elements, relationships, and in the principles of its design and evolution.
- **Architecting -** Process of conceiving, defining, expressing, documenting, communicating, certifying proper implementation of, maintaining, and improving an architecture throughout a system's lifecycle (i.e. "designing").
- **Architecture description -** Work product used to express an architecture.

This overview tells us that, at least from a theoretical perspective, there is a difference between the architecture (of a system) and its architecture description (which could be text, video, boxes and arrows or any form you can think of). In this book, I will simply use the word "architecture".

The above definition also shows an architecture is always made of some system. Systems can be anything, including social systems, information systems, or the combination of these two. Note also, that an architecture of a system can be made and documented as it is now, or as a future version – how we want things to be. With this in mind, capturing the architecture of a system means that two questions must be answered: (1) what is the fundamental organization of that system, and (2) what principles underlie this fundamental organization.

The first aspect suggests that architects worry about "the big picture" and not so much about the details. In our field, these details are usually called the "(detailed) design'" It turns out that it is hard to give an unambiguous rule that defines the demarcation between the two. This is due to human nature: what is fundamental for one stakeholder need not be fundamental for another stakeholder at all. This is best explained by comparing the architectures of two cities (example 29).

Example 29. Architecture of cities

Toronto

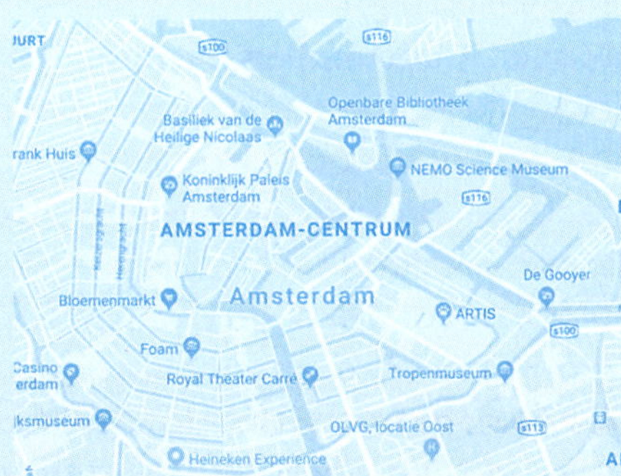

Amsterdam

Please locate a map of the downtown area of a big North American city (e.g. Toronto). If you look closely, you'll quickly notice that the fundamental organization of this city is a grid-like pattern. Note that the pattern is broken in several places: several roads are diagonal, or loop around the waterfront. This doesn't change the fact that the fundamental pattern is a grid. The reason for this structure (the 'principles') likely include ease of navigation.

Compare this with a typical European city (e.g. Amsterdam). The city center of Amsterdam is shaped by canals which are organized in a semi-circle pattern, presumably because of the transportation of goods and defending the city from invaders hundreds of years ago. Here too the pattern is broken in several places which doesn't change the fact that the main pattern is that of nested semi-circles.

Thinking at the architecture/ big picture level has several advantages. For example, it helps to see how the pieces of the puzzle fit together. When working on a specific piece (e.g. fixing up a certain street or neighborhood), it also helps to see how this piece is connected to the bigger whole. Last but not least, it helps stakeholders with different concerns (designing streets and houses, implementing infrastructure such as water and electricity, ensuring mobility across the city) to work from a common operational picture about the domain they are working in, without getting bogged down in the details.

In our context, the same line of reasoning applies:

- **Scope = process:** how are our processes organized and why? Do we structure them as end-to-end value streams[1], or do we organize them mainly per department? Are processes optimized for throughput? For flexibility? For something else?
- **Scope = information systems:** how is our information systems landscape organized and why? Did we opt for a single vendor solution, or are we adopting an approach based on smaller components (for the technically inclined readers: using web services or micro services)?
- **Scope = enterprise:** how do the pieces of the puzzle fit together? How do our processes and systems align? What are we doing centrally, and where do we grant units more autonomy?
- **Scope = data:** how is the data landscape organized? What are the fundamental principles for deciding which data goes in which system and how it flows through the enterprise? This is discussed in more detail in the next section.

Here too the focus is on the big picture level, not the details. Yet the above list also makes another point: the scopes may be nested. The enterprise scope is the biggest scope. For the next level down, you can drill down to business units and then to processes, systems, or data. Once these are understood also, you can drill down again. At some point during this analysis you will transition from "architecture" to "detailed design". This is illustrated in figure 12.1. Note that for the person who works

1 With the term end-to-end I mean: starting at the customer and ending at the customer. For example, the value stream that starts when you order pizza and ends when you have it in your hands. For contrast, another approach would be to consider value streams/ processes per department which would result in a very different structure.

on the architecture of the "details" of the data landscape of one of the units is no longer "architecture" but "detailed design". This does not diminish the value of the architecture of the data landscape of this unit in any way.

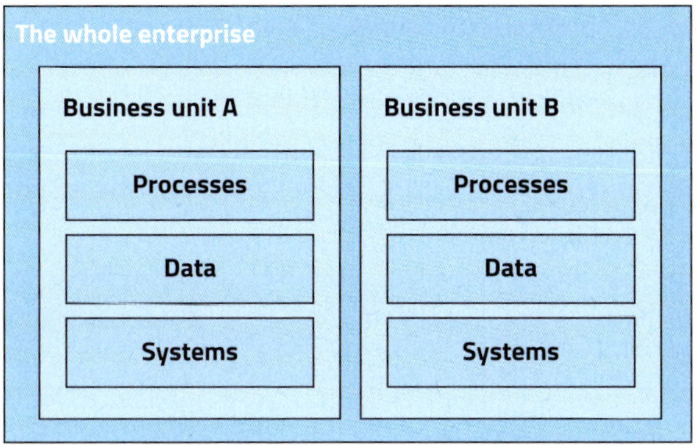

Figure 12.1 Nested scopes

12.2 DATA ARCHITECTURE

The DMBOK defines the data architecture capability as follows: "Identifying the data needs of an enterprise (. . .) and designing and maintaining the master blueprints to meet those needs. Using master blueprints to guide data integration, control data assets, and align data investments with business strategy". In my view, the "data needs" are not so much part of the architecture but a key driver for making an architecture. It does stress that data architecture should focus on two things:

- **Data at rest -** This part of the data architecture is about understanding how data (based on which principles) are grouped together in data clusters and how it is decided which data is stored in which information system.
- **Data in motion -** This part complements the previous part and considers what the essential patterns are for how data flows through information systems and which principles have been used to design these flows.

The approach in the DMBOK is similar to what is advocated by TOGAF [The11]. The *architecture development method* (ADM) is a key part of TOGAF and phase C of this method deals with data architecture. One of the listed goals for this phase is: "Develop the Target Data Architecture that enables the Business Architecture and the Architecture Vision, in a way that addresses . . . stakeholder concerns". In other words, here too the focus is on satisfying the needs of stakeholders, only the wording is different. This discussion is rather abstract. Example 30 serves the purpose of illustrating these two perspectives on data architecture.

Example 30. Data architecture

Suppose you are working for a company that offers *loan* products, *lease* products, and *savings* products. All three business lines are heavily data-driven. You want to manage your data assets well. Grouping data in clusters helps to decide who should own/ be the steward of which data. It also helps in deciding which data should be stored together in which system. Let's say that you decide to organize things per business unit. This means that the architecture will show that each business unit has its own data and presumably also its own systems (data at rest). If desired, data flows can be set up to exchange data so that we can discover shared customers between business units. The following diagram shows the resulting structure.

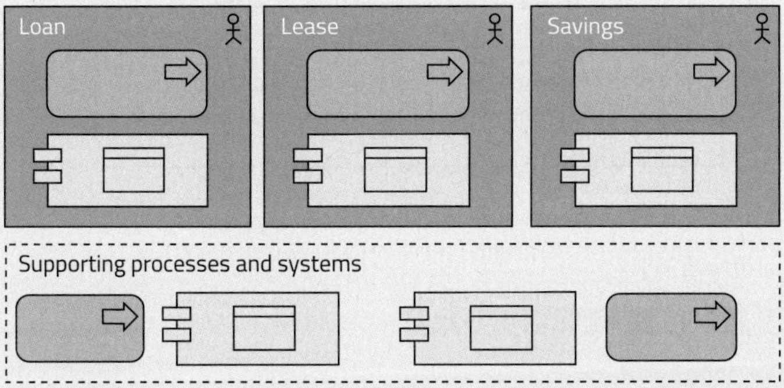

Another approach would be the group data per "category" such as *Customer data, Product data*, and *Location data*. Using this approach would likely lead to systems such as a Customer Relationship Management System (CRM) and a Human Resources System (HRS). Together these systems support the business processes in the units.

This would probably mean less autonomy for business units but would make it easier to optimize individual functions. The following diagram shows the resulting structure.

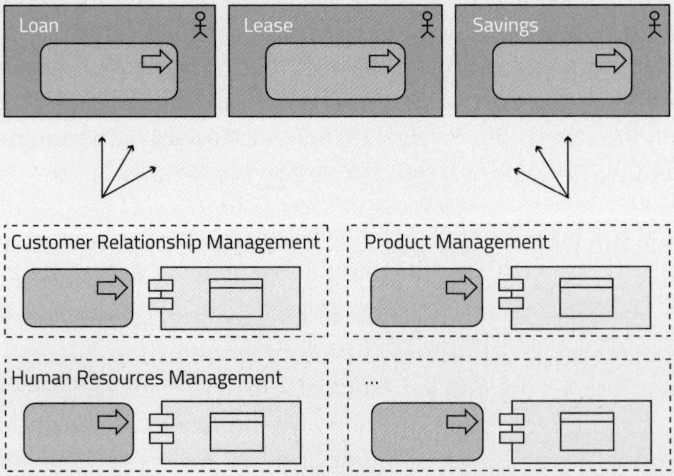

The two diagrams are very different. This illustrates the point that different principles lead to different structures.

This brings me to the last topic of this section: how are data architectures documented? The term "blueprint" was already mentioned in the DMBOK definition of architecture. Blueprints/ diagrams are indeed commonly used to document (data) architectures which means that there is a big overlap with chapter 11 where I discussed modeling techniques.

Modeling languages such as ArchiMate are increasingly popular for documenting data architectures, as they allow the flexibility to capture many perspectives: data at rest/ in motion but also the flow of data and the link to business processes. Often these models are complemented by conceptual data models where more detailed analysis and designs are required.

Whether it makes sense to create one big conceptual data model for the whole organization remains to be seen. For many years this was seen as "the Holy Grail" as it clearly and unambiguously standardizes language and terminology across the enterprise. By now we know that this is never easy (see e.g. [Hop03]). A more popular approach is to standardize terminology within a specific context such as a process or department.

This also goes for *data in motion*. Many organizations have tried to create a (logical) data model that served as a "lingua franca"[2], often called a *canonical data model*. Example 31 illustrates how this works.

Example 31. Canonical data model

The number of potential connections between systems can be calculated with the formula $\frac{n(n-1)}{2}$. This means that with five systems, there are ten potential connections. With ten systems there are 45 potential connections and with 25 systems there are 300 potential connections (see also section 13.3.1).

Suppose you have a dozen or so systems that all store data about employees. However, they use different names (*Staff, Worker*) and data may be structured differently. Rather than figuring out how each two systems can exchange data a good practice is to create a "lingua franca". The idea is that you now have to only figure out how each system interacts with this in-between system. If systems *A* and *B* now wish to exchange data, the process is simple: first translate data from *A* to the lingua franca, and then translate it to *B*.

The big advantage of this approach is that it scales linearly. With three systems there are three mappings to be made. With five systems there are five mappings to be made, and with 20 systems there are 20 mappings to be made.

2 A language that is adopted as a common language between speakers whose native languages are different.

This pattern is still very popular. Its advantages and disadvantages are increasingly well known. In part II – chapter 31, I will discuss this in more detail from a data integration perspective.

12.3 RELATIONSHIP TO OTHER (DATA MANAGEMENT) CAPABILITIES

The relationship to one other discipline is discussed already in the previous section: the techniques from *data modeling* are used heavily in the field of data architecture. Data architecture is also closely related to data integration – which is discussed in the next chapter: it is a good practice to consider the data integration challenge from an architecture perspective before diving into the details. Last but not least, example 32 illustrates the connection with *data governance*: insights in the architecture of the enterprise/ the data landscape of the enterprise may be a good starting point to decide who should fulfil the role of data owner/ data steward.

Example 32. Data architecture & ownership/ stewardship
This example continues where example 30 left off.

Consider the first option where each unit has its own data. From an ownership/ stewardship perspective, it would make sense to ask the person responsible for the business unit to also fulfill the role of data owner. The data owner could be supported by a small army of data stewards to ensure things run smoothly.

Now consider the second option, where data is clustered per category. In this case, the person responsible for a business function could fulfill the role of the data owner, supported by one or two more hands-on data stewards. An advantage of this approach would be that the function- owner is usually very knowledgeable about his/ her function and therefore understands the data well.

■ 12.4 VISUAL SUMMARY

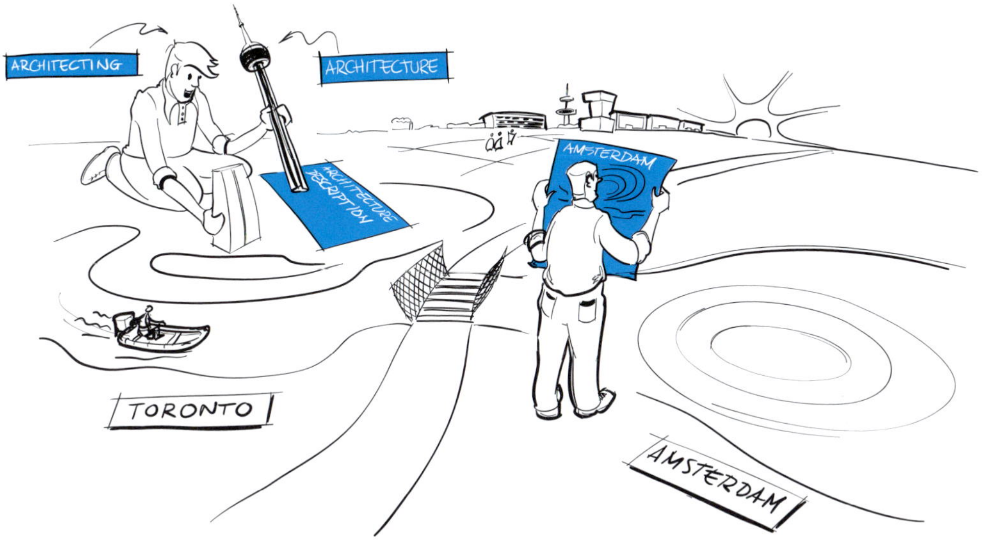

DATA ARCHITECTURE: ARCHITECTURE OF THE DATA LANDSCAPE

13 Integration

Synopsis *- This may be the most technical chapter in this book. I will talk about the integration of multiple data sources/ the flow of data across the enterprise. I will first give a high-level introduction in the field, following the Data Management Body of Knowledge DMBOK [Hen17]. It is impossible to provide a complete overview of integration patterns. I will cover the more common patterns and attempt to do so without scaring off readers who do not have a technical background. In the last section, I will discuss the data integration challenge from an architecture perspective.*

13.1 INTRODUCTION TO DATA INTEGRATION

The notion of data flowing through the organization's processes and systems has been discussed in several places in this book (e.g. example 14 in chapter 7 which discusses the "data river", and in section 12.2 which discusses data at rest/ data in motion). This "movement" of data is the realm of data integration. The DMBOK formally defines this as follows [Hen17]:

> *Managing the movement and consolidation of data within and between applications and organizations.*

This definition highlights that two things should be considered: (1) How do we move data from system A to B? (2) How do we consolidate this new data with the data that is already present in system B? (Example 33 illustrates what these two questions entail.)

Example 33. Data integration

The diagram below shows two systems with data about people in a *Person* table. Let's say that data from system A has to be moved to system B. One aspect that needs to be considered is: how do we do this? There are many options to achieve the same goal. For example, are we going to use a flash drive, or can we perhaps do this via our internal network? How often do we want to send data from A to B?

Another question is: how do we consolidate the data? The diagram already outlines the basic process for how to deal with each of the fields. But what do we do if a person that is in A is already present in B? What do we do if system A claims that the birth year of a person is 1976, while system B claims that it is 1977? Can we simply overwrite the existing data in system B, or are there other solutions? Handling this type of challenge is called consolidation.

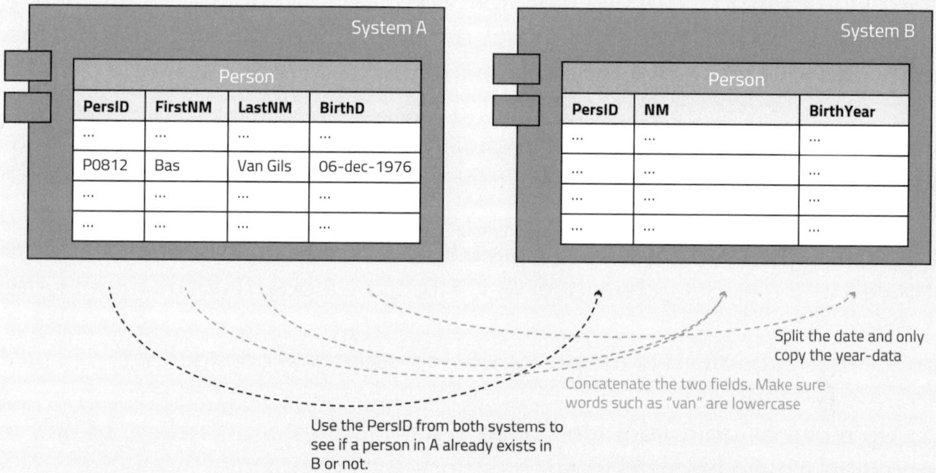

For the readers with a more technical background: there are many cases where you encounter two database designs about the same business domain/ scope that are completely different. Even when both designs are normalized according to the rules of the game, there could still be big differences – often due to different requirements. Finding a good way to *consolidate* data from systems using these conflicting designs can be a challenge.

The type of considerations that are involved are typically technical in nature. For example, it includes the choice of an integration pattern (some of which are discussed in the next section), but it also includes the type of technology that is used to implement the pattern. This type of consideration is made by architects (see chapter 12 and also section 13.3). One word of advice: think about *what* you want (i.e. which integration pattern would work best), before considering *how* you will implement it (i.e. which technology or vendor you will use).

13.2 COMMON INTEGRATION PATTERNS

There are many patterns for *data integration* and several attempts have been made to catalog them ([HW04] is a good, albeit somewhat older, reference work). In this section, I will include a short overview of the more common integration patterns. I will stay away from the technology/ vendor discussion as much as possible.

13.2.1 Batch integration

The first pattern, probably the oldest too, is batch integration. This approach is sometimes called *Extract, Transform, Load* (ETL). The name describes exactly what happens: data is moved in batches from a source system to a target system. Usually this is done at set intervals, e.g. twice per day. Batches are often run in the middle of the night, to make sure that operations are not impacted too much when data is moved around. When databases are large (many records), keeping them synchronized will put a heavy load on systems.

The way this approach works is best explained with the diagram in example 33 in mind. When the process starts, the first thing that is done is to *extract* the specified data from the source system. This gives us a data set with records that are structured to the needs of the source system. The next step is to *transform* the data to a structure that is used by the target system, after which it can be *loaded* into the target system.

There are many variations to this pattern. Some aspects to consider are:

- Do we move all data from the source system to the target system, or only the records that have been updated/ new since the last batch?
- Do we simply overwrite existing data in the target system, or do we have another process in place for handling potential conflicts between source and target systems?
- What do we do if the process breaks during the migration of one of the records? Do we simply abort the whole process, or will we pick up with the next record?

13.2.2 Accessing data through services

One of the disadvantages of the batch approach is that the target system gets its updates only a few times per day, so it will always be just a little bit out of date. A more interactive/ real-time approach to integration is aptly named *Data as a Service* (DaaS) [Sar15].

In this approach, data is not moved from the database of system A to system B. Instead, system B has the opportunity to ask for data on demand. In technical terms this means that system A exposes services (to manipulate data), that system B can use. Example 34 illustrates what a typical conversation between these two systems would look like.

Example 34. Data as a Service
For this example there are two systems. The first system is called *PMS* (short for *Party Management System*) and the second is called *WebTool* which manipulates, among other things, data about people using web forms. Let's say someone wants to add a new person named *Bas* to the system, using *WebTool*. After filling out the webforms, the conversation between the two systems might go as follows: (1) *WebTool* asks *PMS* to add the record about *Bas*; (2) *PMS* discovers it already has information about this person and adds the new details, overwriting old data points (e.g. Bas's Twitter account has been updated and his e-mail address has been added); and (3) the new record is sent back to *WebTool* which shows Bas's record to the user of the system.

The word "service" in this pattern is used deliberately: we don't care *how* the system processes certain requests, we only care *that* it performs the task at hand. In other words, we ask it to perform a service on our behalf.

13.2.3 Change data capture

The *change data capture* (CDC) pattern sits somewhat between the previous two patterns. This pattern is used to make sure that a source system and a target system are in sync. Unlike the batch pattern, the updates are done in real-time. In essence, the working of this pattern is straightforward. Each time an update (new record, update to an existing record, removing a record) happens in the source system, two things happen. First, it is processed in the source system. Second, a separate piece of software picks up the change and sends the details of the update to the target system. The target system then also processes the change. This process only takes microseconds, so the two systems are always synchronized.

A big advantage of this system is that you now have two systems with the same data. The original version is used by the source system but the perfect copy is available for other purposes, such as creating a dashboard or performing statistical analyses. Therefore, this pattern is often used in the context of business intelligence projects (see chapter 18).

13.2.4 Streaming data integration

Once again, the name aptly describes the process: a stream of data is brought to a central point for processing and use – often without storing the data. The question is: what is streaming data? The Wikipedia definition is[1]: "Streaming data is data that is continuously generated by different sources". Example 35 presents two short cases that illustrate what is meant by this definition.

1 https://en.wikipedia.org/wiki/Streaming_data, last checked: 22 June 2019.

Example 35. Streaming data

The first case is about tracking what happens on your website. Every second, thousands of people are clicking on your website. If you want to know what is going on, you have to analyze the *stream* of clicks. Each time someone clicks on a link, you have a new data point (real-time). Analyzing these patterns may be very valuable for your organization.

The second case is where you are managing a large warehouse. All items in your warehouse have electronic tags that allows you to see where everything is in real time. All the movements of items through your warehouse form a *stream* of data. Special software can be used to analyze and visualize this data stream which gives useful insights in how well the warehouse is performing.

A key characteristic for streaming data is that it has a very high *velocity*, meaning that the rate of new data coming in is very high. The "traditional" way to deal with data (structure the data, store it, then analyze it) tends to be too slow for this type of process. Also, there is often no point in *storing* and *retaining* data for longer periods of time since you are only interested in what happens right now/ in the last hour or so. A host of tools and platforms have capabilities to implement this type of process. For a more extensive overview, see [ACL18].

13.2.5 Data virtualization

The last pattern that I will discuss, is *data virtualization* [Lan12]. The idea is to make a "virtual" layer in a separate system that integrates data from different sources. This word "virtual" is used because data stays in the original system but it is accessed *on demand*[2]. Figure 13.1 illustrates this further. The bottom "layer" in the diagram is where we have *integrated* access to the data of source systems. Using advanced technology, this layer makes it look like tables from source systems are also tables in this layer. The middle layer restructures data from tables in the lower layer. For example, a *Person* table from the *HR* system is combined with a *Contact person* table from the *Customer Relationship Management* system to form a new *Party* table. In the top layer, data can be restructured once more to suit the needs of specific stakeholders.

The point is that all these layers are *virtual;* the data stays within the original source system. When a stakeholder accesses the data in his/ her view, the system works through the different virtual layers, pulls the data from the source systems, and then presents them back to the stakeholder. Data virtualization is *state-of-the-art* and requires complex technology. The capabilities of such platforms are extensive and

2 Some data virtualization platforms have the opportunity to "cache" data from source systems. This means that a copy of the data is kept in the data virtualization platform for easy access. This copy is kept up-to-date, for example with algorithms that are similar *change data capture* – which was discussed also in this chapter.

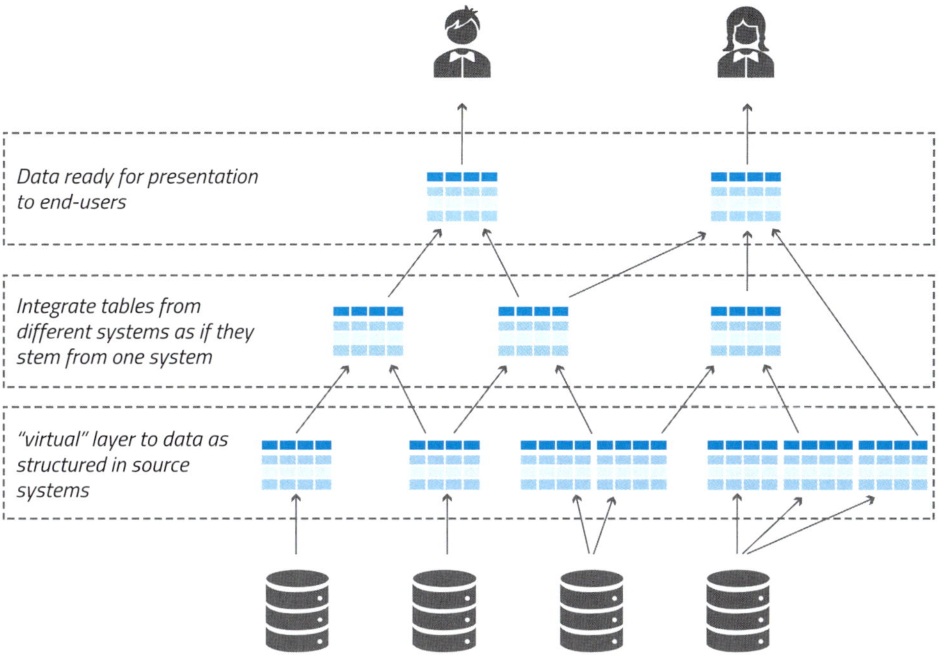

Figure 13.1 Data virtualization

Diagram inspired by [Lan12]

include such things as *caching* (i.e. storing a temporary local copy of data from source systems that is synchronized with the source system in the background), *access control* and other security measures (see chapter 17), and managing metadata (see chapter 10).

13.3 INTEGRATION FROM AN ARCHITECTURE PERSPECTIVE

Choosing which integration pattern to use when is a daunting task. In this section, I will discuss some of the integration challenges from an architecture perspective. See also chapter 12 for more information about data architecture.

13.3.1 Dealing with the number of potential connections

When the number of systems – and therefore the number of data sources – in your landscape grows, the number of potential connections between these data sources also grows. As stated previously (example 31), the formula for calculating the number of connections between n systems is $\frac{n(n-1)}{2}$. This means that for $n = 25$ systems there are 300 connections. Since the number of potential connections grows so fast, we say that there is an exponential relationship between the number of systems n and the number of potential connections between these systems.

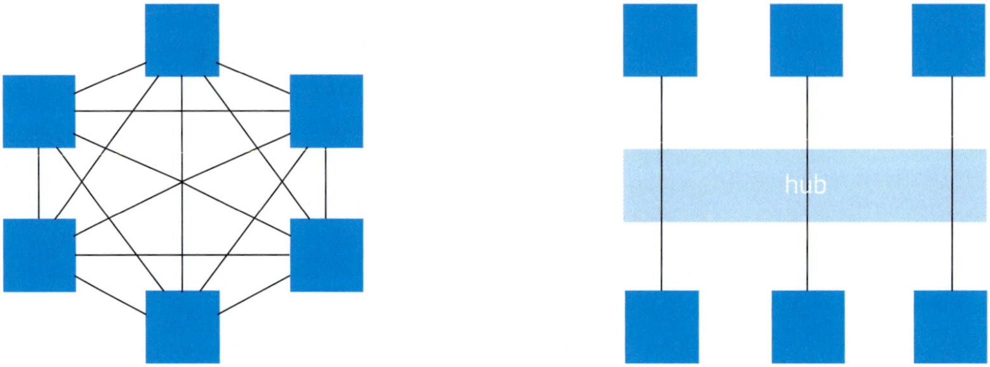

Figure 13.2 Introducing a "hub" to reduce the number of connections between systems

Managing a "spaghetti landscape" (sometimes also called "hairball architecture") where everything is connected to everything else is a big task. To make this more manageable, it may make sense to introduce a "hub" in the landscape: a common connection point in the network. All systems connect to this hub: if two systems want to communicate, they do so via this hub. We say that this "scales linearly": with *n* systems there are now *n* connections to the hub (see figure 13.2). Architects tend to like those numbers as it seriously reduces complexity. A disadvantage of this approach, though, is that the hub becomes a single point of failure: if it fails, then all connections between systems that go via the hub also fail.

13.3.2 Dealing with different names and structures

Somewhat related to the previous topic is the notion of systems that want to communicate but have to deal with different data structures and different meanings of words. In part, this was already discussed in example 31. The challenge can be framed through a set of questions:

- How do you deal with the situation where one system has separate fields for *first name* and *last name*, whereas another system has a single *name* field?
- How do you deal with homonyms and synonyms?
- How do you deal with situations where data types mismatch? For example, one system stores the status of a process as a number ("the process is in state 42!"), whereas another uses a more verbose characterization ("the process is in a fault state because required inputs are missing")?

The list of potential challenges in this category can be extended almost indefinitely. From an architecture perspective, the question is how to solve these challenges. Do we want to use a canonical model such as in example 31, or are we going to create translations between source and target systems on a case by case basis? Can we perhaps (governance!) force everyone to use the same language, or reduce the number of *dialects* that systems use by standardizing language per department/group of systems?

13.3.3 Dealing with different patterns

As discussed in chapter 12, architects tend to worry about translating the (data) needs of the enterprise into master blueprints which will ensure that, when implemented, these needs are met. To that end, architects tend to analyze the needs of different stakeholders and optimize the data/ systems landscape to meet those needs. When not careful, this may lead to over-engineering/ over-structuring the landscape through principles such as "all connections between systems must go via our integration platform", where the integration platform is a complex whole of modules that will take care of integration challenges. In many cases, more freedom is required. Successful integration architecture requires balancing between optimization through standardization on the one hand and freedom/ flexibility of using different patterns on the other.

Years ago, most (if not all) data of an organization was stored in systems that were hosted on premise. These days, organizations make more and more use of *cloud computing*[3]. This means that architects are now faced with additional challenges to figure out how to perform integration between on-premise data sources with cloud data sources, or even between different cloud data sources. Further exploration of this topic is beyond the scope of this chapter. Chapter 31 discusses the practicalities of setting up a successful integration architecture.

13.4 VISUAL SUMMARY

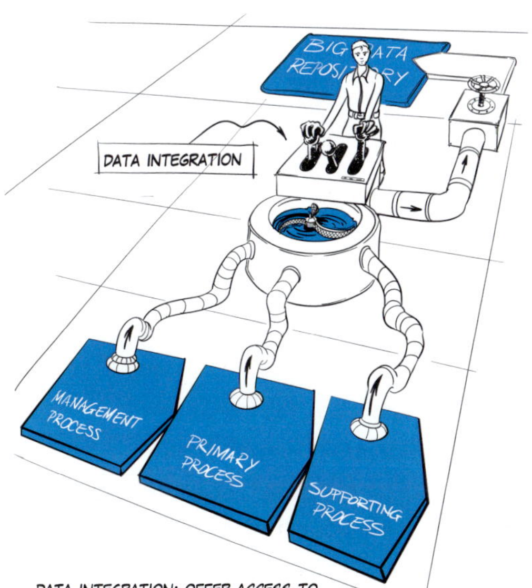

DATA INTEGRATION: OFFER ACCESS TO HIGH QUALITY, INTEGRATED DATA

3 See e.g. the Wikipedia page on Cloud Computing for details. https://en.wikipedia.org/wiki/Cloud_computing, last checked: 22 June 2019.

14 Reference data

***Synopsis** - Reference data is data – often in the form of codes and the interpretation of these codes – that helps to make sense of other data. In this chapter, I will show what reference data management is all about. I will also show that it is a key capability for successfully managing data. I will start with a short exploration of what reference data is. I will then link reference data to business metadata and making the meaning of data more consistent. I will also discuss the challenges around retaining a historic version of reference data sets. Last but not least, I will briefly discuss the link to governance.*

14.1 DEFINITION

The DMBOK defines reference data as follows [Hen17]:

> *Reference data [. . .] is data that is used solely to characterize other data in an organization, or solely to relate data in a database to information beyond the boundaries of the organization. Reference data management entails control over defined domain values and their definitions. The goal of reference data management is to ensure the organization has access to a complete set of accurate and current values for each concept represented.*

These definitions are abstract and confusing at best. My definition is: "reference data is data that is used to understand other data". This type of data typically comes in the form of code lists, such as a list of country codes, as shown in example 36.

Example 36. Reference data

Suppose you have a system where you store data about shipments of your products. You are an international company, so you ship your goods all over the world. You don't want to rely on people typing in their country name correctly, knowing that would be a potential source of data problems. Instead, you want to use a country code list that is internationally accepted. Using such a list, you know that US refers to the United States of America, NL refers to the Netherlands, and DE refers to Germany.

Reference data is often available through (external) data providers. Reference data is available on many different topics, such as country codes, product types, industry classification codes, and book classification codes such as the Dewey Decimal System[1]. If a standard list is not available, organizations can build their own. For example, you may classify your customers as *lead* (code: L), *customer* (code: C), *top customer* (code: T) or *former customer* (code: F).

In some cases, reference data sets are a bit more complex than simple flat lists. More advanced reference data sets contain *hierarchies* of codes, not unlike a family tree, as illustrated in example 37 which is inspired by [Hen17].

Example 37. Reference data hierarchies

Let's say that you are in the *floral* business. Each day you purchase new flowers and sell them to your customers. Together with your partners in the supply chain, you have chosen to use the *Universal Standard Products and Services Classification* (UNSPSC) reference data set for consistency. Part of the code set is listed below.

Code value	Description	Parent code
10161600	Floral plants	10160000
10161601	Rose plants	10161600
10161602	Poinsettias plants	10161600
10161700	Cut flowers	10160000
10161705	Cut roses	10161799

Using these more complex hierarchies has many practical applications. With a few algorithms in your systems, you can now easily query for "all sales records for cut roses" (which would result all records where the code equals 10161705), but also for "all records for cut flowers" (which would result in all records where the code is

1 https://en.wikipedia.org/wiki/Dewey_Decimal_Classification, last checked: 23 June 2019.

101617xx – where "x" stands for a random digit. This would also include all records for cut roses).

14.2 USING REFERENCE DATA TO HARMONIZE THE MEANING OF DATA

Using reference data in a single system can be valuable in and of itself as it helps with consistently identifying things through a set of codes. Consistently using reference data sets across systems, however, increases the value exponentially. This does mean you have to choose your reference data set carefully and use governance mechanisms (see chapter 9) to make sure that everyone uses the same set.

If you want to use reference data, you have to choose whether you want to adopt a standard set, or to create your own reference data set. When there are competing data sets, you also have to choose which one you will go with, as illustrated in example 38.

Example 38. Competing reference data sets

This example continues from example 36. Examining the Wikipedia page for *country code*[a] shows that standard 3166 from the International Standards Organization (ISO) lists country codes in different forms (two letters, three letters, three digits). There are competing standards, for example the *United States Department of Transportation* has its World Area Codes (WAC) list.

Suppose one department uses the ISO standard whereas another uses a home-grown list. Discrepancies between the two lists could cause serious issues. For example, the ISO code for Poland is PL. If the home-grown list has PL for Portugal and chose PO for Poland, then where are you going to send a package with the code PL?

a https://en.wikipedia.org/wiki/Country_code last checked: 23 June 2019.

14.3 HISTORIC VERSIONS OF REFERENCE DATA SETS

Reference data tends to be fairly stable. If you consider the country codes example, this makes sense: the list of countries does not change all that much. The point, though, is that they do change! Every now and then, new countries are formed and old ones disappear. This will have to be reflected in your reference data. The question is: what do you do when the world changes?

Let's assume that you choose to simply upgrade your reference data set to match the new reality. New countries are added to the list and old codes are removed. You'll also have to update the data itself.

Example 39. Fall of the Berlin wall
In 1990 Germany was reunited. Two countries (*Deutsche Demokratische Republik* and *Bundesrepublik Deutschland*) became one country (*Germany*). From a reference data standpoint, this means that two codes have to be removed and one new code has to be added to the list of country codes.

That is not the whole story. In your databases you will still have records that refer to the old codes. These will all have to be updated to the new code to reflect the new reality.

At first sight this may seem like "problem solved". In some cases it might be. However, in many cases, data with old codes will be around a lot longer than you might think and for several reasons. A first reason might be a backup: if your system crashes and you have to restore an old back-up, then suddenly you are faced with old codes again. Another, more regular, case is where data is used in a *business intelligence* (BI) context (chapter 18) where historic data is typically available (section 8.5). You will probably want to be able to do many different types of analyses with queries such as "How many customers did we used to have in Bundesrepublik Deutschland before 1989?", "How many customers do we now have in the unified Germany?", and "Did we lose or gain customers around the time of the reunification of both countries?" This means that your historic data will have to be linked to both the old reference data set and the new reference data set.

14.4 REFERENCE DATA AND GOVERNANCE

I hope that by now it is clear the concept of *reference data* is not complex: it is about understanding data through the use of other data, be it in the form of lists/hierarchies of codes. Handling the implementation of reference data across the landscape is pretty complex, though, and requires good governance practices. In this section, I will cover a few practical considerations.

The first challenge has been discussed briefly already and deals with the question of selecting reference data sets: which set do you want to use and why? Related to this, though, is a more complex question: do we want to *standardize* the use of reference data, or do we allow units to decide this for themselves? This question is closely related to strategic choices that are made in your organization, such as: are we standardizing (doing the same work in the same way) or integrating (sharing data) our processes along the organization? Do we share data across geographic locations, or do they have more freedom to operate? Answers to these questions typically do not come from the data management/ data governance professionals but do have a profound impact on what the data landscape will look like. Consequently, it is important to be aware of these discussions and to have the power to act accordingly.

The second link between reference data management and data governance lies in the need to keep reference data up-to-date: decision-making about when to update reference data – especially when many systems are involved – is a typical data governance task. This does not always get the attention it deserves, especially in situations where there are more potential projects than the organization can handle (funds, availability of resources). It is not uncommon to hear arguments that "upgrading reference data has little business value so we should put our money in other projects". This line of reasoning is false and dangerous: features come and go but data may very well be the most important asset that your organization has. Being able to make sense of it is key to running a successful business.

14.5 VISUAL SUMMARY

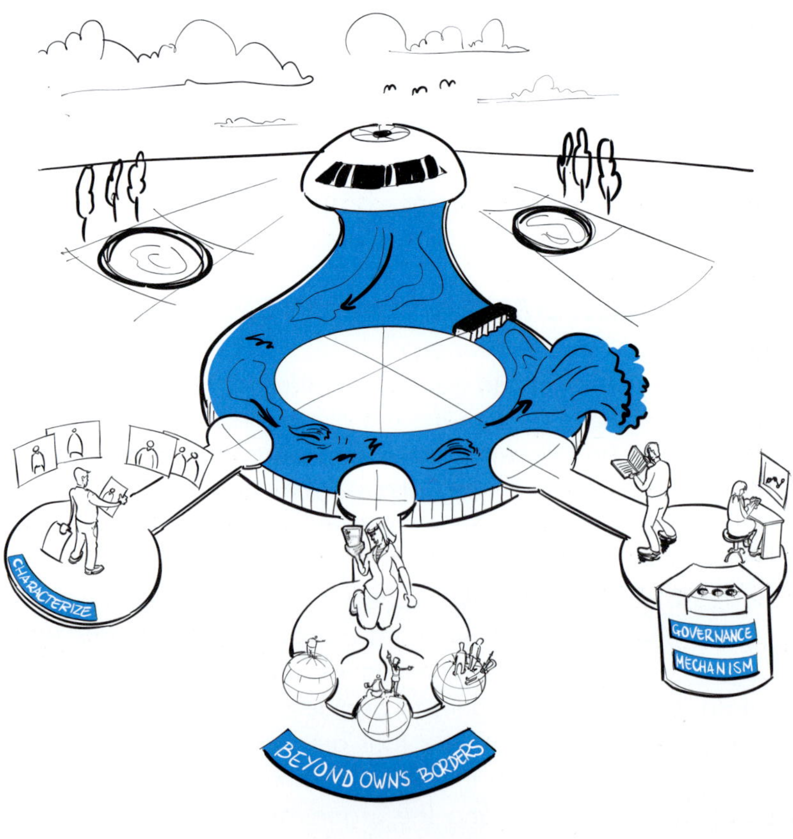

15 Master data

***Synopsis** - Data about a business concept can often be found in many systems around the enterprise and these sources are not always in agreement. Master Data Management (MDM) is a capability that is concerned with the organization of a "best version of the truth" about a business concept, across the information systems landscape of the organization. In this chapter, I will first explain the challenges that MDM tries to solve. Then I will cover the basic concepts and solution patterns to solve these problems. I will conclude this chapter by linking MDM to other data management capabilities.*

15.1 MULTIPLE VERSIONS OF THE TRUTH

Most organizations have multiple systems with more or less the same purpose, and with more or less the same data, often with good reasons. There are many situations where this causes headaches, as illustrated in example 40.

Example 40. Multiple versions of the truth

Consider the above diagram which shows three units with systems that hold data about the business concept *Person*. Assume that someone needs to know the details of one specific person. In which system are you going to look? What will you do if you find that two records from two different systems are almost the same? Are you *sure* that the two records are about the same person? Could it be the case that this person used to have the title of *drs*[1] but has achieved a promotion to full *dr* ? Could it be that this person was born in one city and moved to another?

1 The title *drs* stands for doctorandus, and is the old Dutch equivalent of a Master's Degree.

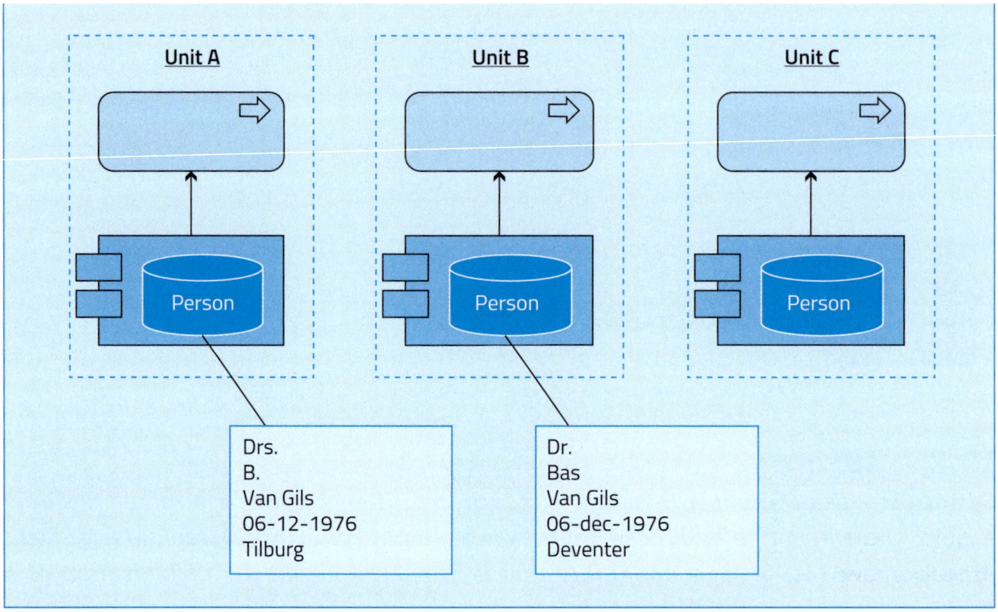

The example shows that having multiple sources of (potential) truth about a business concept may have serious business impact. It is hard to figure out in which information system you should look for data and if you find multiple records then you are faced with the challenge of deciding if these records are about the same "thing" (in this case: person).

Master Data Management (MDM) is a capability that is intended to deal with this type of challenge. The DMBOK definition states that [Hen17]:

> *Master Data Management entails control over Master Data Values and identifiers that enable consistent use, across systems of the most accurate and timely data about essential business [concepts].*

Using MDM techniques (explained in more detail in the next section) entails a significant investment of time/ effort. Therefore, it is common practice to apply them only to the most important business concepts, such as *Person* and *Product* (leading to names such as Customer MDM and Product MDM) [BDPR11, OJ15].

When MDM techniques are applied to a business concept such as *Person*, then we colloquially say that "we are mastering *Person* data". Following the lines of the DMBOK definition, this means we want to make sure that all persons have a unique identifier (e.g. a unique number). If we want to make sure that two records are about the same person, then all we have to do is compare their identifiers: if they match then, according to our data, these records are about the same person.

Being able to *automatically* detect whether two records are about the same "real world thing" is a non-trivial task. Example 40 has two records that appear to be about the same person. As humans we can easily detect this. For computers this is harder. The traditional approach is to use heuristics and business rules but artificial intelligence (AI) and machine learning (ML) approaches are increasingly popular for this type of task.

Systems that implement MDM capabilities are typically called MDM systems (or sometimes an MDM hub). The basic concepts of how these systems operate are explained in the next section[1].

15.2 BASIC MDM CONCEPTS

A quick warning before diving in: this section is somewhat technical in nature and explains how MDMsystems work. Two basic concepts are:

- **System of record** - An authoritative system where data is created/ captured and/ or through a defined set of rules and expectations.
- **System of reference** - An authoritative system where data consumers can obtain reliable data to support transactions and analysis, even if the data did not originate in the system of reference.

Paraphrasing these definitions, a system of record *has* the data, whereas a system of reference knows where to *get* the data. Using these two basic concepts, four common MDM patterns are commonly used (e.g. [DHM+09]), which are illustrated in figure 15.1:

- **Consolidation implementation style** – The consolidation implementation style brings together master data from a variety of existing systems, both databases and application systems, into a single MDM hub. In other words, all systems have their own copy of the data and the MDM hub has an overview. The advantage is that this is simple to realize. A disadvantage is that systems are not synchronized.
- **Registry implementation style** – The registry implementation style can be useful for providing a read-only source of master data as a reference to other systems. In this style, the MDM hub does not have the data itself but it has a link to data in other systems (system of reference). The main difference with the previous style is that the MDM hub does not store the data itself. Other characteristics are largely the same.

1 See also [DHM+09] for a more extensive theoretical exploration.

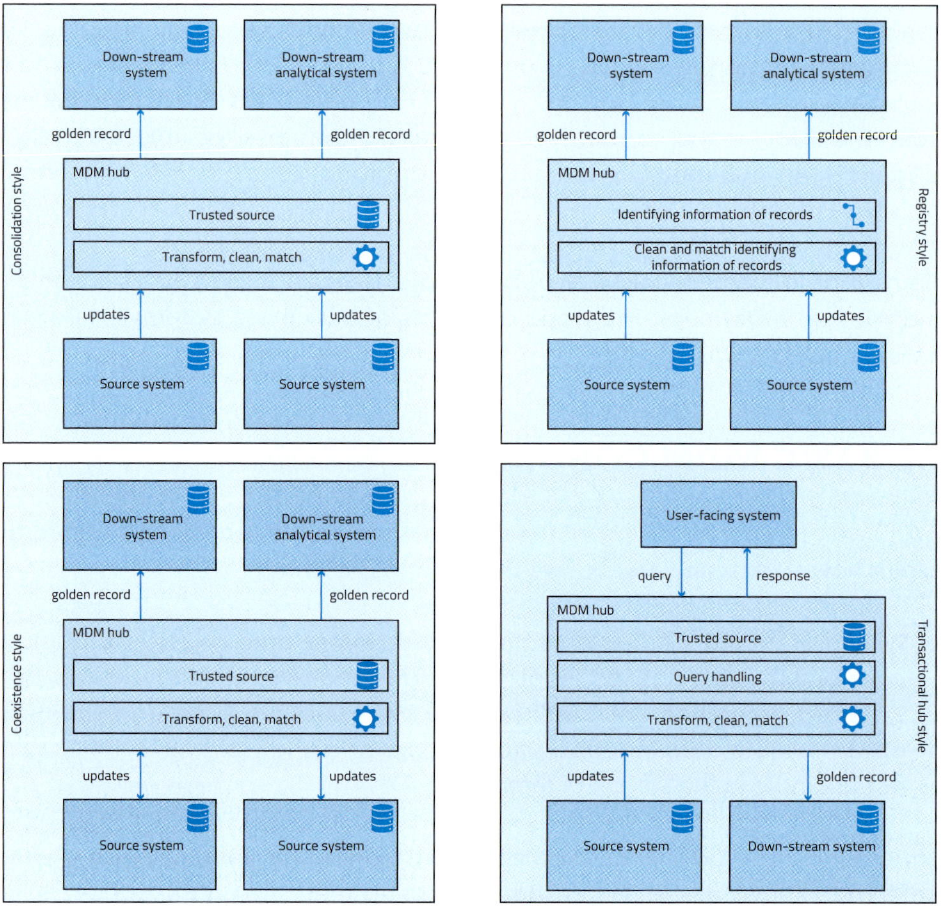

Figure 15.1 Four MDM patterns

- **Coexistence implementation style** – The coexistence style of MDM implementation involves master data that may be authored and stored in numerous systems in such a way that (a) the MDM hub has the golden copy of the data, and (b) all these systems are synchronized. In this style, all connected systems forward their updated data to the MDM hub. The MDM hub then processes the new data and forwards the new golden record to all the connected systems so that they are once more in sync.
- **Transactional hub implementation style** – A transactional hub is part of the operational fabric of an IT environment and is the *only* system in the landscape that has data about a given business concept. All other systems in the landscape will have to connect to the MDM hub when they need access to data. The advantage of this approach is that there is a single place where data is stored (system of record), so it should always be up-to-date and of high quality. A disadvantage of introducing such a system is that it is very invasive: all other systems have to be updated to link to this new hub.

Each of these patterns has advantages and disadvantages. Most vendors of MDM systems have different capabilities and are able to implement multiple styles. The question "which one is best" depends, of course, on the context in which it is used. Example 41 illustrates the MDM style that was implemented by a global company in the financial services industry.

Example 41. MDM case study

This example is based on a project that I did with a global company in the financial services industry. The challenge that this organization faced was using MDM technology to ensure that parties (customers, vendors, etc.) could be uniquely identified across the organization (this company requested to remain anonymous).

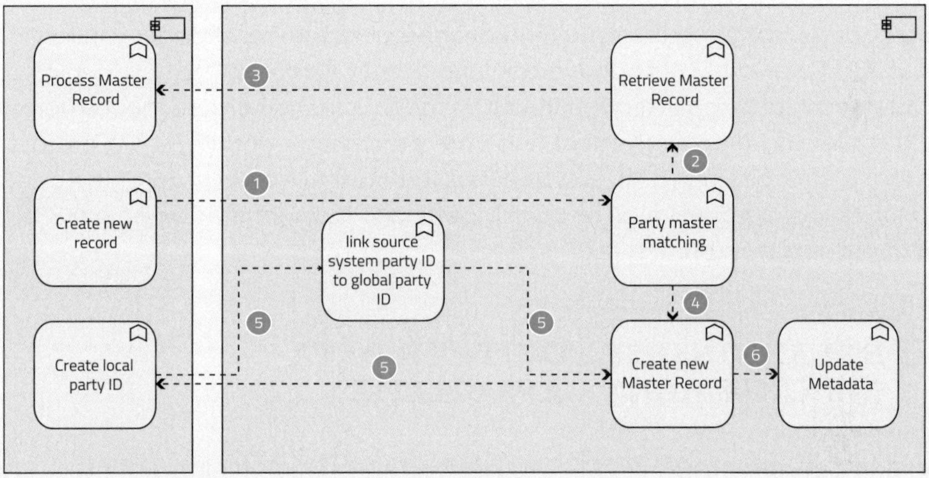

This company had many source systems with *party data* (i.e. data about parties with which the company does business: suppliers, partners, customers, etc.). These systems reside in different countries. The idea was to make sure that all these source systems kept their own local party ID but added an extra field for the global party ID. The MDM hub is responsible for handing out these global ID's.

The diagram illustrates how the process works: (1) The process starts when a source system wants to create a new party record. If this is the case, it forwards the details about this party to the MDM hub. (2) The MDM hub tries to match the party details to the parties that it already knows. If there is a 'match' then (3) The party record is retrieved and sent back to the source system for further processing and the process ends. (4) If there is no match, then this party is as of yet unknown to the organization. If this is the case, a new record will be created in the MDM hub, including the global party ID. (5) This record is sent back to the source system, which creates a local party ID which is sent back to the MDM hub. The local party ID is then linked to the global ID for future reference. (6) The process ends when the relevant metadata is updated.

> The advantage of this approach is that all local source systems can retain their own version of the truth but the MDM hub has an overview across the enterprise. Tongue-in-cheek this could be called a non-invasive MDM solution.

One of the things I like about what is presented in example 41 is the search for a *non-invasive* solution. In this organization it was recognized that it was key to be able to integrate data from different sources and to be absolutely certain whether two records were about the same party or not. Being able to synchronize across data sources was not a requirement and we found a solution that solved the problem without doing much more than that.

In most cases, *mastering* the data for a business concept has stronger implications. As discussed previously, it is about organizing a "best version of the truth" which can be obtained in one spot. Through the MDM techniques you ensure that all updates about something (*Person*, *Product*, etc.) are processed centrally so we are pretty sure that the record in the MDM system has the most up-to-date data. This can be used for various purposes such as quickly getting to the right data when a customer calls or building a "customer 360" system[2].

15.3 RELATIONSHIP TO OTHER DATA MANAGEMENT CAPABILITIES

One of the key challenges that MDM systems perform is matching records to see if they are about the same real-world "thing" (e.g. if two records are about the same person or the same product.). There are smart algorithms to do this but they are not perfect. The records that are a match, or do not match *with sufficient certainty* are processed automatically. The records that are "left over" represent the hard cases and are set aside to be handled by a data steward.

This means that MDM systems typically have a workflow component to assist data stewards in handling these tough cases. This workflow tends to include functionality to prioritize and assign work, to look up metadata about data elements, and to document the resolution for these cases.

2 A customer 360 view is the idea of bringing data from different sources together so the company has a good overview of everything it knows about the customer. This includes structured records from key systems, data about the behavior of this customer on the website, e-mail exchanges and so on.

There are also strong links between the MDM capability and the field of data integration: usually the flow of data between source systems and the MDM hub are real-time in nature but that still keeps the door open for using different integration techniques. An approach based on *services* (section 13.2.2) is most commonly used.

Last but not least, the link between MDM and *architecture* ensures that the MDM solution fits in the overall landscape. MDM is a way to solve the problem of reconciling differences between data sources with respect to key business concepts such as *Party* or *Product*. Other solutions exist as well (e.g. appointing "golden sources" or migrating all data to a single system) and the task to choose among alternatives typically falls to architects.

15.4 VISUAL SUMMARY

16 Quality

Synopsis *- Quality is a tough concept to define. Years ago, I published research which showed that quality is both subjective and situational [Gil06]. This work is relevant for this chapter because determining the quality of data assets also requires a good understanding of the needs of stakeholders and the situation in which data is used. After a short introduction, I will start this chapter with a recap of some of the findings from my earlier research. I will then give an overview of data quality (DQ) and data quality management. I will conclude this chapter by linking DQ to other DM capabilities.*

16.1 INTRODUCTION

Data quality management is concerned with ensuring that stakeholders have access to *fit for purpose* data. Just having a bunch of data available is not very useful in and of itself, it has to be of sufficient quality for business success. A good analogy is: if *processes* are the value creation engine of the enterprise, then *data* is the fuel. If you have the world's best engine but use the world's worst fuel, then overall performance probably will not be very good. Poor data quality has a big impact on organizations and includes customer dissatisfaction due to poor service, increased operational cost, less effective decision-making, and a reduced ability to make and execute strategy [Red98]. Therefore, it is good business practice to invest in data quality.

16.2 THE NOTION OF QUALITY

From 2002–2006, I undertook research about the notion of quality [Gil06]. The line of reasoning in this research was as follows. The first point is that quality is *subjective*. This means that two people can judge the quality of something and they may arrive at a different conclusion.

The second point is that it is hard to quantify value. This means that a statement such as "person *p* asserts that the value of x is *y*" is hard to make. If we use money to represent *y* then the money serves as an indicator for the quality of x. What you are doing in this case is *comparing* the value of two things. In other words, you're saying "person *p* asserts that the value of x equals the value of *y*".

The last aspect is that the *situation* in which a quality assessment is made is relevant: different circumstances lead to different choices. This means that, if you want to be very precise, you would say "in situation s_1 person *p* feels that the value of x equals the value of *y* but in situation s_2 he might make another assessment". Example 42 illustrates this line of thinking.

Example 42. Quality is personal and subjective
The two objects that we are comparing are a bottle of water and $10. The quality assessment of these objects may be very different depending where you are (in the desert, versus in the supermarket) but at the same time it is not unthinkable that other people would make a different assessment than you would.

Switching to the world of data, consider a data set that lists the prices of products. Two stakeholders, depending also on the situation in which this data is to be used, may assess the quality of this data set differently. This could be because one stakeholder is working in an operational process and needs the price information to three decimals and up-to-the-minute accuracy but another stakeholder is creating weekly reports and only uses two decimals.

While the discussion is somewhat abstract, it does show that quality assessment is not a straight- forward process. A thorough understanding of the needs and requirements of stakeholders is key to assessing data quality. I will discuss this further in the following section.

16.3 DATA QUALITY

The quality of data can only be assessed in the context where it is used by stakeholders. This means we should get a good understanding of the processes and systems in which data is used and the needs of the stakeholders in this context. There are two key questions for this:

- What data do we need? In other words, which business concepts and data elements do we need? (See also chapter 6.)
- How good should the data be? In other words, what are our requirements for the quality of the data?

The first question has been covered in chapters 6 and 12; by listing the business concepts/ data elements, potentially supported by a conceptual data model/ logical data model respectively, you get a good understanding of *what* data is needed. The second question requires a more careful exploration of *data quality dimensions*.

A data qualitydimension is a measurable aspect or characteristic of data [SC12, Hen17]. The word *dimension* appeals to the idea that the quality of data can be assessed by looking at different characteristics of the data. There are endless lists of data quality dimensions and a full overview can't be given. Therefore, I will only cover a short list with dimensions that are frequently used in practice (the selection is based on DMBOK and my personal experience).

- **Accuracy** - Accuracy refers to the degree in which data is a correct representation of what is going on in the real world. For example, it would be accurate to say that the author of this book is a person with the name *Bas van Gils*. Accuracy is hard to determine if you only have the data itself at your disposal. For example, if I were to stand in front of you and claim that I am 41 years old - how would you determine if this is true or not[1]? Often you need another source of information to determine accuracy of data.
- **Completeness** - Completeness refers to the degree in which all relevant data about real-world phenomena is present. For example, I could claim that *Koen van Gils* is my son (which is accurate). The dataset about *Kids of Bas van Gils* would not be complete, as my other son – *Stijn van Gils* – would be missing.
- **Consistency** - Consistency refers to the degree in which data "agrees" with other data. A good example here is marriage: it would be *inconsistent* if one record claims that *A* is married to *B* but another record claims that *B* is not married to *A*.
- **Currency** - Currency refers to the degree to which data is still current/ up-to-date. This often has to do with how fast updates to data in source systems travel through your information systems' landscape. For example, say it takes a day for updates to travel from one system to another. If an update occurs in the source system then, at that moment, the data in other systems is no longer current. Whether that is a problem or not is a different matter.
- **Validity** - Validity means: does the data conform to a specific set of rules. You could, for example, state that dates should be formatted *dd-mm-yyyy*. If data comes in that is formatted according to the American standards *(mm-dd-yyyy)* then this data is considered to be not valid (even though it could very well be accurate!).
- **Granularity** - Granularity (or precision) refers to how precise your data is; how many details you have. For example, if I claimed that this chapter is written in

1 It isn't; at the time of writing I am 42 years old.

June of 2019, then that is certainly accurate but is it precise enough? If I need more precision, I could state that it is written on the 29th of June, 2019. Even more precise would be that this sentence was typed on the 29th of June, 2019, at 21:18.

Example 43. DQ problems in a complex landscape

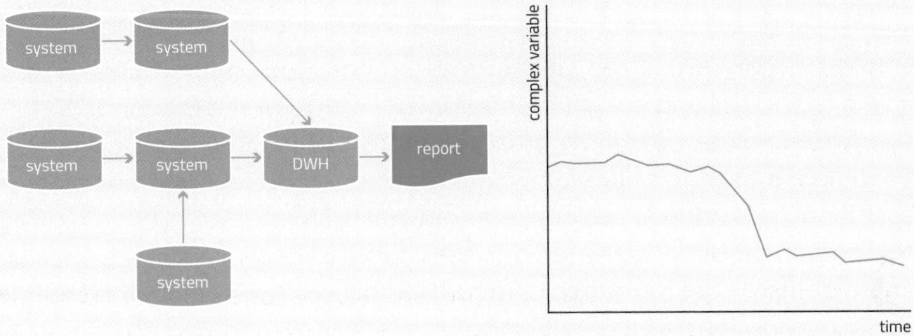

This example comes from a real-world assignment for a large Dutch governmental organization. The example has been anonymized as a result of a non-disclosure agreement that we signed for this project. Consider the above diagram. On the left it shows how data flows between systems until it reaches a data warehouse at the end of the data value chain. From the data warehouse, various reports are generated, giving statistics about a certain complex variable.

The diagram on the right is a rough approximation of what the values for this variable looked like. This data was reported to one of the ministries, who got suspicious because of the break in the trend. The challenge for our team was to assess the quality of the reported data.

In order to deal with this challenge – and the questions from the ministry – we had to determine how the data in the report was generated (in technical terms: determine the lineage of the data). We compared data in the report to data from the various sources and tried to figure out if each of the sources were *accurate* – which turned out to be the case. We then followed a hunch and examined if there was a *timing* problem (which refers to the *currency* dimension). This also wasn't the case. Finally, we checked all the steps between the source system and the final report. This is when we found out that in one of the systems, someone had changed key business rules which had a dramatic impact on how certain situations were handled (i.e. the rules around *validity* had changed). In the end, all it took to "fix" the problem was to discuss these business rules and synchronize them across systems. This also satisfied the auditors that were sent by the ministry.

It took three consultants and over three weeks of hard work to figure out what was wrong with the data. A simple change that was not communicated with stakeholders in the data value chain turned out to be quite costly.

There are only six dimensions you could consider when assessing the quality of data. That can certainly be a daunting task. To illustrate how costly it can be to solve DQ issues after the fact in a complex information systems landscape, consider example 43.

Another way to classify data quality issues comes from the work of David Loshin [Los10, Los12]:

- The simplest quality issues are at the level of individual data values. A good example is to find spelling errors ("Nehterlands" instead of "Netherlands").
- Issues between values but within a single record are (a little) more complex. A good example is to spot a situation where a person aged four also has a driver's license. It is not forbidden to be four years old, nor is it forbidden to have a driver's license. The combination, however, is questionable at best.
- Even more complex are issues across records within a single system. This includes, for example, situations where one record says that *A* and *B* are married but another record claims that they are not.
- The toughest issues occur when data values in many records across many different systems together do not make sense. Example 43 is a good case.

As a general rule, organizations usually start with finding and correcting the category of simple errors. The other levels are more ambitious and require a more mature data quality capability (and thus larger investment by the organization).

16.4 DATA QUALITY MANAGEMENT

This brings me to the topic of *data quality management*. The DMBOK defines this as follows [Hen17]:

> *The planning, implementation, and control of activities that apply quality management techniques to data, in order to assure it is fit for consumption and meets the needs of data consumers.*

A close examination of this definition shows that this is a big task. The *planning* aspect refers to the fact that it takes foresight and careful consideration to design the interplay between processes, data, and systems in such a way that data is fit for purpose when it is used. Sidebar 5 illustrates this point further: responding to problems with data quality after the fact is a costly strategy. "Thinking before doing" is a much more sensible strategy, even if it may seem that "thinking" slows down the realization process a little: this investment tends to pay itself back many times over. The planning aspect includes making agreements about the DQ *requirements* and analyzing which controls are needed in processes and systems to ensure sufficient levels of quality.

The definition also includes the *implementation* aspect. This entails the realization of the aforementioned controls in processes and systems. Finally, the *control* -activities refer to the fact that making agreements and implementing controls is a good thing but you still have to regularly/ continuously monitor if data quality is as specified. It also refers to the fact that corrective action may be required when data quality issues are found.

Sidebar 5. Interview Marc van den Berg (summer 2019)

It is important that staff functions such as *security, privacy, architecture*, and *data management* cooperate. The needs of business and IT stakeholders should be a driving force for all data management initiatives. Only through shared vision and approach can success be achieved. One of the challenges is to get business stakeholders to think about data management in a proactive manner: if you only correct data problems reactively then you are always one step behind. This requires a culture shift: rather than investing time and resources to fix things after the fact, the organization should learn to *think* first (What are we trying to achieve with data, processes, and systems? Which controls do we need?) before changing/ building new capabilities in the organization.

Marc van den Berg is managing director of IT *and Innovation at* PGGM, *a Dutch pension provider.*

In my experience, having good *data agreements* that specify what data is required, at which levels of quality, is the key to success. You can have all the monitoring and profiling tools[2] in place but if you have no shared understanding of what constitutes *fit for purpose* then you might as well throw money down the drain. The data agreements are good input for discussions about required controls and to design effective processes and systems in the organization. As sidebar 5 shows, it is also crucial to help the organization to move to a way of working that balances proactive and reactive DQ activities.

16.5 CRITICAL DATA ELEMENTS

When implementing a data quality management capability in organizations, I often hear that "we are trying to boil the ocean and it won't work". Attempting to boil the

---

2 Profiling, in this context, means analyzing data against requirements, or to search for patterns in the data. Through data profiling you would, for example, be able to detect that low house numbers are more common than high house numbers with the exception of house number 9999 (which could be the escape value "I don't know the house number but the system forces me to specify one anyway").

ocean is definitely not a good idea, so we need a way to find out where to apply this capability more strictly, and where a more "loose" approach is sufficient. This is where the notion of *critical data elements* (CDE) comes in. The term CDE refers to the data sets that are critical for the well-functioning of the organization. These data sets require stringent data quality management processes. Other data may require a less strict approach. Example 44 shows a real-world example of how to deal with this prioritization problem.

Example 44. Critical data elements

This example comes from a real-world assignment that I did in in the financial services sector. Together with a team, we had to come up with an approach to determine which data was "critical". This organization already had sound practices around data security (see chapter 17) where data was classified along three security dimensions on a four-point scale: confidentiality, integrity, and availability. Also, data was tagged as being privacy sensitive or not. We used these classifications to determine how critical data was:

- **if** the data is privacy sensitive **then** it is critical
- **if** the data is classified as a four on either one of the three security dimensions **then** it is critical
- **if** the data is classified with at least two times a three on the security dimensions **then** it is critical
- all other data is not critical

This is a very deterministic process, as data owners (see chapter 9) were obliged to establish these security/ privacy classifications. However, we decided to build in an escape: if data was thought to be "not critical" but a data owner believed it still should be classified as "critical" then the deterministic process can be over-ruled.

At the time of writing, this approach has only just been implemented. The first results and effects are positive: business stakeholders find it hard and time-consuming to use such an elaborate mechanism but are also happy to have a good mechanism that helps them set priorities.

16.6 RELATIONSHIP TO OTHER CAPABILITIES

I will conclude this chapter with a brief discussion about the relationship with other data management capabilities. Several links have already been mentioned, so I will keep this overview brief.

The first link is to metadata: specifying data quality requirements is often done by listing *business concepts* and *data elements*, potentially accompanied by a *conceptual data model* or *logical data model* respectively. Data modeling is a key to getting a sound understanding of data and ties directly into data quality dimensions such as *accuracy, consistency,* and *validity* (see section 16.3).

The second link is to *data governance*. I have already discussed that data owners play a key role in data quality management. This is also true for *data users*: they have to share their requirements with data owners. How else can data owners ensure that the data which is made available is of sufficient quality? Regrettably, a good conversation is usually not sufficient to ensure fit for purpose data. In many cases, we see conflicting requirements or conflicting priorities. To resolve them, it is crucial to have governance structures in place that help address them in a productive manner that does justice to the needs of all stakeholders involved.

Last but not least, there is a link to *data integration*. As example 43 shows, data quality issues can become more visible when comparing data across the information systems landscape. The term *lineage* is used to indicate where (in which system) data originated and how it flowed through the systems landscape. Lineage is a form of metadata. Knowing the lineage of data is key in efficiently resolving data quality issues.

16.7 VISUAL SUMMARY

DATA QUALITY IS SUBJECTIVE AND HAS MANY DIMENSIONS

17 Risk and security

***Synopsis** - Data security management is a topic that has close ties to risk management. Based on the risk appetite[1], requirements around the protection of data assets are translated into an effective set of measures to mitigate risks around data assets. Security measures are often complex and highly technical. In this chapter, I will approach the topic of data security management from a business perspective. I will start with a high-level introduction to concepts such as risk and risk mitigating measures. I will then shed light on the relevant ISO standards and give an overview of data security management based on the DMBOK [Hen17]. I will end this chapter by linking data security management to other data management topics.*

17.1 RISKS AND RISK MITIGATING MEASURES

Security is a very broad topic and typically goes much further than only *data security*, which is the topic of this chapter. The terminology and way of thinking that is introduced in this first section is general enough to fit with the broad scope of security. The remaining sections of this chapter will zoom in on the specifics of *data* security management. This chapter is based on the DMBOK, supplemented by other key publications in the field [Hen17, DH11, WP11, Dis13, HHSB15].

The term *security* should not be used stand-alone. It always requires a context: the security of some *asset* (such as data assets). There may be one or more *threats* that prevent us from using these assets in the way we want to. The operative word is *may*: there is a *risk* that things could go wrong.

The classic formula for *Risk* is *Probability* times *Impact*. In mathematical terms: $R = P \times I$. In theory, probability can be scored as a percentage (i.e. it has values

1 Risk appetite is a measure for how much risk is a stakeholder willing to accept.

between 0 and 100). I find that most people find it very hard to assess risk using this approach, as illustrated by example 45. In practice, these percentages are impossible to determine. The impact can be assessed in different ways. For example, using T-shirt sizing (low/ medium/ high), or by quantifying it with a dollar amount. In my experience most organizations work with low/ medium/ high scores to assess the impact of a risk.

Example 45. Risk assessment

Suppose you want to travel from Amsterdam (Netherlands) to Barcelona (Spain). This is a journey of roughly 1500km (approximately 930 miles). Suppose also that you are a very risk-conscious person and want to choose the safest way to travel. What will you do: train, car, or airplane? Trying to compare the risk of an hour of flying to an hour of driving is probably not the best way to tackle the problem. For a good analysis, you should compare the whole journey. According to a recent article in *The Guardian*, the safest option is to fly [Bal14]. For some people this is surprising, as the *impact* of airplane accidents is so big. However, it turns out that the *probability* is extremely low. The cited article claims that traveling by train is about twice as deadly as flying and that making the journey by car is about 3,000 times more deadly.

How hard can it be to make this type of assessment? Years of experience shows that it is doable as long as the probabilities and impact are not too extreme. When you start thinking about questions such as "which threat has the highest risk for death in the Netherlands", then this becomes much harder. For example, the probability of a flood is extremely low but the impact is extremely high[1]. Typical answers to the aforementioned question are traffic accidents, cancer, and smoking. These are serious threats but in terms of $R = P \times I$, flooding has a much higher risk.

1 To see how high, check a map of the Netherlands that shows what happens when the country is flooded. In the Netherlands, the norm frequency for a major flood has been determined as once every 10.000 years. This norm is used to determine the height of the Dutch dikes. The probability of a flood in the provinces North Holland/ South Holland adds up to $1.7 \cdot 10^{-7}$, which is very low indeed. Note, also, that the western part of the country is densely populated.

To protect against threats, you can choose to implement *controls* (i.e. extra process steps, or verification routines in software) that either lower the risk, lower the impact, or both. This is illustrated in example 46. There is at least *some* risk that the threat still manifests themselves. In more technical terms, there is a *residual risk*. Of course, you can endlessly try to reduce the risk further with a new set of controls. Each time it becomes harder (and more costly) to reduce the risk further[2]. The trick to risk

2 This is a good example of the *law of diminishing returns*. See e.g. https://en.wikipedia.org/wiki/Diminishing_ returns, last checked: 12 October 2019.

management is to find out how much risk an organization is willing to accept (its *risk appetite*).

Example 46. Controls to reduce risk
Suppose you own a big house in a popular location. One of the threats you wish to insure against is fire. You have calculated that the probability of a fire destroying your house is not so high but the impact is simply too big. After comparing options from different insurers, you go with a package that includes two things. First, your house will be fitted with smoke detectors and fire extinguishers. This is an example of a control that reduces the probability somewhat: it helps you to find out sooner rather than later that the house is on fire, so there's a good chance you can get the fire under control. Also, your insurance will financially compensate you if the house does burn down. This is an example of a control that reduces the impact: you will still have lost your home and many of your belongings but at least you will have the funds to rebuild your home.

Another example is in mobile banking. The one thing that most people (in the western world, at least) always carry with them is a phone. In many cases this is a smartphone that is connected to the internet. Being able to make payments from your phone is convenient. But what if the phone is lost? Many banks have added a layer of security to mitigate the risks associated with the theft of your phone. This includes the fact that you have to type in a username and password/ use biometrics to gain access to the application on your phone. This reduces the probability of misuse of your phone. It also may include a rule that prevents you from making large mobile payments, which reduces the impact if "the bad guys" do get access to your phone.

17.2 ISO STANDARDS

In the previous section, I have explained the relationship between *risk* and the *controls* to mitigate those risks. As you can imagine, the range of risks related to data is huge. It would be pointless when each organization tries to reinvent the wheel by brainstorming their own list of viable risks. The same goes for controls: there is a long, but limited, number of controls that are typically used to mitigate these risks. In close cooperation, the *International Standards Organization* (ISO) and *International Electrotechnical Commission* (IEC) are working on a set of widely accepted standards to aid professionals in the field. The series of standards is collectively called the ISO 27000-series of standards. At the time of writing, 46 standards in this series have been published with several more to come. The objective is to provide a standard framework for risk and security management that helps organizations with their risk and security practices as well as providing a basis for auditing. A small selection includes:

- **[ISO18] -** Is titled "Overview and vocabulary" and does just that. This standard presents the general concepts related to risk and security and formally defines key terminology. A standardized language helps professionals to collaborate effectively.
- **[ISO13a] -** Is titled "Requirements". This standard describes a plan-do-check-act cycle for risk and security management. The idea is to develop a *security policy* that is used to mitigate the relevant risks in the organization.
- **[ISO13b] -** Is titled "Code of practice for information security controls". This standard gives an overview of controls in various security categories, such as access control, cryptography, and communications security. These controls are described in detail including a "best practice" guide for implementation.

These standards are invaluable for organizations. Their adoption is growing, still, and they are frequently revised to stay up-to-date with trends and current practices. In chapter 32, I will present a pragmatic approach to implementing a (data) security capability that also leverages these standards.

As further guidance, note that certification is of great professional benefit to students and employees: it gives credibility and provides a good basis for assessing in which area(s) a person is competent [RR13]. Also, Hsu argues that the implementation process of security practices is far from trivial and warns that clear alignment of goals, expectations, and certifications is a key factor for successful implementation [Hsu09].

17.3 DATA SECURITY MANAGEMENT

Data security management is a capability that leverages the risk management approach as outlined in the previous section: classify the risk and seek to mitigate it to acceptable levels. There are, however, other strategies to deal with security risks. Gartner has developed a framework to classify these strategies [Car16][3]:

- **Prevent -** Minimize the potential avenues of attack to prevent incidents.
- **Detect -** Recognize incidents in order to isolate and contain them.
- **Respond -** React to breaches, mitigate the damage, analyze and learn.
- **Predict -** Understand your risk, know where incidents/ attacks could occur, and uncover weak spots to monitor/ improve.

The DMBOK defines data security management as follows [Hen17]:

3 Full coverage of this framework is beyond the scope of this book. Only the highlights are included. In this book, I will focus on the prevention strategy mostly.

Definition, planning, development, and execution of security policies and procedures to provide proper authentication, authorization, access, and auditing of data and information assets.

I am not a big fan of this definition as the emphasis is too much on the *measures* rather than the *objectives* of data security management. My take on a definition is:

Data security management is the capability for managing the risks associated with threats to confidentiality, integrity, and availability of data assets.

This definition refers to threats in three categories: *confidentiality, integrity,* and *availability.* Collectively these are referred to using the CIA acronym. They are defined as follows:

- **Confidentiality** - Refers to keeping data assets confidential – restricted and/ or private – meaning that only authorized people can get access to the data. There are many controls that organizations use to improve the confidentiality of data assets. For example:
  - Requiring a password to get access to data reduces the probability that unauthorized people get their hands on sensitive data.
  - Using a system where more detailed access to data requires additional passwords. This reduces the impact if a password is lost, since only part of the data will become accessible to unauthorized people.

- **Integrity** - Refers to prevention of unauthorized modification of data and protects the accuracy and completeness of data to keep it consistently reliable. Controls to protect the integrity of data assets are:
  - Using a checksum[4]. If you transmit both the data and the checksum of that data, then the receiving party can verify whether the data came across correctly. No doubt this is not a perfect solution but the use of a checksum at least reduces the probability that the integrity of the data assets has been compromised.
  - Installing and using anti-virus software that prevents unauthorized parties from tampering with data assets. This reduces the probability that the integrity of data assets has been compromised.
  - Frequently perform manual checks with respect to the integrity of data and make sure to have a secure backup of data available. Being able to restore a backup reduces the impact when data has been compromised.

4 A checksum is a calculated value using a standardized function. Suppose you have a text ("hello world") when transmitting data. A checksum function could be to summarize the numerical values of all letters (a=1, b=2, etc.). The checksum for "hello world" would be 8+5+12+12+. . .=124.

- **Availability -** Refers to data assets being available when needed and ensures that stakeholders have reliable and timely access to data assets. Controls to protect the availability of data assets are:
  - Using a UPS[5] for systems that hold important data assets. This reduces the probability that systems go down due to a power failure and therefore reduces the probability that data assets are unavailable.
  - Using a failover solution for systems that hold important data. This means that data is replicated across multiple systems in such a way that the data remains available when one system has a high workload. This reduces the probability that data is unavailable.

There are many different data security threats and probably even more ways to exploit them. Specific types of exploits/ attacks often go under impressive sounding names such as *Denial-of-Service attack* (DoS, aimed at availability), or *man-in-the-middle attack* (aimed at confidentiality). As with data quality (chapter 16), a purely *reactive* approach to data security management is not very (cost) effective: the trick is to think before you act.

This brings me to the topic of data security processes. Typically, a discussion about data security processes starts with the definition of a *data security policy* at the strategic level of the enterprise. According to the DMBOK, the data security policy "describes behaviors that are determined to be in the best interest of an organization that wishes to protect its data". These policies are typically very high-level and provide very little concrete guidance on what should be done in the organization. It does, however, provide guidance on *which* controls should be selected to reduce risk to acceptable levels and *how* they should be implemented.

With a security policy in place, a *risk assessment* can be performed. This is an extensive process which consists of identifying which risks are relevant (i.e. which *threats* do we want to take into account?), to analyze/ quantify them (i.e. what are the probability and impact of these risks?), and evaluate whether these risks are acceptable or not (i.e. should the risks be mitigated, and to what extent?). Based on this analysis, controls are selected and implemented.

This is not the end of the process, even though it is a good start. A security management system with all controls in place should still be actively *monitored* and regularly *audited*. Monitoring, in this context, means keeping track of which risks actually manifest themselves and how effective the controls are. An audit can be both *internal* or *external* and is aimed at formally establishing if the selected

5 UPS stands for Uninterruptible Power Supply; a device that provides battery backup when the electrical power fails or drops to an unacceptable voltage level.

controls together are a good implementation of the objectives that were set out in the security policy.

17.4 TRAINING AND CERTIFICATION

The field of risk and security management naturally lends itself to the development of standards in which professionals can be trained and certified. One challenge is that there are so many different certifications that it is very easy to mistake a forest for the trees. In my view, these certifications are valuable, as long as you realize that there is more to being a good risk/ security specialist than being able to pass exams. I will briefly discuss three popular security certifications:

- **CISSP** - The acronym stands for "Certified Information Systems Security Professional". It is recognized globally and is therefore claimed to be the "world's premier cybersecurity certification". Note that the focus is on *cybersecurity*, so the *physical* part of security is not covered. One of the interesting aspects of this certification is that it requires a minimum of five years of experience. This suggests that the training goes well beyond a cursory discussion of security topics and aims to be more in-depth and hands-on.
- **SABSA** - The acronym stands for "Sherwood Applied Business Security Architecture" and was developed by John Sherwood. Development started in the 1990s and it has become a popular standard that aligns well with architecture approaches such as TOGAF and ArchiMate. This stems from the fact that the SABSA framework is built on top of the Zachman framework (e.g. [Zac87]). The framework uses six perspectives: Asset (what), Motivation (why), Process (how), People (who), Location (where), and Time (when) combined with six levels of abstraction (contextual, conceptual, logical, physical, component, and operational) to provide a total of 6x6 = 36 viewpoints on the security architecture of the organization.
- **CISM** - The acronym stands for "Certified Information Security Manager" and is aimed at those managing teams of information security specialists. The certification is overseen by an independent and not for profit organization (ISACA) and is intended to show an all-around knowledge of technical competence and an understanding of business objectives around data security.

17.5 RELATIONSHIP TO OTHER CAPABILITIES

Data security management is one of the most technically complex disciplines in the field of data management. The field is ever-changing (if only because hackers are always seeking new and creative ways to get access to your data!) and is hard to keep up with. In my opinion, the only way for data security management to be successful is when it is strongly linked to other capabilities, most notably risk management, architecture, and governance.

The links with risk management should be obvious: data security management is about managing a specific set of risks associated with your data. Many organizations – especially those in the financial services industry – have departments whose sole responsibility is *enterprise risk management* (ERM), which is the capability that defines the methods and processes used by organizations to manage risks associated with the achievement of their objectives. Working side by side with the ERM department should give the data security professionals much more grip on risks and the concerns of key stakeholders. This, in turn, should help find the optimal set of controls to be implemented.

As a quick side note: many *users* of information systems perceive security controls as annoying, if not outright unnecessary. Because of these controls, users have to perform extra actions such as typing in credentials (username/ password). Typing in credentials is perceived to have low added value by most business users. Indeed, controls do tend to have that effect: it may take extra effort to keep data assets safe. There is a delicate trade-off between *safety* of assets and *usability* from a user perspective.

This brings me to the link with architecture: enterprise architects (see chapter 12) have a good overview of the interplay between processes, data, and systems. This insight – often in the form of models and blueprints – provides a good starting point for both analyzing (the impact of) risks and mapping out an effective set of controls to mitigate these risks.

■ 17.6 VISUAL SUMMARY

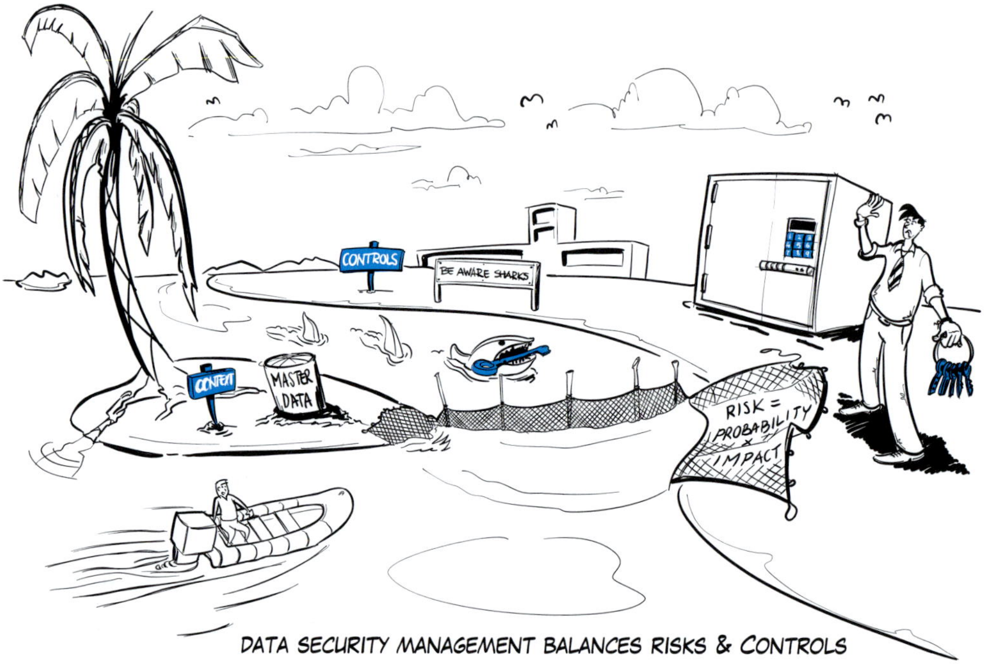

18 Business intelligence & analytics

Synopsis *- Most of the chapters that I have covered so far dealt with the defensive side of data management (see section 3.2). In this chapter (and the next), I will shift gears and discuss value creation with data. I will zoom in on business intelligence (BI) and analytics here, and cover big data in the next chapter. I will start by defining BI and analytics and discuss different types of systems that are commonly found in a BI context. In the next section, I will show how data should be structured for BI and analytical purposes, which relates to the discussion in chapter 11 about data modeling. I will then review self-service BI, which is an important trend in the field. I will end the chapter with an overview of relationships to other data management capabilities.*

18.1 DEFINING BUSINESS INTELLIGENCE AND ANALYTICS

The DMBOK discusses *business intelligence* (BI) and *data warehousing* (DW) in a single chapter [Hen17]. I have chosen to focus on BI in this chapter. The DMBOK defines the field of business intelligence and data warehousing as follows:

> *Planning, implementation, and control processes to provide decision support data and support knowledge workers engaged in reporting, query, and analysis.*

Digging a little deeper, DMBOK lists the following goals for this field:

> *(1) To build and maintain the technical environment and technical and business processes needed to deliver integrated data in support of operational functions, compliance requirements, and business intelligence activities; and (2) To support and enable effective business analysis and decision-making by knowledge workers.*

In this chapter, I will leave out the technical aspects and focus on the purpose of the field instead: to support decision makers with fit for purpose data and analysis/ visualization capabilities. I will use the name *business intelligence & analytics* for this, and use BI as its acronym. In section 18.2, I will very briefly discuss data warehouses and other common system types, mainly from a functional perspective. Example 47 illustrates the distinction between querying, reporting, and analysis to further explain the DMBOK definition of BI.

Example 47. Querying, reporting, and (predictive) analysis

Suppose there is a data set that integrates all of the data your company has on its customers. This includes past and current addresses, purchases, complaints, etc. This data set can be *analyzed* through many different types of queries, such as "find all customers that have filed a complaint shortly after moving to another city". The one-time answer to such a question can satisfy the curiosity of a decision-maker, or help in making a decision about some course of action.

This can be extended to reports which show the *historic trends and patterns* in answers to this query. These reports can be published daily/ weekly/ monthly, or perhaps even shown on a real-time dashboard. By having this data available at all times, it can serve as an early warning system, and signal to decision-makers what the effect is of their actions.

By analyzing the effect of past changes to processes and procedures, the data set can also be used to make *predictions* that show the effect of new interventions, helping management to choose between different courses of action.

The examples show different types of analysis that fall in the realm of BI. Querying and reporting are considered "backward looking" and tend to be cut-and-dry analyses where data is analyzed to give a 100% correct answer. Predictive analyses are considered to be "forward looking" and tend to use statistics to make an educated guess about what *might* happen in the future. There are also situations where statistical analyses are used in backward looking situations, for example when trying to answer questions of the sort "why did xyz happen?".

The key point is to recognize that BI is about supporting decision makers and knowledge workers in their tasks by managing and analyzing data in order to make better decisions.

18.2 COMMON SYSTEM TYPES

A business intelligence capability requires a specific type of tooling. A lot has been written about this. Two often-cited authors and pundits are Inmon (who coined the term *corporate information factory*) and Kimball (who introduced the *dimensional data warehouse*) [Hen17, CS09]. A full exploration of the two approaches is beyond the scope of this chapter, so I will focus on the commonalities rather than the differences.

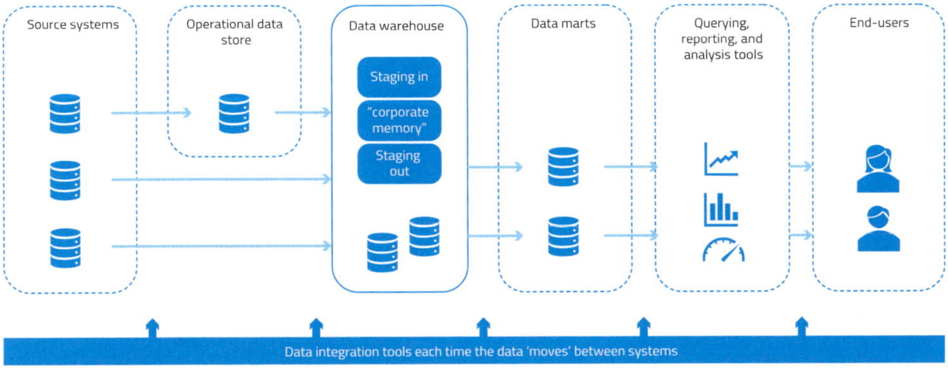

Figure 18.1 Typical BI architecture, from source systems to end-users

Figure 18.1 shows a typical BI architecture and introduces different types of components: source systems, operational data store, data warehouse, data marts, and various types of analytical tools[1].

- **Operational data store (ODS) -** Most IT professionals have come to the conclusion that it is a good practice to use transaction systems only for what they were originally intended: supporting primary business processes by handling these transactions. Running advanced (BI) analyses and reports on such systems should be avoided, as these tend to cause a high load[2] which may hamper the normal operation of the system. An ODS is essentially a fully functional copy of the data from a transaction system. It is also a common practice that an ODS has the data of multiple transaction systems. Typically, an ODS has atomic data (e.g. it has not been aggregated/ summarized) and does not maintain history.
- **Data warehouse (DW) -** The DMBOK states that "The DW provides a single integration point for corporate data to support management decision-making and strategic analysis and planning". This definition still doesn't say much about what a DW is, yet it does give a good indication of its purpose. Key characteristics of a DW are: (1) a DW is a central repository of integrated data from one or more sources; (2) a DW typically holds *historic* copies of data, making it possible to perform analysis of how certain things change over time; (3) a DW does not always have the "atomic" data from source systems but may keep "aggregated" or "summarized" data instead; and (4) a DW typically

1 Whether these are hosted *in the cloud* or, more traditionally, in the data centers of the company itself is not relevant for this discussion.
2 The system load indicates the amount of computational work (the "stress level") that a computer system performs.

has several technical layers as indicated in figure 18.1 – these layers help to manage (the quality of) incoming and outgoing data.

- **Data marts -** Different stakeholders tend to have different needs with respect to (the same) BI-data. For example, both the *finance department* and the *marketing department* may be interested in analysis of *sales data* but with different purposes. Different purposes may lead to different requirements (for example, the finance department may be interested in total sales per month per region for the last six months, whereas the marketing department is only interested in sales per product type per region in more detail, for the last six weeks). Both departments may want their BI data to be structured in a different way. This is where *data marts* come in. A data mart tends to hold a subset of the data in a DW and is usually oriented to a specific business line or team.

On top of these three categories of system types, end-users (e.g. business analysts and "quants") use querying, reporting, and analysis tools to build the insights that are needed by knowledge workers and decision makers.

18.3 STRUCTURING DATA

Data that is used in a BI context is called BI-data. This type of data is often (1) historic and (2) aggregated in nature. Historic, in this context, means that we not only consider the latest version of data about some business concept (e.g. Bas lives in the city of Deventer) but also in past data (e.g. Bas used to live in the beautiful city of Tilburg). This is required to be able to see and analyze patterns and for making predictions. Aggregated, in this context, means that we're usually not interested in individual data points ("Bas has bought a new phone of type X on the 30th of June at store Y") but more in different *aggregates* of those data points (e.g. all transactions on some date, all transactions for a specific store, etc.). Example 48 illustrates this further.

Example 48. BI report

The diagram above shows a BI report for a fictitious company with two stores, A and B. This company sells two types of products, phones and tablets. The sales figures for both stores, for both product types, have been brought together for the first five months of the year and the results are presented in tabular form as well as in a diagram. The analysis shows that there has been a significant increase in sales with the exception of the last month. More specifically, the phone business has been doing well, whereas the tablet business is stable. This report could be used to devise a course of action that would help this company to achieve its goals. Key questions would be: should we invest more in the tablet business? Can we capture a bigger market share for the phone business? What should the next marketing campaign focus on?

	A		B		
	Phone	Tablet	Phone	Tablet	
Jan	200	120	100	80	500
Feb	240	100	190	110	640
March	290	120	290	80	780
April	295	105	300	100	800
May	250	90	275	85	700
	1275	535	1155	455	

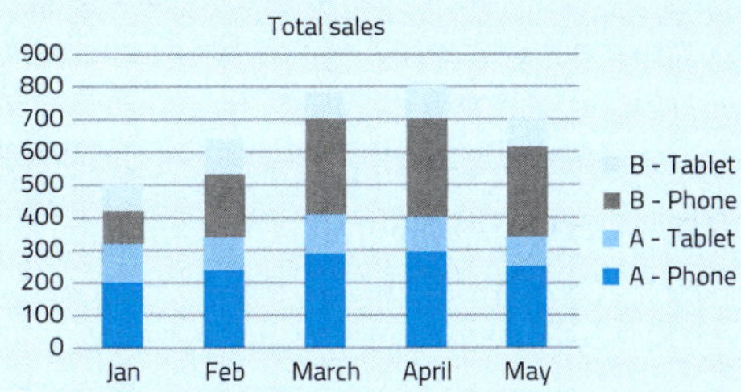

In section 6.3, I discussed storage of data. In sections 8.3 and 11.2, I expanded that discussion and explained that transaction data is typically *normalized*. The purpose of normalization is to ensure that each fact about the real world is stored as data in a consistent manner, to reduce data redundancy (storing facts about the real world more than once) and to make sure no anomalies occur upon adding new data, or updating/ removing existing data.

This does not hold for BI-data: here the purpose is not to avoid redundancy but to make sure that data can be analyzed in a meaningful way. Many different approaches have been developed to structure data effectively for analyses, such as *star schemas*, *snowflake schemas*, and *data vault* [CS09, LO15, Kni15]. Discussing these in great detail would shift the focus of this chapter too much onto data modeling. Therefore, I will discuss only *star schemas* in example 49 since this is the most common/ widely adopted approach for structuring data for BI purposes.

There is more to say about using models for structuring BI-data. I highly recommend *Agile Data Warehouse Design* and *Enterprise Data Architecture – How to navigate its landscape* for a more in- depth treatment of this topic, as these both give a practical and pragmatic overview [CS09, Kni15]. One further topic has not been thoroughly discussed: BI-data is typically *integrated* data, which means that it comes from many data sources. This means that there is a strong relationship with data integration (chapter 13) which I will discuss in more detail in section 18.5.

Example 49. Star schema

The diagram below shows a *star schema*, which consists of one *fact table* in the middle, and four *dimension tables* around it. The approach is sometimes also called *dimensional modeling*, because the focus is on analyzing *facts* (in the fact table) from different *dimensions* (in the dimension tables).

Facts are events that can be observed in the real world. Here the facts are about *Orders*, and we record the *Order ID*, *Order quantity*, *Revenue*, and *Discount* of each order. Each *Order* can be analyzed from the four listed dimensions. The 'keys' are used to create links between the fact table and the dimension table. Consider the link between the *Order* fact table and the *Calendar* dimension table. This link allows us to analyze which date orders occurred on but also (to list but a few options) which day of the week the order occurred on, or which orders were placed on a holiday.

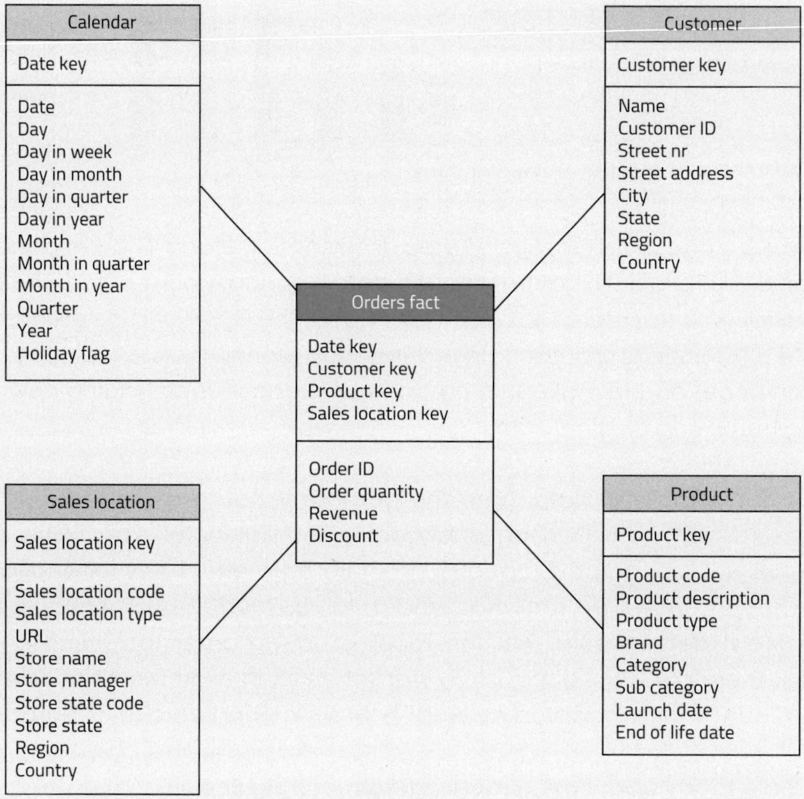

18.4 SELF-SERVICE BI

So far, I have not discussed the different roles that are involved in the BI process. It stands to reason that a group of professionals is involved in gathering, querying, reporting and analyzing data in such a way that knowledge workers/ decision makers can do their job. This at least suggests that knowledge workers/ decision makers are mainly involved as consumers of data. In this approach, the way to build a BI solution[3] is usually as follows. First, you analyze what data you need and from which data sources, for example by studying your data architecture (chapter 12). Then you find a way to bring this data together using one of the integration techniques (chapter 13). This requires, among other things, that data is transformed into a format where it is suitable for analyses (e.g. example 49). Once this is done,

3 Here I am using the word "solution" colloquially to indicate a BI tool and the available data to use in the tool.

questions and business problems are translated into queries and reports, which are often built by the IT department.

Now, assume that you have done all this hard work and a new report is sitting on your desk. You study it and come up with follow-up questions that require new reports. What do you do then? Starting the process again may take too long and with impending deadlines it may not be feasible. This is exactly where self-service BI comes in. Self-service BI tools are advanced software packages where knowledge workers and decision makers have access to BI data in such a way that they can query, analyze, and report data themselves. Figure 18.2 shows an overview of the architecture.

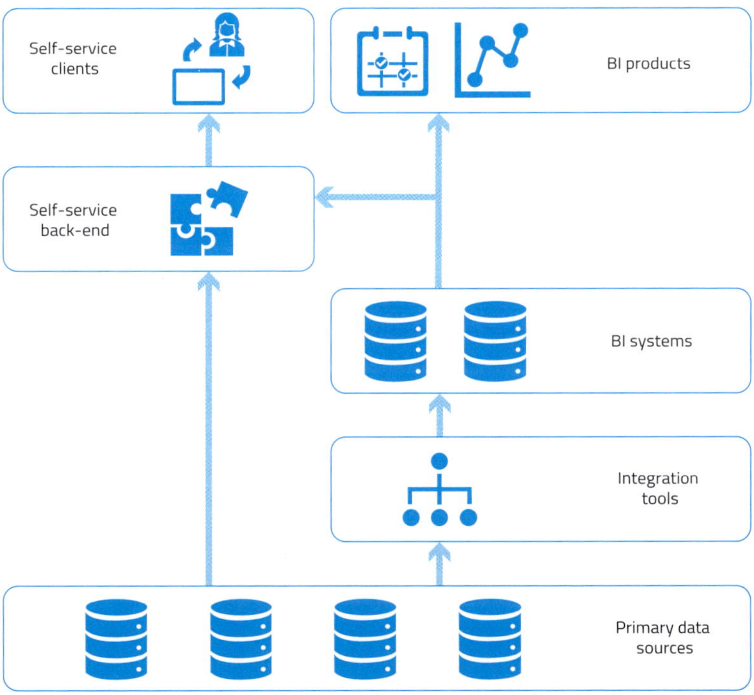

Figure 18.2 Example BI architecture, including self-service

The diagram should be read from the bottom to the top. The bottom shows the primary data sources. These are the "normal" systems of the organization, such as its customer relationship management system (CRM), its enterprise resource planning system (ERP), etc. The right-hand side of the diagram shows the "traditional" approach of BI, using integration tools (e.g. ETL tools – see chapter 13) which feed BI-systems. These systems use data structures as discussed in example 49. The top layer on the right-hand side shows the BI products such as reports and dashboards, as discussed.

The left-hand side of the diagram is different. Both primary data sources and the results from the BI systems on the right-hand side are integrated in a self-service back-end system. On top of this type of system, users can perform their own analysis. When results lead to a new question, users can immediately follow-up with more detailed analyses.

One of the advantages of using a self-service BI tool is speed: users can perform their own analysis and immediately move on to follow-up analyses. Experience in practice shows that there are also serious disadvantages. First of all, IT professionals are trained in dealing with the complexities of integrating data from different data sources (especially in how to deal with data that may look like it is about the same business concept but in fact is about something vaguely the same but precisely different). Business users typically do not have this formal training which may lead to awkward results. Another aspect has to do with statistics and how easy they are to use in typical self-service BI-tools: it becomes very easy to click-and-create fancy dashboards based on advanced statistical analyses. The question is: do you really know what your analyses mean and how these advanced statistics should be interpreted? Example 50 illustrates how this topic can influence the outcome of an investment decision.

Example 50. Statistics & investment decisions
This example is based on a real-world case of an (anonymous) organization. For this governmental organization, I was involved in building the BI capability. There was a proposal on the table where a certain group of managers would get access to a self-service BI tool. The solution wasn't purchased yet and we were in a meeting where the investment decision was discussed.

The architect who was leading this initiative presented his proposal and did a good job at showing what the end-result would look like. Advantages and disadvantages were discussed and one of the team members asked the crucial question: "Are our managers equipped to successfully and meaningfully use this type of tooling?" It remained quiet for a long time in the meeting room until someone spoke again. It was then argued that the group of managers was definitely *not* equipped for this type of analysis. It took another meeting to find the final solution which was implemented successfully: the self-service BI-tooling was purchased and installed, and the organization trained a small group of specialists whose sole task was to work with management to answer their questions, working side-by-side.

18.5 RELATIONSHIP TO OTHER CAPABILITIES

The BI capability has relationships with pretty much all the other data management capabilities. In this section, I will highlight the key ones. Some of these have already been mentioned in this chapter.

First of all, there is a relationship with *architecture* and with *integration*. Architects tend to have a good overview of what data can be found where in the landscape. They also have a good overview of how data flows through the landscape. Since BI analyses require access to a lot of data, potentially from many different sources, it is crucial to have this information at hand when designing BI solutions. The inverse is also true: involving architects may prevent your systems landscape from evolving into a "hairball architecture" where everything is connected to everything else. Good architects are very much aware of the different integration patterns and techniques that are at their disposal and use this to deliver effective BI solutions while at the same time avoiding the aforementioned hairball architectures.

There is also a strong link to *reference data*. Data from different sources, potentially with different reference data, is integrated in BI solutions. Having good reference data will help in getting a sound understanding of the data and improves the data integration processes. Even more, from a BI perspective it would be beneficial to ensure that source systems use *the same* reference data sets. This stresses the link with *governance*: it helps to have good governance in place for the whole of the data value chain – from source systems to final reports. Through governance processes the organization can balance "local" needs of people working with source systems, with "enterprise" needs of people working with data either at the source, or in a BI context.

The *governance* aspect is also important when you consider the combination of *data quality* and BI. Data flows from source systems to BI-systems. A lot can happen along the way. Typically, there are quality checks before data is imported in a BI-system. It would be illogical/ irresponsible to load data for analysis purposes without first checking data quality. Making decisions based on reports that are based on poor data would be pointless. Problems with data quality that are discovered at the end of the data value chain (at the BI system) should be fixed at the source because in that way everybody who uses that data can benefit from the fix. The thing is: people (e.g. data stewards) concerned with these source systems may not be aware of these problems or may have other priorities. Only through good conversations and effective governance processes can we make sound decisions on why/ when/ where data quality problems are resolved (for a further discussion, see also the analogy of the *data river* in example 14).

18.6 VISUAL SUMMARY

19 Big data

Synopsis *- Big data is a topic that is frequently discussed in many different contexts: in business circles the discussion is mainly about the application and benefits of big data, whereas the techies mainly talk about the (new/ novel) technical capabilities that are required to handle big data effectively. It appears that big data is still somewhat in the buzzword phase, meaning that there is no standard, widely agreed, upon its definition yet. In this chapter, I will present an overview of the field of big data. I will base the chapter on frequently cited works, including the DMBOK [ZEDR+11, MSC13, KM16, Kle17, Hen17]. I will start with the definition of big data, including examples about the application of big data. Then, I will provide a high-level overview of the technical capabilities and architecture that are required to implement big data systems. I will end the chapter with a discussion about big data and ethics.*

19.1 DEFINITION OF BIG DATA

The term "big data" was introduced in the mid-1990s and has been used in many different contexts (the first mention of the term appears to be [Mas97]). A quick review of the available literature suggests that there is no single, clear definition of what "big data" is, exactly. The term has been hijacked and hyped in the industry to emphasize the new insights that can be gained by use of new types of technology. This makes it difficult to use the term in a meaningful way (see sidebar 6). In my view, a definition of big data should say something about what it means from a *data* perspective but most definitions are about its use and the technology that is required. The following is a good introduction [DMGG16]:

> *Big data is the information asset characterized by such a high volume, velocity and variety to require specific technology and analytical methods for its transformation into value.*

As the name already suggests, one of the characteristics of big data is that it concerns *a lot* of data. The technical term for this is *volume*. In the realm of big data, the volume of data tends to be high, up to an order of magnitude higher than what we are used to in "normal" information systems.

A second characteristic of big data is its *velocity*: this refers to the rate/ speed with which data is generated. In big data, data tends to come in at very high speeds. In many cases it comes in continually. Sensor data is a good example: sensors can measure something (temperature, traffic movement, number of people in a certain location, etc.) continually, which results in a constantly changing data stream.

The third characteristic of big data is *variety*, which says something about the types of data that are considered. So far in this book, I have mainly focused on *structured* data[1]. Big data deals with many different types of data, including structured data, video, images, audio, etc.

Sidebar 6. Interview with Ronald Damhof (summer 2019)

Big data as a phrase is to be positioned in the same category as "data-driven", "data warehouse", "business intelligence", "data science", "data governance", "master data", and so on. What do they have in common? They have become words that are hollow, empty and above all, ambiguous. We tend to use them abundantly in our work, even relate them to one another and state over and over again a dire future for the organization if they are not implemented or adopted. And in so doing we break some vital communication principles. Is it clear to the recipient what the terms actually mean? In the context of the organization is it validated how the sender defined it and how the recipient interpreted it?

Ronald Damhof, "just a data-guy", self-employed, often in the role of enterprise (data) architect in large (mostly public) organizations.

19.2 DEALING WITH BIG DATA

Dealing with high velocity data can be challenging. A good way to understand why is to make a comparison with a physical production line. In the physical world, there is a limit to how fast a single line can work and this limit is determined by the speed of the workers (human/ robotic) that collaborate on this line. Trying to yield more production from a line that is already at maximum capacity will likely result in work piling up, failures in production, etc. The only way to improve the production

1 Structured data tends to follow the *relational model*, where data is structured in tabular form. See also chapters 6 and 11.

capacity is to reorganize the work, for example by using better resources (e.g. moving from manual labor to robots) or to scale up by adding a second production line. The same is true for data processing. At some point, traditional systems of storing data before analyzing it will no longer work. New technical capabilities for handling this type of (streaming) data are required.

The fact that a data set is large is by itself not enough reason to speak of big data, if only because dealing with large data sets is not new. Think, for example, about all the data that the government (or law enforcement agencies) have about their citizens. Processing huge amounts of data may be technically complex but it is a problem that has been solved: we know how to do this. Similarly, dealing with fast changing data is not new. It is something that we have been doing for years, for example in the realm of signal processing in which a signal of one or more sensors is continually monitored and appropriate action is taken when something changes. The same holds for variety: image or video search/ manipulation are not new and capabilities in these areas continue to improve.

What makes big data special is that it is characterized by all three: high volume, high velocity, and high variety. Using more data (volume) of many types (variety) that changes frequently/ comes in at a high speed (velocity) all increase complexity. To be able to deal with data that has all three characteristics, organizations need novel technical capabilities. These are discussed in section 19.3. Example 51 gives examples of big data use cases in different contexts.

Example 51. Big data use cases

Fraud detection

Many companies, e.g. insurance companies, want to detect fraud early on in order to minimize risk. Automatically detecting fraudulent behavior is a non-trivial task. Insurance companies are experimenting with how big data can help to make *predictive models* to detect fraud as early as possible. These predictive models use many different types of data (*variety*), both historical and real-time (*velocity*), including wages, medical claims, weather data, call center data, clickstream data that shows how people navigate through the website, etc. The first (research) papers on the effectiveness of such an approach are appearing with moderately positive results. At the same time, the first case studies are also appearing. One case study[a] concluded that:

> *The big data architecture enables the insurance agency's fraud detection effort to be more scalable, faster, and more accurate. Because the system really processes and analyzes every record of the available data, it also gives investigators more confidence in their findings (we like this better than sampling techniques and plain hunches!).*

My best guess would be that there is a new arms race between fraudsters and insurance companies, and the one with the best data will win in the end.

Health care

Time is of the essence in healthcare. Being able to quickly respond to changing conditions of patients can save lives. Here too, experiments with big data approaches have promising results. For example, "regular" medical data about patients, combined with real-time data from wearables (such as smart watches that monitor temperature and heart rate) and conditions about the patient's environment can be correlated with historical cases (the same type of data from patients with similar conditions and characteristics) to create an early warning system that predicts when care is urgently required. When blood pressure goes up and there are no indicators of increased physical activity nor of increased temperature in the room then this may be an indicator that something is wrong. The example is perhaps somewhat trivial but being able to do this at scale for many different indicators is an interesting technique with a lot of potential for improving health care. Here too the results are promising[b].

Dynamic pricing

It is a well-known fact that there is a relationship between the price and demand of a good/ service. This relationship is known as *price elasticity*[c]. For companies, the trick is to find a price level where sales, and thus revenue, are maximized. The process of finding this sweet spot can be drastically improved through the use of (big) data. On the one hand zooming out and trying to understand patterns in data (with variables such as price, weather, day of the week, location of the store, marketing campaign, sales strategy) leads to insights about strategy. Along the same lines, zooming in on the characteristics of a specific customer maximizes the chances of an individual sale. Through the use of big data, companies can follow a dynamic pricing strategy. In many branches this proves to be both feasible and successful[d].

—

a https://www.searchtechnologies.com/blog/fraud-detection-big-data, last checked: 9 July 2019.

b See e.g. [RBD+18] for an interesting student paper in this area.

c https://www.investopedia.com/terms/p/priceelasticity.asp, last checked: 10 July 2019.

d See e.g. [BKW14] for a case by McKinsey.

There are many use cases for big data. As the above examples show, some of these have shown great potential, or have already reached the stage of maturity. Big data is, justly, associated with the *offensive/ value creation* side of data management. The name big data is considered to be "sexy" by many, and professionals tend to rally to projects involving this topic. As a result, these projects typically attract people with many different backgrounds, ranging from statistics (being able to perform analysis is key), computer science and engineering (the next section will discuss technical capabilities), as well as strategy and innovation.

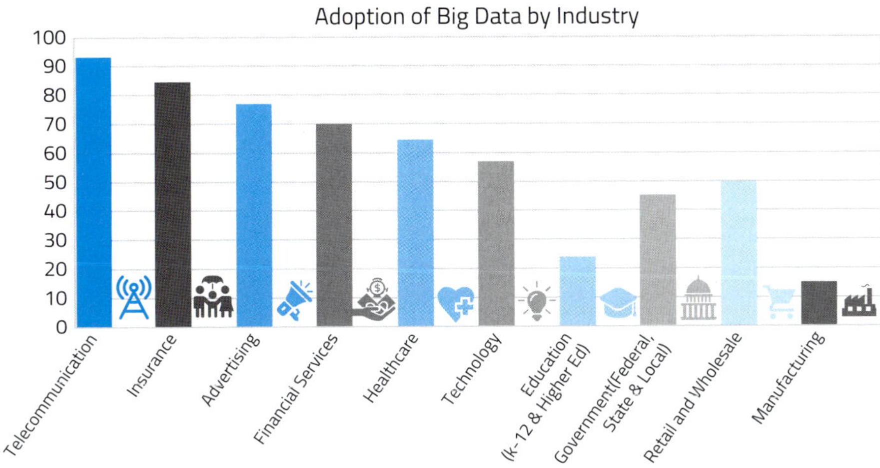

Figure 19.1 Big data adoption (taken from [Agr19] and based on research by Dresner Advisory)

Big data adoption is increasing. In some industries it increases faster than in others. Figure 19.1 shows that use of big data in telecommunications and insurance is already quite common, whereas it is still in its infancy in sectors such as manufacturing and education.

Whether the adoption of big data and its associated technologies continues to grow is, in my view, not a done deal. There is an increasingly strong (public) debate about the ethical use of data (see chapter 21), especially where big data is concerned. The concern is that the abundance of data, in combination with powerful algorithms (e.g. artificial intelligence) will lead to undesirable situations.

As an illustration, consider the mortgage industry. In 2019 there were several news items that discussed a situation where an artificial intelligence system (AI) decided whether to grant a mortgage to customers (e.g. [Kle19]). The AI used all the data it could get its hands on (both its own structured data, through to big data from various sources). As it turns out, the AI discovered all sorts of correlations between characteristics found via big data on the one hand, and the potential outcome (is this a good or a bad customer to lend money to?) on the other. Some are definitely unethical: discrimination based on where someone was born and raised, as well as the social network of a potential customer are dubious factors for a credit model, at least from an ethical perspective.

19.3 TECHNICAL CAPABILITIES AND ARCHITECTURE

One of the things that makes big data special lies in the underlying technology, which enables business users to gain new insights through the smart use of data. As discussed, the traditional model of creating structured databases where data is stored for further analysis is no longer feasible. New technological capabilities are required.

Figure 19.2 gives a high-level overview of a big data architecture and shies away from using specific brands or technology names[2].

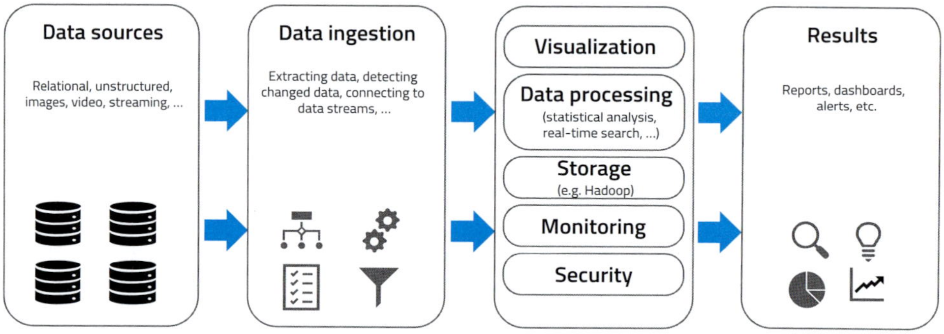

Figure 19.2 Example big data architecture

In this architecture, there are several (types of) data sources – which refers to the *variety* aspect of the definition of big data. The normal/ relational data sources provide but one type of input. Often we see unstructured data (e.g. e-mail, word documents, web pages, social media data), images, videos and streaming data (e.g. sensor data which show temperature, the number of people in a location, etc.). Any type of data can be used in this architecture. The motto is: if you can query/ analyze the data then use it.

The second "layer" is about getting access to the many different types of data sources. We're dealing with a lot of data (*volume*) that changes at high speed (*velocity*) and may take many different forms (*variety*). To gain access, many different techniques can be used. This ranges from techniques that have been around for years (such as ETL to access data in batches – see e.g. section 13.2.1) to modern techniques that are capable of accessing high volume data streams and filtering potentially relevant data from these streams.

The third layer contains a lot of functionality that was also discussed in chapter 18 on BI but with a twist. All the listed functions are important and similar to before but they require a different style of implementation because of the big data characteristics. As an example, sifting through fast changing data in many different forms from many different sources is completely different from analyzing relatively static data that sits on a computer hard drive. The *functions* (security, monitoring, storage, etc.) are the same but their implementation is more complex given the nature of the

2 This book is intended to be vendor- and technology neutral.

data that is used. I expect these capabilities to continue to evolve and become both more powerful and more user-friendly.

In the end, it is about advanced data processes and visualization of the results of these analyses, publishing them to decision makers and knowledge users in such a way that they can use the data insights to their advantage.

Before moving on to the discussion on ethics in relation to big data, I want to offer a brief reflection based on my experience with big data. It may appear that the fields of (the more traditional) BI and the field of big data are pretty much the same with some (relatively minor) variations on a theme. This view is, in my opinion, wrong because the nature of the data is fundamentally different, the technological capabilities are more advanced, the insights are much more powerful, and the way people with different backgrounds collaborate is fundamentally different too.

19.4 RELATIONSHIP TO OTHER CAPABILITIES

The fact that *technologies* continue to change, introducing new capabilities at a dazzling speed, should not come as a surprise. A colleague recently said: "by the time we fully understand a new technology and are ready to put it into production – it will have become obsolete again". I expect that in years to come there will be even more focus on the integration of data from different sources (chapter 13). I also expect that the link to data handling ethics (chapter 21) continues to grow more and more important.

Because of the tension between what is possible with (big) data – and what is "right and proper" – data governance will also be increasingly important: there will be a trade-off between how much *control* the organization really wants in reigning in undesirable use of data, while at the same time fighting to continue to use data to stay at the forefront in the competitive arena. Chapter 34 will discuss the practical issues of working with big data.

19.5 VISUAL SUMMARY

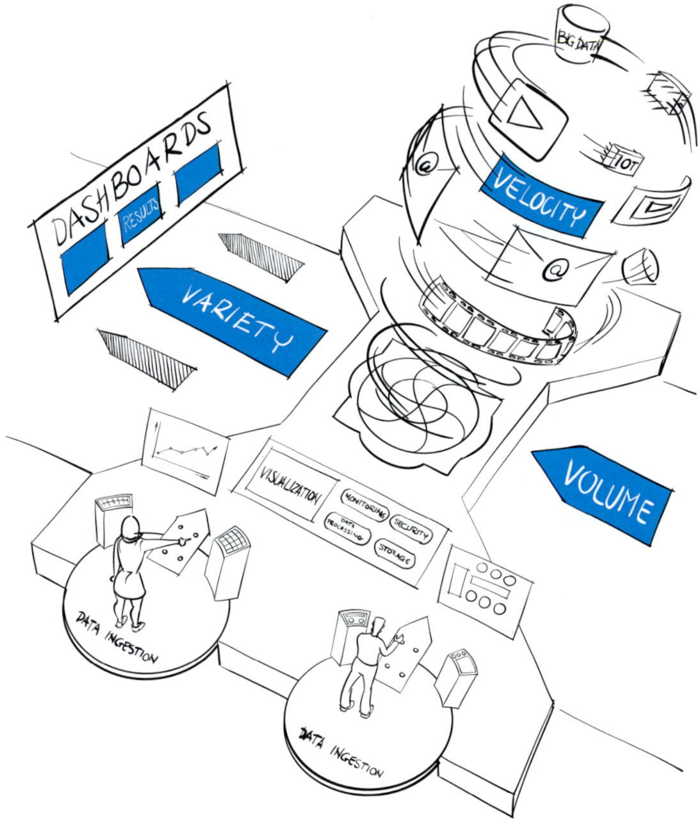

20 Technology

Synopsis *- I have avoided most discussions about technology in this book so far. On the one hand, this is to deliberately signify that data management is a business capability, and on the other hand because technologies come and go. Yet, it cannot be denied that technology is important for data management. I will start the chapter by once more emphasizing my firm belief that, in data management, focusing on people is key. I will then share some observations about technology, including two sidebars by experts in the field. Finally, I will give a high-level overview of technological capabilities that are relevant for data management based on an analysis of the DMBOK [Hen17].*

20.1 PEOPLE ARE KEY

You can buy all the technology in the world in an attempt to solve the data management problems of your organization and still not make much progress in achieving your goals with respect to data management. In this section, I will argue that this is because *people* are the key to success. Technology is a big part of it, but *in an increasingly digital world, you have to put the people first.* In [KNPCA19], it is argued that:

> *The main problem posed by digital disruption is not the rapid pace of technological innovation, but the uneven rates of assimilating these technologies into different levels of human organization. Thus, companies can effectively navigate the challenges of digital disruption by undertaking initiatives that are far more organizational and managerial than technological. Only by fundamentally changing the way the organization works – through flattening organizational hierarchies, speeding up decision-making, helping employees develop the required skills, and successfully understanding both opportunities and threats in the environment – can an organization truly adapt to a digital world.*

To me, this quote captures the essence of both *digital transformation* of organizations and building key capabilities such as *data management*. This is also confirmed by Westerman et al., who speak of a digital culture as a key enabler for successful organizations [WSE19]. Such a culture should be built on several practices, which include data-driven decision-making, but also include self-organization and empowerment of people through an open culture with a high-level of autonomy for employees. As a further example, sidebar 7 illustrates how the people perspective is a prominent factor for building a data quality management capability.

Sidebar 7. Interview with Jan Robat (summer 2019)

People (still) play a large role in data quality management. Skills, knowledge and maybe most of all *awareness* are key. Within ABN AMRO, awareness and education are the prime capabilities we focus on.

Jan Robat is head of data quality management at ABN AMRO.

The simple truth is that technology alone does not do much that is useful: it is an enabler and should be embedded in sound processes and an organizational system. In data management, this means that the *goals and objectives* with respect to data management offense and defense should lead to building a capability that balances the people who do the real work, supported by effective processes, (meta) data, and systems. This is illustrated in figure 20.1. There are two takeaways from this. First, always consider the big picture of people, process, data, and technology through an architecture approach (chapter 12) when considering data management technology, and second always put the needs of your data management professionals first.

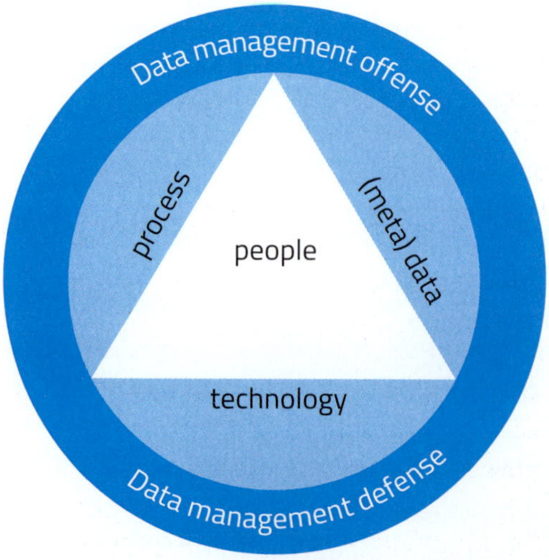

Figure 20.1 Balancing DM offense and defense with people, process, (meta)data, and technology

20.2 OBSERVATIONS ABOUT TECHNOLOGY

While preparing for this book, I was wondering about the perspective of people in the field on changes in technology in general and data (management) in particular. To this end, I have interviewed several people. Sidebar 8 contains excerpts from those interviews.

Sidebar 8. Observations from the field (interviews conducted summer 2019)

In his interview, Marc van den Berg (working at PGGM) zooms in on standardization of technology. He said:

> IT *should support data management initiatives. It is an enabler. However, people should not wait for tools to be in place before getting in action. You can start with simple tools and scale up as you mature. All in all, I believe that standardizing data management technology is a smart way forward that requires a mix of careful planning and experimentation in practice.*

This point of view is supported also by Fanny Vuillemin and Céline Lescop (both working at AXA). When talking about building a data management capability, they argued that "it is difficult at AXA because we don't impose anything on teams for data management". They explained that they have defined an overall framework for data management which lists roles and responsibilities, as well as high-level processes. The actual implementation and selection of supportive tooling is the prerogative of business units.

I discussed several technological issues with Eric D. Schabell (working at Red Hat). He has extensive experience with technology in corporate and open source settings. When asked about the evolution of technology in data storage, he said:

> *I started working at IBM while at the university, on DB2 and mainframe storage*[a]*. The actual changes you see in data are not so much how it's stored, but in how to leverage it. Nobody talks about the problems of "old stuff" but more about how to leverage the existing data within the newer cloud-native development*[b] *and application delivery concepts. Everyone has legacy architecture elements to deal with, so the trick is to use open technologies to expose them to your development teams [. . .]. There are wonderful ways to do this but it requires a strategic organizational transformation as much as the technical cloud-native way of developing/ delivering application and services to your customers.*

It is striking to see that a discussion about data storage immediately includes the human-factor when Eric speaks of making sure that teams gain access to (legacy) data. Later in the interview, we discussed data integration:

> *I see so many different approaches but the best seems to be incremental and thereby gaining experience in your teams as you go with regards to*

the integration of services, data and existing infrastructure/ architecture. Organizations have so many legacy choices to deal with that they are unique in almost every single case. One of the tasks I currently have is to examine successful solutions in certain use cases using our open source technology portfolio. If I look at three successful customers, it's then possible to a certain degree, to elevate a generic architecture that somewhat describes the architectural blueprint for future customers looking to do the same solutions. I always find unique and different approaches in this research as each customer has a completely different playing field, often dictated by resources, past architectural choices, legacy technologies, etc.

Last but not least, I also interviewed Piethein Strengholt (working at ABN AMRO). The main topic of the interview was data integration (chapter 13). When asked about standardization, the use of integration patterns, and technology, he said:

Standardization on integration patterns is extremely important. Integration is very complex and the data integration capability is intertwined with many of the other data management subjects, e.g. metadata, governance, security, etc. Within ABN AMRO we have decided to standardize on three patterns: batches with ETL, APIs[c] *and streaming. These integration capabilities are deployed on all platforms, including public cloud. We also distinguish between enterprise data integration (integration of data across business domains) and local data integration (integration of data within a business domain). Distribution and integration between domains always have to use the enterprise data integration capabilities. Within the domain itself we are more reluctant to enforce standards, because the use case requirements typically have different patterns and needs.*

Piethein also made a link with the human/ organizational aspect of data management. In my view, the essence of his argument is that developing standardized patterns supported by technology is important, but the key to success is to decide when to use them/ enforce their use and where to allow more freedom.

—

a See https://en.wikipedia.org/wiki/IBM_Db2_Family, last checked: 14 July 2019.

b Cloud-native refers to the development of systems "in the cloud". See e.g. section 13.3.3.

c See https://en.wikipedia.org/wiki/Application_programming_interface, last checked: 14 July 2019.

Marc van den Berg is managing director of IT and Innovation at PGGM, a Dutch pension provider.

Fanny Vuillemin is senior data manager at AXA and Céline Lescop is lead data architect at AXA.

Eric D. Schabell is global technology evangelist and portfolio architect director at Red Hat. Piethein Strengholt is principle data architect at ABN AMRO.

The interviews and quotes from the above sidebar confirm a key point about technology that I also made in the opening section of this chapter: technology is important for successful data management, but it can only be used effectively when considering the context (people, process, data) in which it is to be used.

20.3 TECHNOLOGY AND THE FUNCTIONAL AREAS OF DMBOK

One of the strong points of the DMBOK is that all data management topics are discussed in a very structured manner, including an overview of tools/ technology to be used in each area. The overview of data management tools and technologies presented in this section are based on the DMBOK. I have taken the liberty of renaming some technologies to create a more consistent overview and to leave out those elements that appear to be outdated or plain wrong. Note that some tools and technologies appear more than once in the paragraphs to come. This highlights the interconnectedness of all the data management topics.

20.3.1 Data governance and stewardship

Data governance was discussed in chapter 9. The tools and technologies that were listed for this topic are:

- **Websites** - Data governance activities deal with communication and awareness about data management with stakeholders. Websites could be a useful tool. These could be generic websites, or perhaps in a more advanced form such as a Wiki.
- **Business glossary** - A business glossary lists the business concepts/ business terms that are used in an organization, together with formal definitions (which are a form of metadata). Often a glossary also includes information about who is the data owner/ steward for any given concept.
- **Document management tools** - A large part of the formal data governance processes and procedures deal with policy. Policies tend to be documented in formal documents. Maintaining them (and their history) is best done through document management tools.

20.3.2 Metadata

Metadata was discussed in chapter 10. The tools and technologies that were listed for this topic are:

- **Metadata repositories** - This category deliberately uses a plural noun to indicate that it is not necessary per se to implement a single integrated repository in which all enterprise metadata is collected. Metadata is often collected in a variety of tools (such as data modeling tools). The DMBOK also explicitly mentions the aforementioned *business glossary, data dictionaries* that capture the structure and content of data sets, and *data catalogs* that indicate where access to data sets can be obtained.

- **Metadata repository management tools -** This category alludes to the fact that metadata may be distributed across systems and being able to manipulate (collect, integrate, visualize, etc.) metadata is a key capability for effective data management.

In my view, one category of tools is missing:

- **Lineage tools -** Lineage refers to the origination of data and its flow through the information systems landscape. Being able to (automatically) detect the lineage of data is an important capability.

20.3.3 Modeling

Modeling was discussed in chapter 11. The tools and technologies that were listed for this topic are:

- **Data modeling tools -** This is a broad category of tools that should include all the abstraction levels that were discussed in chapter 11: conceptual/ logical/ physical data modeling. Ideally the models for each abstraction level are linked (which is sometimes called "vertical lineage"). Modeling should also include the flow of data through the information systems landscape.
- **Metadata repositories -** One the one hand, metadata repositories are a key input for data modeling. These repositories provide a wealth of information for the data modeler. Also, the results of data modeling should be linked to the repositories. For example, the documentation with a business concept in a data modeling tool should include a link to the glossary in which it is formally defined.

20.3.4 Architecture

Architecture was discussed in chapter 12. The tools and technologies that were listed for this topic are:

- **Data modeling tools -** These were discussed already in the previous paragraph. Architects both produce and reuse existing data models.

In my view, two categories of tools are missing:

- **Enterprise architecture modeling tools -** These types of tool are capable of modeling the relationship between process, data, and systems. ArchiMate is a good standard for architecture modeling and tools in this category should at least support this modeling language.

- **Configuration Management Database Systems (CMDB) -** A CMDB contains all relevant information about the hardware and software components used in an organization. This information is key to designing/ understanding/ checking architecture models.

20.3.5 Integration

Integration was discussed in chapter 13. The tools and technologies that were listed for this topic are:

- **ETL tool -** The ETL pattern for moving data between systems was discussed in chapter 13. Organizations usually have one or more ETL tools at their disposal.
- **Data virtualization server** – Data virtualization was also discussed in chapter 13. This is high-end and pretty advanced software that not all organizations will want to use.
- **Enterprise Service Bus (ESB) -** An ESB implements a communication system between mutually interacting software applications and assists in keeping connections between systems in a landscape manageable[1]. Most ESBs have advanced capabilities that guarantee data is delivered when systems are temporarily down.
- **Metadata repository -** Metadata repositories are used in data integration projects to document how data moves through the landscape (lineage, data structures, data mappings, etc.).

In my opinion, the overview in the DMBOK is a good one. At the same time, it can never be complete. When other/ new integration patterns are used then different tools are required too.

20.3.6 Reference and master data

Reference data was discussed in chapter 14, whereas master data was discussed in chapter 15. The DMBOK lumps these two topics together. The tools and technologies that were listed are:

- **Data modeling tools -** Modeling tools help to understand the data and its use in processes and systems. This is key for designing and implementing good reference data management systems as well as master data management systems.
- **Data integration tools -** Integration tools are needed especially for master data management and may use different integration patterns.
- **Reference data repositories -** Reference data is stored in a reference data repository. This can be a stand-alone tool, or it can be a capability of other tools (e.g. a metadata tool, or a data modeling tool).

1 See e.g. https://en.wikipedia.org/wiki/Enterprise_service_bus. Last checked: 14 July 2019.

- **Master data management systems** - Master data is often stored in a "master data hub" using one of the patterns which were discussed in chapter 15. These systems can be highly complex.
- **Data profiling and quality tools** - Data quality requirements for both reference data and master data are usually (extremely) high. In particular, when integrating data from different sources in a master data management system it is key to profile/ verify its quality. Along the same lines, when verifying the quality in other systems, having access to reference data and master data is key.

20.3.7 Quality

Data quality was discussed in chapter 16. The tools and technologies that were listed for this topic are:

- **Profiling engines, query tools** - Data profiling is the process of examining data against predefined criteria such as data quality requirements. Often this involves statistical analysis and visualization tools. Tools in this category come in many shapes and forms. Some organizations choose to build their own using common programming tools. Others opt for commercial off the shelf products.

I believe that this overview is far from complete, as profiling is only the beginning of the data quality process. The following group of tools is also indispensable:

- **Issue management tools** - Once data quality issues are discovered, it is key to monitoring whether/ when they will be resolved. These types of tools typically involve capabilities to assign data quality issues to stakeholders in the organization, to plan/ schedule their resolution, and to create metrics about the efficiency of the data quality process.

20.3.8 Security

Data security was discussed in chapter 17. The tools and technologies that were listed for this topic are:

- **Access control systems** - This class of tools help in managing who has access to what data in various systems of the organization. There are many different patterns for implementing access control which are beyond the scope of this brief discussion.
- **Protective software** - This is a broad category of tools to protect data from undesirable manipulation. This includes, but is not limited to, firewalls, virus scanners, and backup tools.
- **Intrusion detection systems** - This category of systems has a similar role to data profiling engines used for data quality management. These systems monitor all other systems and will signal security professionals when these other systems have been compromised.

- **Encryption software** - Encryption is a capability that can be used in different settings. The purpose is to safe guard the confidentiality of data. Two key areas where it is used are: (1) when storing data in a system, and (2) when moving data between systems.

20.3.9 Business intelligence

Business intelligence (BI) was discussed in chapter 18. The tools and technologies that were listed for this topic are:

- **BI systems** - This is a broad category of tools that integrate and store BI data. Typical examples are *data warehouses* and *operational data stores*[2].
- **Metadata repositories and data modeling tools** - Metadata and data models are key for finding data that is to be moved to BI systems, as well as the meaning and structure of data.
- **Data integration tools** - These types of tools help to move data from source systems to BI systems.
- **Analytical applications** - This group of tools includes the logic to process data and analyze it in order to generate reports and dashboards for knowledge workers and decision makers. These tools basically come in two categories: those that are operated by IT professionals, and self-service tools that are used by knowledge workers and decision makers themselves.

20.3.10 Big data

Big data was discussed in chapter 19. The DMBOK lists several tools and technologies that are required for big data solutions, such as *distributed file-based solutions, columnar compression*, and *in-memory computing and databases*. Follow-up research shows (1) that these tools and technologies are known under different names, and (2) that the list of capabilities for big data change rapidly. Because of this, I have decided not to give an overview of required capabilities for big data and recommend looking up more up-to-date literature when needed.

20.4 TECHNOLOGY ADOPTION

At the beginning of this chapter, I argued that data management is a business capability where people are the key to success. In part this can be explained by the *technology acceptance model* (TAM), which was first published in 1989 and states that the acceptance of technology largely depends on two factors [Dav89]:

2 See https://en.wikipedia.org/wiki/Data_warehouse and https://en.wikipedia.org/wiki/Operational_data_store respectively. Last checked: 14 July 2019.

- **Perceived usefulness -** Which attempts to measure/ quantify whether users of technology perceive this technology to be useful.
- **Perceived ease of use -** Which attempts to measure/ quantify whether users of technology expect that the use of this technology is free from effort.

Each of the technologies that are mentioned in this chapter can be useful, depending on the context. There is no single best solution that specifies which technologies should be implemented when. My best recommendation would twofold. First, I believe in the power of experimentation: work with simple tools (e.g. office functionality, or simple intranet websites) before purchasing expensive tools. Second, involve your data management professionals as well as a broad representation of business users to make technology choices and take the TAM considerations into account when making a choice.

20.5 VISUAL SUMMARY

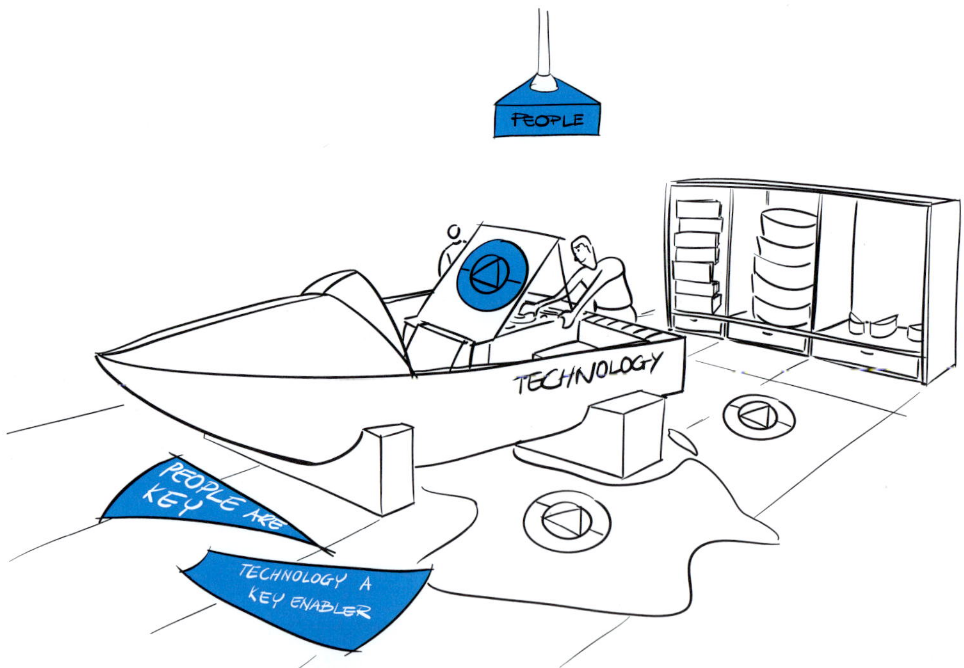

TECHNOLOGY IS A KEY ENABLER FOR DATA MANAGEMENT

21 Data (handling) ethics & compliance

***Synopsis** - Ethics is a big topic, deserving a chapter of its own. Below, I will first expand on the DMBOK's definition of data ethics. I will then discuss an approach to ethical handling of data based on principles related to the data lifecycle. I will conclude this chapter by discussing the relationship between data handling ethics and data governance.*

21.1 ETHICS IN DATA

Ethics is the discipline that is concerned with what is good and bad and mainly pertains to (human) behavior. A key question is: "is this the right thing to do?" Ethics is a topic that has been around for many years and continues to grow in importance in organizations, not only from a data perspective, but also from a business/ IT perspective. For example, many organizations have an onboarding program for new employees and a continuous education program for existing employees in which the corporate norms and values are shared. The idea behind this program is that continued attention to proper behavior and good values will help to ensure that people do the right thing (and prevent fraud, or other undesired behaviors). The DMBOK states that [Hen17]:

> *Data handling ethics are concerned with how to procure, store, manage, interpret, analyze/ apply and dispose of data in ways that are aligned with ethical principles, including community responsibility.*

Ethics is a big topic and, in my opinion the DMBOK definition does not do it justice. Ethics deals with the question of "what is right/ wrong?", whereas the DMBOK tends to focus mostly on the question of "how do we ensure that people do what we believe to be right?" (i.e. compliance). A good understanding is important for all professionals but data management professionals in particular. I have chosen to focus mainly on ethical principles (which can be linked to data management topics such as data ownership and stewardship) and avoid the topic of how to build a culture in which these principles are embedded. To frame the ethics discussion in a big data context, consider the following quote taken from [CMG14]:

> *In an "informatics of domination" that gathers all the data it can to unlock some presumed or as yet-unknown value down the road, data generation and collection are equated with innovation and scientific breakthroughs. As such, participation in the big data project—offering up the data we generate through the social interactions that shape our everyday lives—becomes the responsibility of all good citizens. To contribute one's data to the pool is to contribute to the advancement of science, innovation, and learning. This rhetoric can be seen most clearly with regard to health data. To be concerned about individual risk is equated with hindering progress; why be concerned about releasing data if it could help others, in the aggregate? Of course, this fails to acknowledge the ways in which our data can reveal much about us that we cannot know or intend and can be used to discriminate against individuals and groups. And how much trust should we have in the custodianship of data? The repositories of data are characteristically unstable; data is leaky, and it escapes in unexpected ways, be it through errors, hacks, or whistleblowing.*

As the above quote mentions, in many cases it is obvious that data could be used in a certain case (e.g. for assessing health risks) but the unintended consequences are often hard to foresee. The line of thinking becomes: if we allow an organization to collect data to do x (where x is one of these obvious cases), what will they be able to do in the future with that data? What is the risk (probability and impact) of doing things that are unethical?

21.2 ETHICAL HANDLING OF DATA

The DMBOK has a definition of data handling ethics and continues to cite activities such as (1) review data-handling practices, (2) identify risk factors, (3) create an ethical data handling strategy, (4) address gaps, (5) educate staff, and (6) monitor and maintain alignment. While useful as general guidance, this doesn't help practitioners much. More pragmatical approaches and frameworks have been developed, many of which start with the *data value chain* and link these to ethical principles.

21.2.1 Ethical principles behind data protection

Many organizations have chosen to develop and advocate a set of ethical principles, often inspired by/ linked to legislation around data handling and use (e.g. the General Data Protection Regulation (GDPR)[1]). The following principles are based on the DMBOK and sidebar 9 shows ethical principles in practice:

- **Respect for people** - Treat people in a way that respects their dignity and autonomy as human individuals.
- **Beneficence** - Do no harm, and maximize possible benefits while minimizing possible harms.
- **Justice** - Consider the fair and equal treatment of people.

Sidebar 9. Interview with Lisa Gaudette (summer 2019)

A lot of data is used and created in research. Working at the grants office of the university, the ethical principles that we use in my field are focused on the protection of the rights of different stakeholders:

- Protecting the creator of data (ownership). With ownership comes the "exclusivity" of the data (i.e. ideas, personal research). An owner has the right to decide who to share/ not to share the data with.
- Protecting the data itself. Research data itself should be protected from mishandling or maliciousness (intended or unintended) so as to ensure the privacy of the subjects. There are five main concerns regarding research data protection: (1) There needs to be controls regarding how data is collected; (2) It needs to be known who has access to the data; (3) How will the data be communicated; (4) How can we ensure that the data is accurate; and (5) How will the data be archived or destroyed.
- Protecting the subjects that are listed in the data. There are ethical issues in conducting research with "subjects". Subjects must always give their consent. Beneficence – we must not harm our subjects in any way. Subjects have the right to be anonymous and their data to be confidential. Subjects have the right to privacy.

Lisa Gaudette is director in the Office of Sponsored Programs and Research of Clark University.

Principles, in this context, are general statements that are intended to guide the behavior of people. The general statements that are cited in the examples above are generally complemented by more extensive descriptions and sometimes even specific instructions that show how to behave in certain situations. This is illustrated in example 52. Simply documenting them is not enough and organizations tend to spend time and effort on training staff on how to internalize these principles.

1 https://en.wikipedia.org/wiki/General_Data_Protection_Regulation, last checked: 11 July 2019.

Example 52. Detailed description of an ethical principle
The principles in this example are taken from a research report by Altimeter, which focuses on data handling ethics in the context of big data [EG15]. The following principles are listed in this report:

Beneficial - Data scientists, along with others in an organization, should be able to define the usefulness or merit that comes from solving the problem so it might be evaluated appropriately.
Progressive - If the anticipated improvements can be achieved in a less data-intensive manner, then less intensive processing should be pursued.
Sustainable - Big data insights, when placed into production, should provide value that is sustainable over a reasonable time frame.
Respectful - Big data analytics may affect many parties in many different ways. Those parties include individuals to whom the data pertains, organizations that originate the data, organizations that aggregate the data, and those that might regulate the data.
Fair - In lending and employment, United States law prohibits discrimination based on gender, race, genetics, or age. Yet, big data processes can predict all of those characteristics without actually looking for fields labeled gender, race, or age.

Under the explanation of the *Beneficial* principle, it says:

> *Risk mitigation is also an element of the benefit equation. The Information Ac- countability Foundation (IAF) recommends that, "if the benefits that will be created are limited, uncertain, or if the parties that benefit are not the ones at risk from the processing, those circumstances should be taken into consideration, and appropriate mitigation for the risk should be developed before the analysis begins".*

This statement is a good example of guidance that is given on how to implement a specific principle.

21.2.2 The data lifecycle

As stated previously, ethical principles are typically linked to the lifecycle of data. This gives a framework that helps to assess what type of behavior is fitting and right in a given context. A typical lifecycle model for data is as follows (taken from [Acc16]):

- **Disclose data** - A person, process, or system creates and publishes/ shares data. Activities in this phase include:
  - **Acquire** - Ingest data from sensors, systems, or humans, recording its provenance and consent for use wherever possible.
  - **Store** - Record data to a trusted location that is both secure and easily accessible for further manipulation.

- **Manipulating data** - A person, process, or system transforms, moves, or analyzes data. Activities in this phase include:
  - **Aggregate** - Combine disparate datasets to create a larger dataset that is greater than the sum of its parts
  - **Analyze** - Examine and transform data with the purpose of extracting information and discovering new insights.
- **Consuming data** - A person, process, or system benefits from manipulated data. Activities in this phase include:
  - **Use** - Apply the insights gained from data analysis toward making decisions, achieving change, or delivering a product or service.
  - **Share/ sell** - Provide access to datasets or data insights to new sets of data manipulators or consumers.
  - **Dispose** - Remove data from servers to prevent future release or use.

21.2.3 Using ethical principles in the data lifecycle

A framework for data handling ethics can be created by combining the ethical principles with the data lifecycle. The idea is that each of the principles may have an impact on the phases in the lifecycle.

As an example, take the *fairness* principle which suggests equal treatment of people. This principle can be assessed against the three phases in the above-mentioned lifecycle. In the *disclose* phase, a question is: "What data do we want to collect about people?" There may be legitimate business use for collecting data such as *name* and *address*. But do we really have a legitimate business use for *gender* or *skin color*? And if we do have legitimate business uses for this type of data, should we store it for future reference?

Let's say that *age, skin color,* and *gender* data is relevant for reporting purposes only: we want to be able to see the effect of campaigns on different groups of customers. Therefore, it is decided to *anonymize* the data before storing it.

The next phase is the *manipulating phase*. In this phase, a key question is: if we try really hard, are we still able to reconstruct who is who in the anonymized data set? For example, can we cross reference the moment data was created with an overview of who was in the building at that specific time and perhaps even which computer station that person was logged in from?

Last but not least, consider the *consumption phase*. If we do store this data – either anonymized or not, what is to prevent someone from sending out a marketing mailing to "all white males over the age of 45" for a certain campaign? Perhaps a marketing campaign is still ok but what if this type of data is used in customer service – perhaps in a way where staff discriminate based on gender, skin color, or age group? Would that still be acceptable?

The above process is sometimes called *profiling* and this is a commonly used technique in sales and marketing and related processes. The idea behind this is that more data about customers leads to more/ better sales opportunities which, from the perspective of the company, is a good thing. Whether it is a good thing from the perspective of the customer, however, remains to be seen.

21.3 THE RELATIONSHIP BETWEEN ETHICS AND GOVERNANCE

In this section, I will discuss the relationship between *data handling ethics* and *data governance* (see chapter 9). Ethics, as defined above, are the moral principles (right versus wrong/ good versus bad) that control a person's behavior. With respect to ethics, governance regulates how an organization remains ethical by creating policies and procedures, as well as putting controls in place, thereby ensuring the organization is responsible and accountable for its actions with the data it handles.

Simplified, making a wrong choice could lead to severe repercussions for an organization. Educating employees within an organization regarding the policies and procedures is a critical step in the safeguarding of data and the organization itself. Trainings (which will be discussed in more detail in chapter 26) is essential and key to employee awareness. Many employees see governance as a way to control and punish, thereby leading them to be resentful for their accountability in the organization. This, in turn, may hamper rather than improve the adoption of ethical principles. In other words: introducing too many controls will have the opposite effect of what you are trying to achieve.

There needs to be a balance between training and awareness, or even rewarding ethical behavior ("the carrot") and enforcing ethical behavior through controls and strict governance ("the stick") so that an employee will "want to do the right thing". When done right, this will lead to better/ more ethical employee decision-making, better productivity, and less turnover–and also an enjoyable working environment for the employees within the organization.

Example 53. Ethical protocols
There are policies and protocols in place for research involving human subjects. Institutional Review Boards (IRB) are charged with ensuring that the welfare and rights of human subjects are protected as mandated by federal and state laws, local and internal policies, and ethical principles. Their main concern is to keep human subjects from physical or psychological harm. Procedures were put into place after a series of abominable abuses on human subjects in the early 20th century. Most prominent were the experiments done by Nazi physicians during World War II and the human radiation experiments during the Cold War.
This example illustrates how governance/ controls (i.e. the use of an IRB) was deemed necessary to avoid any risk of an undesirable outcome (to say the least) ever happening again.

21.4 VISUAL SUMMARY

PART II

Practice

22 Introduction

Part I of this book focused on the theory of data management by providing an overview of the relevant terminology and a discussion of key data management topics. In part II, the focus shifts to practice: what does it take to build an effective data management capability for an organization.

In my opinion, there is no single best approach to building an effective and sustainable data management capability. Sustainability, in this context, is closely-related to *antifragility* : the idea is that the data management capability gets better when it is actively used. I also believe that there is no fixed "roadmap" that specifies the order in which key topics should be addressed. In most cases it may make sense to at least include governance aspects at the beginning of the journey. However, the "best" starting point is largely situational. Because of this, I have chosen to discuss a number of *use cases* in part II, using the following principles:

- Each chapter discusses a single use case and each use case focuses on a single topic/ question.
- There is no single best way to tackle a use case. I will offer different perspectives whenever possible, for example by contrasting/ complementing the practices that I propose with the perspective of other professionals through sidebars, similar to part I.
- There will be less citations to other works (books, articles) as this part is mainly about *practice* and a *pragmatic approach* to data management. I will refer to earlier chapters in part I.
- The practices that are proposed are all tested in the real world. When "borrowing" a practice from another professional, I will, of course, include citations (credits where credits are due).

Before diving in, the last part to discuss is the selection of the use cases themselves. This selection is not arbitrary: the use cases are selected based on an analysis of (1) the topics that came up in the consultancy assignments that I have done over the last few years, (2) questions that I have received during training sessions, and (3) the topics that were presented in key data management conferences.

23 Building the business case for data management

***Synopsis** - Building or improving a data management capability requires the investment of time, energy, and resources that are already scarce. Before resources are committed, you should make it really clear what the expected benefits are. In this chapter, I will discuss the need to build a good business case. I will touch upon quantitative and qualitative aspects of business cases. I will end this chapter with a discussion on a strategy for a more agile approach, working with a series of small business cases for each next step, rather than building one large over-arching business case. Throughout this chapter, I will assume that the business case for data management is "stand alone", in the sense that it is not a part of a bigger initiative.*

23.1 THE NEED FOR A BUSINESS CASE

When organizations embark on their data management journey, it is almost inevitable that someone will start asking questions along the line of: What is the added value of data management (DM)? Why should we invest in this new thing? Are you saying that we are currently not doing our job well enough? These are valid questions.

In my experience, many organizations already manage their data fairly effectively, even when they do not have formal processes and procedures in place that show this is done in a structured, proactive manner. Sidebar 10 (which picks up where sidebar 3 left off) illustrates this point. Furthermore, most organizations have enough work on their plates that they should make it really clear what the added value of their data management initiative will be before resources are committed to support them. In other words, DM is seen as something "extra" that must be done, on top of ""normal" business activities. The most common response that I have seen throughout the years is a call for a *business case*.

Sidebar 10. Interview with Marco van der Winden (summer 2019)

I asked Marco the question: What would you recommend to organizations who are just now getting started on the data management journey? His reply was: "My experience is that's it not an easy job. Think big, start small. Start where there is most to win, but also create a bigger picture. Try to fit in your "small" accomplishments in the bigger picture". Further in the interview, Marco stated: "Data management for me is about finding your own way in what works and what doesn't work. On that road you'll have to find partners helping you to keep your lane. Data management is doing it by yourself. Like learning how to drive… and experience how much fun driving by yourself can be.

Marco van der Winden is manager of the corporate data management office at PGGM, a Dutch pension provider.

A business case is a (formal) document or statement that captures the rationale for undertaking a project or initiative. Typically, a business case is written when a decision maker has to make a judgement call on whether to embark on a certain project or initiative, specifically in light of having to commit scarce resources. A business case compares expected costs with expected benefits, as well as the timing of these costs and benefits.

There are several challenges associated with the use of business cases, most importantly that it is very hard to make accurate predictions about the future in general and expected costs/ benefits in particular (see e.g. [Hub14]). Experience has shown that – especially when IT is involved – many projects go over budget, are delivered late, and realize only a fraction of the expected benefits. Still, the practice of requesting business cases for investment decisions prevails: it is better to have a (potentially flawed) indication of costs and benefits over having to make a judgement call based solely on gut feeling.

Another critique of the use of business cases lies in the fact that business cases tend to focus mostly on financial impact alone. Costs and benefits are specified purely in monetary terms and more "soft" factors (e.g. employee satisfaction) are left out of the consideration. In part this is because these factors are hard to quantify: what dollar amount would you associate with the increased confidence in business decisions because they are now based on better data? Or, what dollar amount would you associate with employee satisfaction for having to do less rework and having more effective data at their disposal?

An important question is: who makes the business case and who gets to decide on whether to move forward or not? This is a tricky question and very much context-dependent. I have seen situations where the business case came from the IT department, but also from business teams. It really depends on where the "pain" of poor data management is felt the most. The same applies to decision-making: I have seen cases where a decision was made by the CIO, but also by management within a single business line. If you want to start a data management journey in your own company, the best recommendation I can give is: try to find out who has enough power/ influence to make a decision and stick with it and aim your business case at this person (or group of persons).

23.2 QUALITATIVE AND QUANTITATIVE BUSINESS CASE

There are roughly two ways to present a business case: qualitatively and quantitatively. The former relies mainly on sound reasoning and good argumentation (how and why), whereas the latter relies on financial analysis (how much and how many). The line of reasoning in a business case is generally as follows:

> *I propose we do A because I believe that the effect of doing B is C. When doing A, the benefits D would outweigh the costs E.*

In a qualitative business case, the idea is to convince the reader of the business case to decide through a sound (logical) analysis in which the projected benefits outweigh the costs. When building a business case along these lines, it makes sense to take a *systemic approach* in which many (ideally all) relevant variables and perspectives are considered. System dynamics [Gon17] and group model building [Sco18] are ideal tools to get a shared understanding of a domain. A full discussion is beyond the scope of this book, but the following short introduction, combined with the example in figure 23.1 illustrates the line of thinking.

System dynamics is an approach to understanding the behavior of (complex) systems over time. One of the key tools in this approach is the *causal loop diagram* which shows the relationship between variables associated with the system. Independent variables are the variables that you can influence directly and which have an effect on dependent variables. For example, in figure 23.1 it is shown that the *availability of a business glossary* is an independent variable, meaning that it is something we have under our control. It is also shown that having a business glossary has a positive effect on (the independent variable) *understanding of what our data assets are*. Following the relationships in the diagram shows that this, in turn, has a positive effect on *our understanding the quality of data*, which has a negative effect on *the number of errors in our data*, which reduces *rework*, which reduces *cost*.

System dynamics models in general, and causal loop diagrams in particular, can become large and complex. When done well, they can be analyzed for long-term effects of manipulating the independent variables. While useful from a *scientific* point of view, the practical relevance is low. For purposes of the business case, it

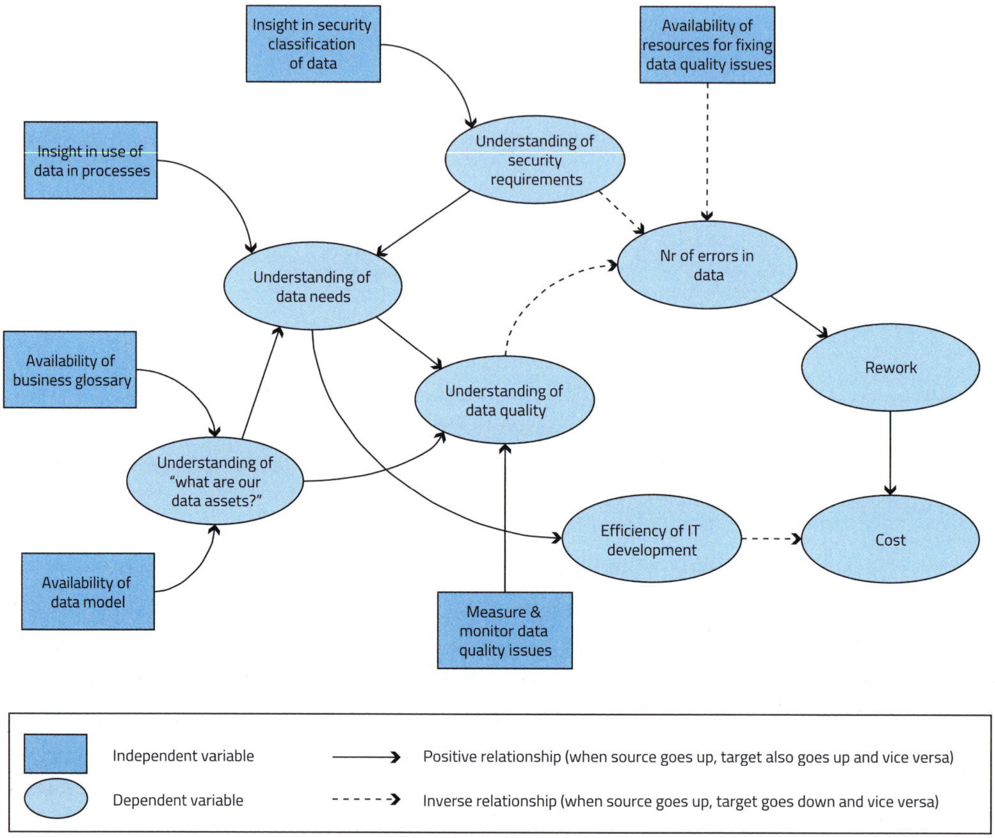

Figure 23.1 System dynamics model as input for a business case

helps to gain an understanding of the effect of interventions and that is where the analysis should stop. When creating these models, one should also be aware of some limitations of using causal loop diagrams in such a "casual" manner. The main limitation is that the effect of changing a variable is limited. Take the example of the glossary: at some point you will come to the conclusion that "good is good enough" and that investing in an even better glossary is of little value[1].

This brings me to *group model building*, which is an approach to getting a *shared* understanding of (the behavior of) a system, often using system dynamics models. As said, causal loop diagrams can become big and complex. The *quality* and level of *acceptance* of the model will improve greatly by building the model with a large group of stakeholders (ideally representing all the main concerns involved). Whether you use a formal process or "grow your own" is beside the point: the key is to build a shared understanding together with stakeholders.

1 See also section 17.1 in which I mentioned the *law of diminishing returns* which also applies here.

Quantitative business cases are all about running the numbers. The idea is to collect data and attempt to create an accurate projection of costs and benefits of a certain project. Example 1 on page 2 provides an illustration (the illustration is loosely based on [Soa11]).

Experience in practice shows that building sound business cases for problems that are relatively well understood is very doable. In [SB07] a distinction is made between *complicated* and *complex* problems. Problems that are relatively well understood are *complicated*, which means that they can be analyzed – even when that may take a lot of time. Building a quantitative business case for complicated problems is feasible. Introduction/ improving the data management capability is *complex*, which means that by its very nature it is impossible to be fully analyzed. This is mainly due to the fact that there are so many variables and interactions between variables – as figure 23.1 clearly illustrates.

When tackling the "build a business case for data management" challenge head-on, I would recommend using a mix of both approaches. The recommended steps are as follows. Start with a stakeholder analysis: who are the key players when it comes to data and data management? Who do you think will be impacted the most? Who will have to do the work and who will benefit from stakeholder management? Based on this analysis, try to collect a group of approximately ten stakeholders with regard to data management and who are willing to invest some time in building a business case (a "coalition of the willing").

With this group, start by building the causal loop diagram in a few short sessions. Using this model, you can do two things. First, you can start building a narrative that shows the expected effects of building/ improving the data management capability. Second, the causal loop diagram gives you the *variables* that you need for your quantitative analysis. Together with the group of stakeholders that you are working with, attempt to make honest assessments of costs and benefits using these variables and convert these to the business case template that your organization uses.

Example 54. Building a business case
Assume you have conducted a workshop that has resulted in the causal loop diagram shown in figure 23.1. Together with your team, you decide that you want to build a business case for a six month pilot project in which you introduce data management to the organization. Based on this, you start your quantitative analysis.

In these six months, we will invest 26 weeks × 3 people × 2 days per week = 156 man days in the listed independent variables. This leads to a total cost of approximately $150,000 (A). The estimates of our experts suggest that we can reduce the number of errors in data by 35% in this period. The benefit associated with rework that will not be required is estimated at $100,000 (*B*). We have three big in-flight projects that will benefit from having good data definitions. We expect the effectiveness of our IT teams to increase.

The effect is hard to estimate, but we believe we can save approximately $ 30,000 (*B*) in direct man hours, and another $30,000 (*B*) in rework that we prevent after the projects are completed because we now have a better understanding of the data. This leads to a positive business case of *B* – *A*, which totals $160,000 – $150,000 = $10,000. If the savings ($30,000 + $30,000) are annual savings, then this strengthens the business case further.

To illustrate the second step, the analysis could go as shown in example 54. This is, of course, a very limited and fictitious example but at least it shows the line of thinking: you will build a sound line of reasoning that is supported by financial analysis.

23.3 INCREMENTAL APPROACH TO BUILDING A BUSINESS CASE

From the previous section you may have guessed that building and selling a business case for data management is far from easy. At the very least it takes time and effort by a lot of stakeholders involved. Given that the task of building/ improving a data management capability is complex, and the observation that estimation (of required time, effort, resources) is so hard, it is not unreasonable to avoid creating a big and complex business case and adopt a more *agile* approach. The line of reasoning could be as follows:

> *We want to achieve A. We know it is very complex so we will avoid building a big and complex business case. We suspect that doing B will contribute to this goal. B is a small step, requiring limited investment. Therefore, it is a safe bet which could possibly bring us closer to A, plus it gives us a better way to estimate what a good next step would be.*

In our case, *A* would be to build or improve a data management capability. This is a rather vague goal, yet it is good enough to give a sense of what we want to achieve. As a rule, try to formulate your goals and objectives as precisely as possible. *B* could be many different things. To stay with the data quality theme that I have used in this chapter, it could be "verify the validity of a weekly business intelligence report by checking the quality of the data that is used".

If you choose *B* such that it immediately adds value to key stakeholders, then it will be very easy for them to agree to the limited investment that is required. Doing such a small project has several advantages. First of all, the scope of the project is limited so the complexity should be manageable. This should make it easier to complete the project successfully (on time, on budget, with good results). Second, you will most likely touch upon data management topics while performing the project. In this case, it is likely that you'll have to define the business concepts that are used in the report. You'll also have to compare (or even create) data models of the source systems and the system where the report is created. You'll probably have to talk to stakeholders about their data quality requirements and analyze if they are met. Third, the results will be threefold: (1) you will have tackled problem *B*; (2) you will have learned more about what it takes to implement a program that gets you closer to achieving *A*; and (3) you will have created a success-experience which is something people will remember. This will make it easier for them to support your next initiative.

I believe that this approach works well in most organizations. It does justice to the fact that there two fundamental challenges to be solved: (1) it reduces complexity of a large project by solving it one piece at a time, and (2) it makes it easier to fund and staff which is key when the change portfolio of the organization is already stretched beyond capacity.

24 Kick-starting data quality management

Synopsis - *In section 16.3, I discussed the fact that there are different types of data quality issues, ranging from simple spelling errors, to inconsistencies within a data set, inconsistencies across data sets in a single system, and inconsistencies across different systems. In section 16.4, I presented a high-level introduction into data quality management processes, including the issue management process. In this chapter, I will zoom in on a simple question: "How do you start with a data quality management program?" As the title of this chapter suggests, the solution lies in starting with small experiments and building the capability one step at a time.*

One of the first topics that people think of when embarking on a data management journey is *data quality*. Quite often there had been an incident with data quality that induced high cost, either directly or through loss of reputation, that sparked such an initiative. This is a good illustration of the *reactive* mindset that many organizations have when it comes to data management. Regardless of that fact, let's assume there is a sound reason for working on data quality improvement in the organization: improving the data quality management capability directly contributes to efficient processes as well as the quality of products and services of the organization.

24.1 TOP-DOWN APPROACH

To me, most of the literature on data quality management – the DMBOK included – seems to advocate a top-down approach, meaning: start by forming a data quality program and articulate a data quality policy. This forms a foundation on which data quality activities can be built across the enterprise, as it ensures (top) management support. While this is sound advice and would work in some organizations, my experience is that a more bottom-up approach has better chances of success. Small and local initiatives empower people which results in more robust/ antifragile solutions. There's nothing wrong with defining a program and setting up a policy, but it might not be the best place to start your data quality initiative.

24.2 A MOTIVATION FOR STARTING SMALL

In chapter 23, I have shown good practices for building a business case using qualitative and quantitative elements. My main recommendation was to try to find a way to start small and grow the initiative from there. This approach is particularly useful for starting on the data quality journey. Unlike the practice that is advocated in much of the literature, I believe that such a journey should not start with a *data quality policy*, but should start with small experiments that add value to the organization:

> *An experiment in this context is the process of trying to solve a (small) data quality issue while at the same time also learning what data quality management entails.*

There are several advantages to starting small and adopting an *agile approach*. First, a small experiment tends to cost less time – perhaps even up to the point where you do not have to ask for permission. Second, an experiment is exactly that: it is a good way to learn the mechanics of data quality management and since this "learning" is labelled as an experiment, it is "ok" if something doesn't go as expected. Third, success sells. When you have conducted a few successful experiments which clearly add value, then it should be easier to get traction for a bigger project. That might be the time where thinking about a *policy* actually makes sense. Last but not least, experience shows that most professionals are more willing to implement their own solutions to common (data quality) problems, rather than be forced to follow the instructions that were devised by someone else: this is easier to implement when tackling small(er) challenges.

24.3 SETTING UP YOUR FIRST EXPERIMENTS WITH DATA QUALITY MANAGEMENT

To start your first experiments with data quality management, you need some organization sensitivity and a good eye for details. The idea is to spot an opportunity where (potentially small) errors in data lead to discomfort/ problems in business processes. It would be ideal if someone *asks* you to help solve one of these issues. To help you spot a good problem to start with, consider the following questions:

- How many processes and systems do you think are involved in solving the problem that you have spotted? In this case, less is more! Less dependencies means a bigger chance of (quick) success.

- How many people do you expect to involve in solving the problem? More coordination tends to make it harder to solve the problem at hand. You may, for example, have to include others if you do not have the technical (programming) skills to perform your experiment yourself, or if you need help from someone who has access to certain data.
- Do you expect to have enough power/ influence to actually make changes or will this be a paper exercise? In other words, do you have the good will factor? Making a real impact has more value.
- Is this something you expect to be able to complete in a limited amount of time or will this last weeks if not months? A short and focused experiment tends to be best. It will also help to "sell" data quality management in the organization when people see that the amount of time that was used in initial experiments was limited.

When you have found a good problem to get started on, then it is key to get started quickly, to stay focused, and to keep it small. Example 55 provides a fictitious setting and simple case for a first experiment in data quality management.

Example 55. Data quality experiment

Consider the diagram below. The top part of the diagram shows a simple (partial) business function model of a company. It shows that the *Sales* function receives *Orders* from *Customers*. The *Customer details* that are listed in the order are passed on to the Customer Relationship Management (*CRM*) function, while the *Order details* themselves are sent to the *Warehouse*. There, the *Shipment* is sent to the *Customer* and the *Packing slip* is sent to *Finance* to create the *Invoice* that is sent to the *customer*.

You have discovered that there are many complaints from customers who received their *Shipment*, but never received the *Invoice* that goes with it. Your hypothesis is that things go wrong in the CRM function: if the *Customer details* from an *Order* are not mapped on the right *Customer*, then *Finance* is very likely to use an incorrect address!

To tackle this problem, you want to compare data from *Shipments* to data from *Invoices*. The complexity is low and if you can get your hands on these data sets (a sample of two months should be enough) then you are good to go. Even with limited programming/ spreadsheet skills this should be enough to do basic analyses.

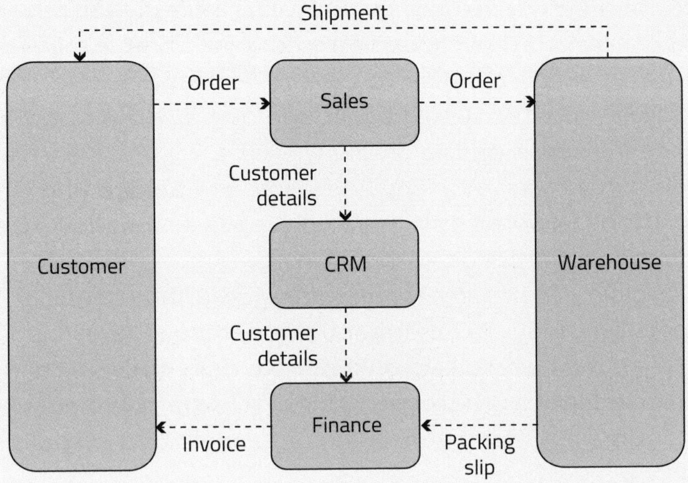

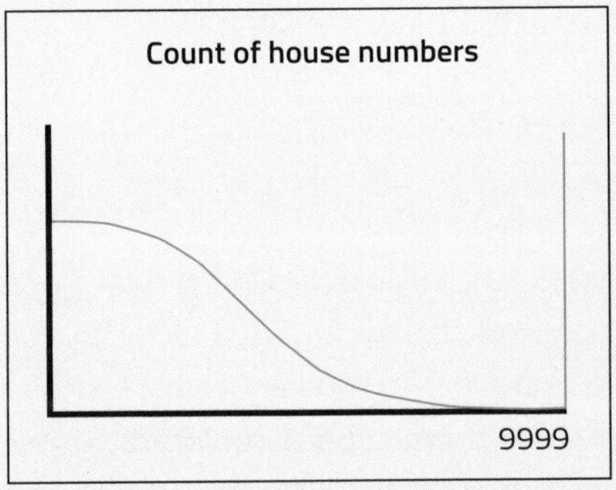

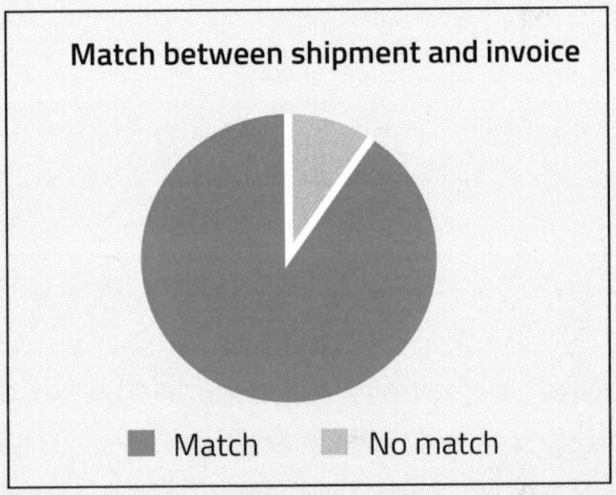

After requesting and receiving the data, you first run some basic tests to get a sense of what the data looks like. The graph at the bottom left shows the distribution of house numbers in your sample. The diagram suggests that low house numbers occur frequently and that high house numbers occur less frequently. There is one exception: number 9999 has a big spike and apparently shows up frequently in your data set. This is your first good finding: apparently 9999 is used as a placeholder for "we don't know the house number".

After this test, you also run more advanced tests, comparing *Shipments* to *Invoices*. The pie chart at the bottom right shows the results. You discover that about 6% of the shipments do not match the invoice. Investigating this further might be beyond your technical skill, but at least you have a good argument to start a small project: these mismatches are having a bad effect on the company: (1) customers don't like it, and (2) it is the cause of quite a bit of rework.

The example above is fictitious but is close to several real-world scenarios that I have seen in practice. Little experiments with small but tangible results lead to good press and eventually the idea that data quality management is valuable starts to take root in the organization.

This brings me to another key point: communication. Let's say you have done a data quality experiment and you have found an issue. Now what? In many organizations it appears to be common practice to *cover it up*: having data quality issues is perceived as *failure* and that should be *hidden* as it does no good to reputation, key performance indicators and so on. In my view, this is the *wrong* way to look at it. Spotting a data quality issue before it does (more) damage (than it has already done in the past) is an opportunity to learn and improve, and should be recognized as such. My recommendation is to bring things out into the open and discuss them – while avoiding the shame-and-blame-game that does occur from time to time. An open discussion about data quality can have several positive effects. For example, others may be working on the same data quality issue as you are, so you can team up to tackle a challenge. Or, your experiments may inspire others to try something similar, thus strengthening the arguments for a corporate-wide data quality program.

24.4 SCALING UP AFTER SUCCESSFUL EXPERIMENTATION

With a few successes under your belt, it is time to start considering how to *scale up* your data quality program. I'm going to assume that you have conducted a few (successful) experiments and that you are working to scale up by solidifying the data management capability. This phase should be about formalizing how data quality management is embedded while at the same time continuing to add value to the organization. I recommend considering the POPIT[1]-factors:

- **Process -** Now that you have performed some experiments, you should have a good understanding of which processes you should introduce/ formalize to take the next step. Good candidates are the *issue management process* and the *data quality reporting process*. The *issue management process* deals with reporting new data quality issues, making sure they are prioritized and resolved. The *data quality reporting process* improves transparency by showing which data quality issues were found and resolved. You should also consider whether you want to formalize the process for *resolving data quality issues*. In my experience it works best to let teams know which issues they have to resolve but leave it to them to find a fitting solution.
- **Organization -** In your experiments you will have figured out what kind of challenges you have to solve to improve data quality in your organization. Data quality is about ensuring data meets a given *norm*, so you need people to define and document that norm, you need people to sign off/ uphold the

1 POPIT standards for Process, Organization, People, Information, and Technology. The mnemonic was suggested to me by Carl Chilley whom I had the pleasure of working with in 2012 and 2013.

norm, people to get their hands dirty by working with the data, and so on. With this experience under your belt, you can start defining roles and how they collaborate in data quality management processes. Example roles that I come across frequently are data owners, data stewards, business analysts, and technical analysts.

- **People** - The people aspect has two sides to it: (1) do we have enough people available to do the data quality management work, and (2) do they have the right skills? The former point is something to discuss with management. Insufficient capacity tends to be an indicator of the fact that data quality management doesn't have the priority (yet) that it deserves. Without support and proper staffing, you can have the best processes and systems in the world, but nothing will get done. The latter aspect refers to training, which I will discuss in chapter 26.
- **Information** - You'll need two types of information for your data quality management initiative. First, you need metadata (see chapter 10) to tell you which data the organization has, where it can be found etc. You will also need information about the data quality issues that were found: who reported the issue, what went wrong, and how bad is it? You'll need this as input for the processes that you have defined and to help the people to play their part in managing data quality across the enterprise.
- **Technology** - Ideally your data quality capability is supported by an effective set of tools. Initially you may get away with using readily available tools (office functionality, internal websites) but at some point you will want to switch to more specific tools. One of the first tools to consider is a good issue management tool to support registering and prioritizing data quality issues across the enterprise.

When scaling up, it is a good idea to perform a *capability gap assessment* which shows (a) where you want to go/ what you want to achieve with data quality management in the long run, (b) what the gap is with the way things are organized presently, and (c) what the first step is that you propose to take. It might be a good idea to also include a business case (chapter 23) which also mentions your victories so far.

25 Finding data owners and data stewards

Synopsis - In chapter 9, I discussed the theory behind data governance, highlighting data ownership and data stewardship roles. The topic came up in many interviews. I will kick off the chapter with two quotes from Tanja Glisin to set the stage from a top-down/ bottom-up perspective. I will then follow-up with a short discussion about five ways to organize data stewardship, based on a talk by Analise Polsky in 2013. I will use these perspectives to discuss how to find good data owners and data stewards.

25.1 TOP-DOWN AND BOTTOM-UP

I will start this chapter with quotes from an interview with Tanja Glisin, as she aptly summarizes a few key points about finding data owners/ stewards for the organization.

Sidebar 11. Interview Tanja Glisin (summer 2019)

When asked about the central position of *data governance* in the DMBOK, Tanja replied:

> *There is a continuous debate on this topic in circles of data governance enablement practitioners: is data governance in the center, or around all other data management functions? Every organization has a number of different governance capabilities and collectively their purpose should be to enable business to go from an idea to a product in the most efficient, safe and meaningful way. Data governance is the same from that perspective with a unique set of concerns – privacy, ethics, bias and 'creepiness' factor have given data governance another dimension in the past five to six years.*

Later in the interview we discussed the top-down/ bottom-up approaches to data governance in general and the role of data stewardship in particular. Tanja responded:

The DMBOK and other available work on governance are emphasizing the top-down approach but mostly from the perspective of securing sponsorship and funding as a means of sustaining an on-going program[a]*. The DMBOK and other available work are completely right to still push for the fact that if you don't get the top- down understanding of enterprise data needs, there will be no long-term program sustainment – and that is where most data governance programs fizzle-out and die on the vine. The realization that bottom-up is as important as top-down is not exactly new: it came slowly but surely as organizations started to realize that data governance is* not what you say you do *(data policies, data standards, decision-making bodies and decision-making rights) but what you actually* do and practice consistently*. The idea is to successfully connect top-down and bottom-up in a strong* data stewardship program *that puts data governance in action to create the system that is not only sustainable but also renewable.*

a By contrast, some programs aim at producing some big deliverable and then end.

Tanja Glisin is an experienced data management professional and frequent collaborator of the author of this book.

Sidebar 11 highlights several key points about finding data owners and data stewards which also tie in with the discussion in the previous chapter about starting a data quality program. First, it stresses the need to make sure there is both top-down support from management (e.g. in the form of time, money and other resources) as well as the need to empower people to do data management work in a bottom-up fashion. Experience shows that it is generally more effective to *invite* professionals to be owners/ stewards than it is to *appoint* them. Second, it also stresses that data governance is a *program* with no clear endpoint: it is the on-going effort to govern the data management initiatives in the organization. The third, and perhaps most important point, is that data governance should be *meaningful:* data governance professionals should always keep their eye on the ball and act in the (long-term) best interests of the enterprise.

The implication for finding data owners and data stewards is that this is not a matter of finding *individuals* but a matter of assembling a *group* of people. This group should have the support of management (top-down support), as well as have the skills and connections to get things done (bottom- up traction). Example 56 illustrates these points further.

Example 56. Seattle Public Utilities

Seattle public utilities provide 124 million gallons of water daily and manage 1800+ miles of water pipes, with two watersheds and water treatment plants in the Cascade mountains. They also deal with 300,000 tons of garbage in two legacy landfills and two in-city "transfer stations". Even more, they manage 1,400 miles of sewer pipes, 485 miles of storm drains and 181 storm water flow control structures. Managing all these *assets* effectively requires a lot of data.

The organization dealt with three types of pain[a]: (1) data was hard to access, (2) data was hard to leverage, and (3) data stewardship was informal. Moving forward, an "interface" was built between stewardship and governance: governance establishes a model for maturing the data management practice and helps to prioritize within the overall program. For formal governance there is a *council* with enough decision-making power to articulate principles and drive results. Stewardship is more hands-on and focuses on making sure that stakeholders get access to high quality data when they need it. Stewards *interface* with the council when there is a desire to formalize practices and roles, or when key (tooling) decisions are to be made. The approach that was taken combines opportunism and an incremental growth model with a focus on sustainable outcomes.

a In his presentation, Duncan used the word 'pain' to describe undesirable situations.

This example is based on the presentation of Duncan Munro and Helen Welborn at Enterprise Data World in Boston in March 2019.

25.2 OWNERSHIP/STEWARDSHIP MODELS

The second topic source of inspiration comes from a 2013 talk by Analise Polsky. Figure 25.1 provides a visual overview of five types of data stewardship models that she sees in practice.

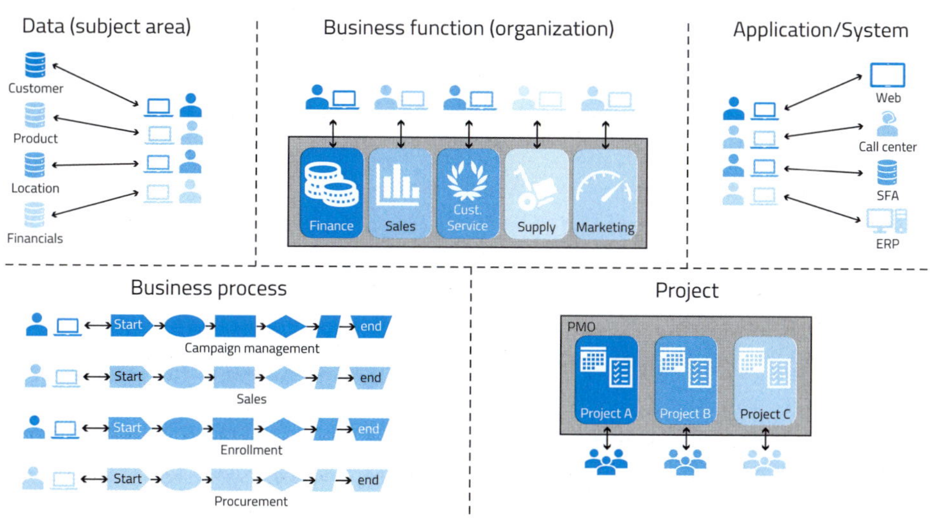

Figure 25.1 Stewardship models, inspired by [Pol13]

These stewardship models are as follows:

- **Data (subject area) -** In this model, data stewards are assigned to/ recognized as experts for clusters of data that "are about the same real-world thing". These clusters are called *subject areas*. Typical subject areas are customer, product, location, and for financial data. The idea is that the steward for a data cluster is responsible for all the data associated with business concepts in that cluster. When data is used in multiple processes or systems, the steward has to collaborate with process/ system owners to ensure that all interests are addressed.
- **Business process -** In this model, the process owner is also responsible for managing the data in the process. The challenge here is to coordinate across processes. For example, several processes may produce/ consume customer data. Process owners will therefore have to coordinate their actions and together define business concepts, business rules, requirements etc.
- **Business function (organization) -** This model is similar to the process model but now the owners/ managers of a business function are responsible for their data. This still requires a lot of coordination.
- **Application/ System -** In this model, the application/ system owner is also responsible for the data in systems. There are two coordination challenges. First of all, several systems may hold similar data, so system owners have to coordinate their definitions. Also, multiple processes may require access to these systems, so system owners have to collaborate with process owners to ensure that all interests are addressed.
- **Project -** This appears to be a catch-all model, where the organization only performs data stewardship activities in projects (e.g. IT projects, or process improvement projects).

It is easy to see that no matter which model you choose, there is always a need for collaboration and coordination. There is no single best solution that always works, so organizations should pick a model that best suits their local needs and situation. Data management literature (especially the DMBOK [Hen17]) at least suggests that the subject area model works best. While I believe this to be an elegant model, it seems that business stakeholders tend to find such a model too theoretical to be useful.

25.3 FINDING OWNERS AND STEWARDS

The key elements for a good approach to finding data owners and data stewards have been presented in the previous sections. First, the interview with Tanja Glisin in sidebar 11, as well as example 56 illustrate the need to balance top-down/ formal governance with bottom-up/ hands-on stewardship. Figure 25.1 illustrates the five common models for organizing data stewardship.

One topic that has not yet been addressed is: are we talking about *functions* (meaning the work to be performed) or *roles* (meaning the organizational position) for professionals? I believe the latter works best (a more detailed discussion can be found in chapter 33). The two ground rules that should be followed are:

- Data ownership is a role that should be assigned to the organizational unit or process where data is created, as this is the only place where the correctness of data can be verified.
  Consider the situation of a retail bank. Interaction with the customer is done in the front office. The chain of command would probably be something along the lines of: clerk, branch manager, district manager, or chief retail banking officer. Who should be accountable for data? If the bank aims for standardization across districts, then the chief retail banking officer seems to be a logical choice since customer data is created under his responsibility. If the bank does not have a standardization goal, then one level down would be a good place to start.
- Professionals should be *recognized as data stewards* because they already have shown that they take care of data in their regular work. Assigning a data stewardship role should be a recognition of this hard work and is intended to empower them to continue their good work. Assigning a stewardship role should come with decision-making power.
  Continuing the retail bank example: there are probably several people who know everything there is to know about customer data. Typical roles are business analysts and business information managers. When you find someone who understands the data well, and "acts like an owner" by taking care of the data, then this person should be assigned the data stewardship role.

As a general rule, data owners should be accountable for data whereas data stewards are responsible for most of the work. Therefore, data owners tend to have a management function already, whereas data stewards tend to be in the team of the data owner. This is not a hard rule but occurs frequently enough to mention here. Owners are often supported by a *team* of stewards, some with more business focus (writing business definitions, supporting their owners in formulating policies) and others with a more technical focus (hands-on manipulation of data, checking quality, and implementing controls).

This leaves one element undiscussed: a list of data owners and data stewards does not create itself, so who creates it? The answer ties in with the recommendations in the previous chapter: start with small experiments (e.g. around data quality management) and grow from there. Initial experiments tend to result in the need to formalize things (processes, roles, procedures). This would be a good time to start a data governance program and launch a *data council* or a *data management office*. This is generally a good place to coordinate the work around finding good data stewards and data owners, as well as approve the appointment of new people in these roles.

Subject Area	Key business concepts
Customer	Customer id
	Customer name
	Customer type
	Customer contact person
	Customer visiting address
	Customer shipping address
	Customer invoice address
Product	Product number
	Product name
	Product series
	Product vendor
...	...
...	...

Subject Area	Data owner	Data steward	Business	Technical
Customer	John	Erica	X	
		Rick		X
Product	Carl	Lisa	X	
		Ron		X
		Mick		X
Location	Mary	Tony	X	X
Vendor	Mike	Stephen	X	X
	Carl			
...	...	...	...	...
...	...	...	...	...

Figure 25.2 Publishing an overview of data owners and data stewards

The list of data stewards and data owners should be publicly available. Figure 25.2 is a simplified version of a structure that we used in a consultancy assignment years ago. Using the table on the left, people were very quickly able to locate which subject area certain data belonged to. The table on the right quickly showed who the owners/ stewards were and also whether the stewards had a business/ technical background. This was implemented in a simple webpage that was freely accessible for anyone in the organization. One of the biggest advantages of publishing this overview is that it tends to self-correct: people will come to you when they see that data is wrong. Also, it may help to find new volunteers who also want to join the ranks of data owners and stewards. It certainly helps to get the conversation going.

26 The role of training

Synopsis - The chapters in part II deal with use cases for building an effective, sustainable data management capability. In several places I have argued that this can only succeed by carefully considering the needs of key stakeholders. In this chapter I will go a step further and argue that the people aspect should be front and center of your approach. More specifically, I will discuss the need for training at all levels of the organization.

26.1 PEOPLE FIRST, AND THE NEED FOR TRAINING

In [KNPCA19], it is argued that *people* are the real key to digital transformation of organizations. On page 34 of this book, the authors aptly formulate that:

> *The main problem posed by digital disruption is not the rapid pace of technological innovation but the uneven rates of assimilating these technologies into different levels of human organizations. [. . .] Only by fundamentally changing the way the organization works [. . .] can an organization truly adapt to a digital world.*

I more than agree with this analysis and would like to extend it to the realm of data management. In my view, data management is one of the key capabilities that successful organizations need in order to survive in an increasingly digital world. Introducing/ improving the data management capability requires changing the way the organization works and this, in turn, should entail adopting a people- first perspective.

Even in organizations where more and more processes are performed by machines and computer systems, it is still all about the people: they are your shareholders, employees, working for the regulators, your customers (or work for your customers), etc. At the very least, I suspect it will take years before we have reached the stage where robots and artificial intelligence systems can start their own companies without involving humans[1]. No matter how technologically advanced your organization is, it is still people that make key decisions on all levels of the organization. From a data management standpoint:

- People articulate their data needs;
- People architect and design processes, systems, and data (flows) to meet those needs;
- People will complain when data does not meet their needs;
- People design and use data management processes to get to grips with the data landscape;
- People design and use processes, systems, and data (flows) to create value with data.

Given that people are key, it is apparent that training is important. This is true for all levels of the organization. Sidebar 12 illustrates this further.

Sidebar 12. Training (interviews conducted during summer 2019)

While discussing the need for training at the executive and work-floor level, Fanny and Céline, both working at AXA, replied:

> *Training is really important at both levels but it has to be differentiated. At the executive level, training should be about awareness. At the work-floor level, training should be more about the hands-on data management activities. This type of training tends to be more in-depth. Despite a high education level for most people in a modern-day workforce, data management training is very much needed. It is not something that is taught at school. Yes, there is a lot of education about big data and data science but not (no longer) enough about the fundamentals.*

When I spoke with Marc van den Berg, working at PGGM, about this, he also supported this point of view and added a few key points:

> *A lot of training should be about awareness. People are smart and tend to be able to figure it out when they have to do something new. Even more, I believe it is important that people across the organization have the same (theoretical) basis; that they work from the same playbook. A staff function[a] will not be the big differentiator in and of itself. Staff functions create the enablers that help business stakeholders to be successful. Key to success is that the data management conversation is started. When there is an open and productive*

1 In November 2019, Ron Tolido gave a talk at the Open Group conference in Amsterdam with the title "Alexa, run my business", which suggests that at least some people believe this scenario might come true.

conversation about data and data management, the organization will learn faster.

a E.g. a corporate data management office, or data management program.

Fanny Vuillemin is senior data manager at AXA *and Céline Lescop is lead data architect at* AXA.

Marc van den Berg is managing director of IT *and Innovation at* PGGM, *a Dutch pension provider.*

26.2 TYPES OF TRAINING

There are several *competence frameworks* available that form a good basis for structuring a training program, such as the *European e-Competence Framework* (e-CF) and the SFIA framework (see [fS16] and [SFI19] respectively). In this chapter, I will use the principles behind the e-CF framework to develop an understanding of the *types* of training that are required to build a good data management capability. I will also use the SFIA framework in chapter 33 where I discuss the roles and responsibilities of data management professionals.

The e-CF framework distinguishes between four dimensions:

1. Five e-Competence areas, derived from the ICT business processes plan/ build/ run/ enable/ manage.
2. A set of reference e-Competences for each area, with a generic description for each competence. The forty competences identified in total provide the European generic reference definitions of the framework.
3. Proficiency levels of each e-Competence provide European reference level specifications on e- Competence levels e-1 to e-5.
4. Samples of knowledge and skills relate to e-Competences in dimension 2. They are provided to add value and context and are not intended to be exhaustive.

Loosely following this framework, I would argue that the five areas (from plan to manage) are also appropriate for data management: it is a capability that should be carefully managed. This is the premise for this book. Drilling down, one could argue that the functional areas of the DMBOK (see section 7.3) map onto the second item in the list above: these functional areas are the data management competences that an organization needs. The degree of proficiency (third item) depends on the situation and ambition of the organization. The degree of proficiency of the organization, in turn, depends on the *knowledge* and the *skills* that the organization has.

It stands to reason that there are two *types* of training that can be used. One type of training focuses on *knowledge*, the other on *skills*. Typical topics for each are listed in table 26.1.

Table 26.1 Data management knowledge and skills

Knowledge	Skills
What is data?	How do I write a good definition for a business concept?
What is data management?	How do I write data quality requirements?
Why is data management important?	How do I document the flow of data through our systems?
Who is involved in data management in our organization?	How do I create a logical data model?
What is the effect of good data management on the organization?	How do I design an effective master data management solution?
Etc.	Etc.

26.3 HOW TO DESIGN A TRAINING PROGRAM

It is rare to find a "pure" training program that focuses on one of the two perspectives. It is more common to find a mix of both. To identify which elements should be part of your training, I recommend following a simple process:

- **Stakeholders -** The first step should be to identify *who* will join the training and *in which capacity*. This gives a good understanding of the playing field.
- **Interviews -** If at all possible, try to interview as many stakeholders as you can. Try to identify (1) what they believe the organization is trying to achieve, and (2) where they think they stand. This gives a good understanding of the *gap* in skills/ knowledge that you are trying to bridge with the training.
- **Synthesize -** Try to capture the results of the previous step in a structured form. I recommend formulating training requirements as: "for role . . . stakeholders should know/ be able to . . . ". This gives the base elements of your training.
- **Elaborate -** The base elements should be expanded in two ways. First, for "skills", you should decide whether a "knowledge component" is also required. Second, if any base components have dependencies on other components then these are included in such a way that the "story" flows naturally. For example, a component on "documenting data contracts between two parties" could depend on a component on "documenting data flows".
- **Design -** The last step is to design the full program. This includes deciding on the order of the components, assigning timeslots and determining the work forms for each component.

Typically, this is a process that a training/ consultancy company does for its clients: they have the expertise and know-how that is necessary to design a good program. This requires both an understanding of the field (in this case data management) but also didactic skills. See example 57 for an illustration of how this process plays out in practice.

Example 57. Designing a training for data stewards

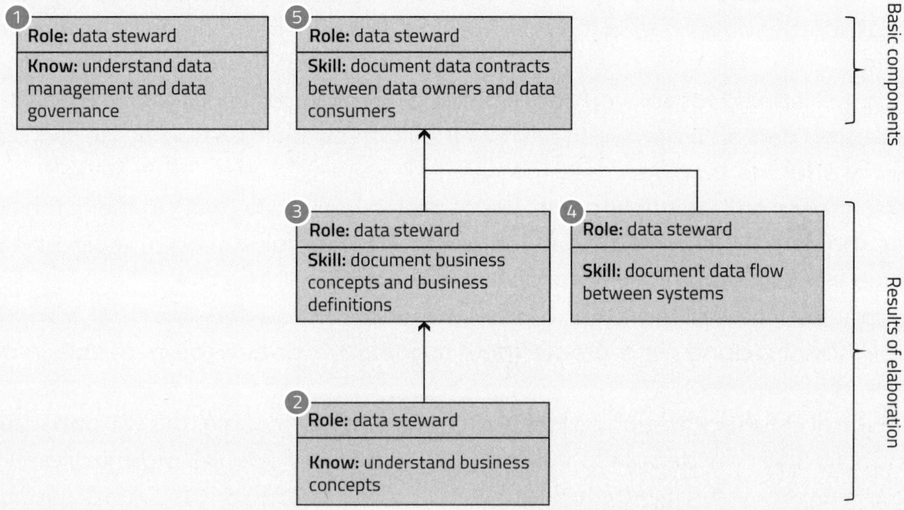

Consider the above diagram. Let's say you are asked to design some training for data stewards. Step 1 suggests you first check whether all participants play this role. Let's assume that this is the case. For steps 2 and 3 you set up interviews to gain an understanding of where they think the organization is going and where they believe they stand currently. From this you derive the two base components that are listed at the top of the diagram.

Using this as input, you start your elaboration. You discover that three more components are required, also drawn in the diagram. An arrow is intended to mean: "to successfully teach the component at the arrowhead, you should first have an understanding of the component at the tail-end of the arrow". In this case, that is a good starting point for deciding the order in which the topics are discussed – as indicated by the numbered circles.

The last step would be to design work forms and an itinerary for the training. In this case, you start with two "know" components and follow-up with three "skill" components. This may suggest starting the training with an interactive work-form to get the creative juices flowing and set a productive atmosphere.

Every organization is different and I do not think there is a standard curriculum that can always be used. So much depends on the type of organization and its goals, the culture in the organization, and the skills already present in the organization. The following principles should help to get you started in an effective manner:

- Don't try to "boil the ocean" and do everything at once. Start with small groups. It is ok to deliver the same training more than once.
- Train both people at the top of the organization and people from the work-floor, ideally at the same time/ in the same period. This will help to get the conversations going.
- Try to link training to real work that has to be done. Participants will be much more interested and active when they know they can apply the results in the real world shortly after the training.
- Try to create multi-disciplinary teams of professionals who work in the same area (the same unit, the same system, the same process/ value stream). A side-benefit of the training is that collaboration within this area will improve.
- Recognize that training is not a one-time effort. Follow the model of training → show how it is done → co-create (do it together) → coach (be available in case there are questions).
- Use (open) standards such as the DMBOK whenever possible. This will also make it easier to add new people to the team, even from outside the organization.

27 Setting up a data management policy

Synopsis *- One of the documents that (eventually) shows up in data management initiatives is a data management policy. The document is not clearly defined by the DMBOK but plays an important role in building/ improving the data management capability of organizations. In this chapter, I will firstly define what a data management policy is. I will then discuss typical elements in a data management policy. I will end this chapter with an overview of the merits of a top-down versus a bottom-up approach to creating a data management policy.*

27.1 DATA MANAGEMENT POLICY

Studying the DMBOK closely will reveal that a key recommendation for many functional areas is to create a *policy* document: a metadata policy, a data quality management policy, etc. Unfortunately, documentation about these policies is sparse. The DMBOK offers the following guidance [Hen17, chapter 13]:

> *All data management knowledge areas require some level of policy [. . .]. Each policy should include:*
> - *Purpose, scope, and applicability of the policy;*
> - *Definitions of terms;*
> - *Responsibilities of stakeholders;*
> - *Reporting;*
> - *Implementation of the policy, including links to risk, preventative measures, compliance, data protection, and security.*

While a good starting point, this guidance doesn't reveal much about why a policy is needed, or what it should actually entail. In my view, a policy is a formal statement that offers a framework for guiding behavior and decision-making across the organization. A first point to note is that a policy is a *formal* statement. This means that it has "power": it has been signed off by (top) management and lays down the law for a certain area. New policies should also be in line with other policies already in place and are potentially derived from more top-level documents such as a strategy or vision statement. This point is illustrated by sidebar 13.

Sidebar 13. Interview with Norbert van de Ven (summer 2019)

When discussing the relationship between data management and other capabilities, the conversation turned to the role of policies. Norbert replied: "It is increasingly important that policies, standards, guidelines, and procedures are developed and promoted across the enterprise. Training is an essential element in this, as it increases awareness". I very much agree with this point. In several places throughout this book, I have advocated that people are the key factor in building a successful data management capability. Training increases awareness and helps to build an effective mindset. Without this, policies, standards, guidelines and procedures are doomed to fail.

Later, we discussed the relationship between "top-down" and "bottom-up" data management initiatives. Norbert's take on this dilemma is: "Top-down approaches – which includes laying down the law in policies – are still necessary, if only because of the investment decisions that are involved. But also, with resources (time, money) available, bottom-up initiatives empower and motivate people to do their job better, at least from a data management perspective".

Norbert van de Ven is data governance consultant at Hot ITem.

A second point to note is that policies tend to have a big "what" focus, not a "how" focus: they answer questions such as *what* is the policy about, *what* are key terms, *what* is the overall purpose of the policy, *what* are the roles involved, etc. A policy tends to shy away from prescribing how a process should be implemented, or how controls are to be implemented in systems. Figure 27.1 clarifies this further.

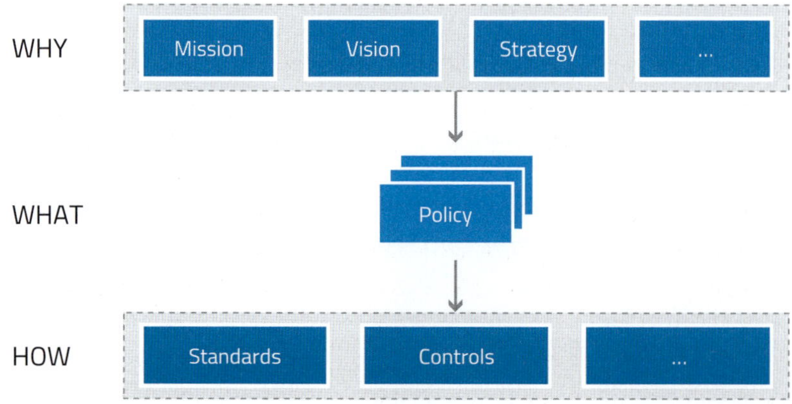

Figure 27.1 Position of policies

In this chapter, I will focus mainly on the *what*-level. Translating policies to more concrete standards, controls, etc., is out of scope for this chapter.

27.2 TYPICAL STRUCTURE FOR A DATA MANAGEMENT POLICY

The data management policy is about *what*, and a recommendation for its structure according to the DMBOK was presented in the opening section of this chapter. Based on my experience with consultancy assignments over the last decade (in financial services, government, and telecommunications)

I have found that there is no single best structure for data management policies. In this section, I will present a consolidated view of what I have learned, which is consistent with the DMBOK recommendation.

- **Purpose -** The first section is about the purpose of the policy: why do we bother in the first place? Typically, this relates to the documents from the why-section of figure 27.1. Often there is a link to a business case (chapter 23) or a link to legislation that mandates the creation of the policy. A good example of this is the *Solvency II*[1] directive for insurance organizations. As a result of this directive, many organizations have started working on a data quality policy. Whatever the motivation for writing the policy, it should be clear about what initiated the work.
- **Goals and objectives -** One of the key sections is about goals and objectives. The two terms are not interchangeable: *goals* are more long-term, whereas *objectives* are more short-term oriented. Since the purpose of the DM policy is to offer guidance for the DM capability, it should be clear what is to be achieved through this capability. Adding *objectives* to the policy document is somewhat unorthodox. However, it can serve two purposes. First, it makes it clear what current priorities are. Second, it ensures that the document is periodically reviewed and updated as objectives are achieved and priorities shift.
- **Scope -** Especially in large organizations, it may be that different units/ departments have their own set of policies. This is ok, not everything has to be standardized. The corollary is that the policy document should clearly define the scope by expressing who/ which part of the organization is affected.
- **Key terms -** Many of the terms that are used in the field of data management are likely to be unfamiliar to people who are not from this field (the number of pages in this book that are used to explain key terms is testimony to that fact). Defining key terms serves two purposes: first, it helps to make sure people understand your policy document. Second, it sets a good example which will yield the much-needed credits to ask business stakeholders to also define their terms.

1 https://en.wikipedia.org/wiki/Solvency_II_Directive_2009, last checked: 27 July 2019.

I recommend against simply referring to a reference work such as the DMBOK for these terms. First, because experience shows that business stakeholders will not look up the document, even when terms are unclear, and second, because you want to show you made an effort to tailor the language to what is customary in the organization.

- **Guiding statements -** This section is the core of the document. It should contain the guidance that the organization needs for building a successful DM capability. I will expand on this later in this section. The focus of the policy is on *what* should be achieved. Details are fleshed out elsewhere, in standards and controls. Whenever possible, add references to these standards and controls in the policy document. This will make it easier for business stakeholders to locate the information they need.

There isn't much content that *must* be in this section for each and every organization. One aspect that consistently shows up in policy documents is a description of roles and responsibilities (see e.g. section 9.3).

- **Indicators & reporting -** When defining goals, it makes sense to also indicate how you intend to measure whether they are achieved. This is usually done through (key) performance indicators. These serve two purposes that align with the carrot and stick[2]: (1) they are intended to motivate the organization to achieve the desired outcomes, and (2) they give an indication which type of behavior should be penalized as it works against the goals and objectives of the policy.
- **Revisions -** This last item addresses the need to keep the policy document up-to-date. The idea is to set clear guidelines for when the policy document should be updated. This should at least be an annual event, though other reasons could trigger an update as well.

I have seen many variations on the same theme, yet most policies seem to follow this structure. Beyond that, two setups are common. The first setup is one large policy that covers all data management topics/ functional areas of the DMBOK. The other is the opposite: one policy document per topic/ functional area. Both can work but experience shows that it is easier to keep a consistent line with the former setup.

This leaves the matter of the actual guidance. As previously mentioned, one of the things that should be included is a clear definition of roles and responsibilities. In the list below, I have included some topics/ questions that I have seen in policy statements. As a general rule, put statements in there that (1) help the organization to achieve its goals, and (2) that you are willing to enforce.

---

2 The "carrot and stick approach" is an idiom that refers to offering a combination of reward and punishment to induce good behavior. It is named in reference to a cart driver dangling a carrot in front of a mule and holding a stick behind it.

- What are the data quality dimensions that you intend to use and how are they defined?
- What are the ground rules for assigning data management roles, such as data owner and data steward?
- What are the ground rules around getting/ gaining access to data?
- What are the ground rules for assigning security classification of data?
- How do you decide what the *critical data elements* are for your organization?
- What are the ground rules for reporting and resolving data quality issues?
- What is the position of metadata in relationship to governance? What metadata should be collected centrally for governance purposes?
- What (type of) reference data is under strict governance?
- What are the ground rules for handling privacy sensitive data, and how is it determined whether data is privacy sensitive?

27.3 SETTING UP A DATA MANAGEMENT POLICY

Setting up a data management policy is a big task. As with so many tasks in data management, there are many approaches to tackling the challenge. The trick is to balance between top-down implementation of a vision and discovering bottom-up what actually works in practice. I believe there is no right or wrong between the two approaches: the circumstances dictate which approach works best in a given situation. I will discuss both perspectives in isolation as much as possible and then move on to recommendations.

27.3.1 Top-down

I think the top-down approach is the most frequently used in practice. In this approach, a small group of professionals – typically staff members from a data management office or similar group – are tasked with the development of the policy. Sometimes the mandate to develop the policy is very broad, with little guidance on what is expected in terms of scope and content. In many cases this is clearer. Example 58 comes from an assignment a few years back, where a team was asked by the *chief information officer* of the organization to develop a data management policy.

Example 58. Mandate to develop a policy

We have been recently audited by an external regulator. One finding in this audit is that our data management processes are insufficiently formalized. We hope to fix this in the next 18 months. We would like you and your team to develop a data management policy that covers (1) roles and responsibilities, (2) a framework for classifying which data is critical for our operations, and (3) how we will deal with data quality management in our organization.

The potential advantage of a top-down approach is speed: a small group is tasked to create a policy and if they can focus on this task (prioritize) then the document could be ready in no time. However, there is also a big risk of the "ivory tower" syndrome[3]: the team could develop a policy that, even when consistent and sound, is not practical and not sufficiently aligned with the needs of, and situation in the organization. To reap speed-benefits and create a counter-balance for the key risk, I recommend the following:

- Work with a small core-team and a review-team. Make sure the members in the review-team address the concerns across the enterprise. There's no such thing as an ideal team-size but to give a rough indication: 3-4 for the core team and 10-15 for the review team should work well.
- Start with a kick-off session in which all team members can voice their concerns and *record these concerns* for future reference. It is key to show that all concerns are heard and that the final policy is checked against them.
- Work in iterations. Make sure that everyone understands what the overall scope is, as well as what the scope of the current situation is. A good loop for an iteration is: (1) communicate the scope for the current iteration in light of the overall goal of the initiative, (2) the core team creates a first draft, after which (3) the review team offers its honest feedback, preferably both oral (meeting) and in writing, then (4) the core team updates the draft and sends the update to the sponsor of the initiative, making sure there is an opportunity for management to clarify their intent, or offer further guidance.
- End each iteration by checking the results against the concerns that were addressed at the beginning of the project.

The advantage of this approach is that you have an improved draft after each iteration. Also, by keeping the sponsor in the loop, there are frequent opportunities for feedback and additional guidance. By addressing the concerns of people from the work-floor, you will likely end up with a workable, pragmatic policy statement.

27.3.2 Bottom-up

Bottom-up is the inverse of the top-down approach and the advantages and disadvantages are mirrored. The potential advantage of a bottom-up approach is that it will fit perfectly with what is needed in the organization. One of the disadvantages is that it may be time-consuming to create a policy in this manner. There are, however, other risks to take into account.

The very nature of a bottom-up approach is to look for solutions that fit the current (local) context. These tend to focus on the "how", rather than that "what" which

3 The "ivory tower syndrome" refers to situations where (top) management loses track of what happens in reality at the work-floor level; they only know what is going on in the "ivory tower" of reports and management meetings.

is the normal abstraction level of the policy. At the same time, there is a risk of divergence: different teams and solutions going off in different directions that are hard to reconcile. Translating solutions – especially when different units/ teams in the organization have found conflicting solutions – to the level of policy may feel like "reverse engineering" the policy and may be harder than it seems. Some would even argue that it defeats the purpose of the policy, which is *guidance* in finding and implementing solutions. For a bottom-up approach, the recommended process would be as follows:

- Work with the sponsor of the initiative to set down a strong vision of what the policy should be about. Be very strict in making sure that all effort goes into solving the puzzle of developing a policy that meets this vision. This will prevent teams and team members from going off on a tangent and focus too much on local needs and solutions.
- In the bottom-up approach, there is frequent interaction with the work-floor. The trick is to keep management up to speed on development of the policy. Try to schedule time with management teams (both top management and middle management) to hear their concerns. Make sure to share these concerns with your team and check the policy against these concerns.
- As with the top-down approach, make sure you form a team of professionals that collaborate on writing the policy. Make sure to select people with (1) a good understanding of the local situation in which they work, but (2) who also have good abstraction skills to help understand the situation in different areas of the organization.
- Accept that it is ok to reverse engineer solutions that are already in place as input for writing the policy. Balance this with tough questions: where do we want to standardize? Where do we allow more freedom? Work with your sponsor to answer these questions.

The advantage of this approach is that the work-floor (especially the people in your working team) will support the policy. The policy effectively documents the type of solutions that the work-floor needs. Keeping both the sponsor and management teams in the loop ensures that the policy aligns with the vision of (top) management and contributes to achieving the strategic/ tactical goals of the organization.

27.4 RECOMMENDATIONS

In the previous section, I have discussed the top-down and bottom-up approaches to developing a policy. I have also listed advantages and disadvantages of both. As in most situations, the best approach depends on the local situation. For example, when a policy initiative is driven by a recent audit (as illustrated in example 58), a top-down approach might work best. However, when you are on a journey to improve the data management capability of your organization one step at a time, then a bottom-up approach might be more feasible, especially in a culture/ setting where empowering people is key.

This brings me back to the philosophical discussion of section 4.7 where I explained that building or improving a data management capability is a *complex* task, especially when striving for an *antifragile* solution that gets stronger when it is used and tested in practice. The proposed approaches, both in the top-down and bottom-up settings, are intended to ensure that the DM-capability has characteristics similar to *antifragility* by focusing on the concerns and perspectives of professionals in the organization. Keep in mind that embedding the ideas behind the policy into the culture of the organization is one of the biggest success factors for an effective implementation of DM.

28 Business concepts and the conceptual data model

Synopsis *- Writing good definitions is an art as much as a science. If definitions are too broad or vague then they are hardly usable. If they are too narrow, then there will be many exceptions when trying to match data elements to these definitions. In this chapter, I will argue that definitions of key terms used by the organization should always be considered in the context of where they are used which means that there may be many definitions of the same term for different contexts. This context is often a process, or system where the term (or, more precisely, the business concept) is used. Furthermore, I will show the relationships between developing a good set of definitions and a conceptual data model that matches it (see chapter 11).*

28.1 FREEZING LANGUAGE

Writing definitions of business concepts (or terms) helps to ensure that they are correctly understood. Definitions help to standardize *meaning*. In the context of data management, definitions help to ensure that data is stored, interpreted, and used correctly and consistently. This requires strong linguistic skills (as well as the skill to design sound data structures, among other things). One of the eminent scholars in this field is Stijn Hoppenbrouwers who wrote a dissertation on *Freezing Language* [Hop03]. Sidebar 14 presents his current thoughts on this topic.

Sidebar 14. Interview with Stijn Hoppenbrouwers (summer 2019)

Language, or languaging, is a very useful trick humans have developed. It is a tool that is highly adaptive: people change the words they use, and the meaning of those words, to fit the specific situation they use them in. This could, for example, be a specific department; many departments, fields, or domains. Each may have their own specific "dialect", shared by the people involved in and communicating about it. Together they change the language if a changing situation requires it. The natural state of language is "liquid".

However, if such a specific dialect is to be adopted as part of an information system, or some other standardized, stable construct, it cannot so easily be changed any more. A ship's telegraph[a] is a simple example of an unproblematic construct involving frozen language. In any situation in which language is subject to some change, there is a dilemma: adapt or maintain the standard? And what should the standard be in the first place? How to design it, how to manage it?

"Freezing language" is a continuous "background challenge" in both society and engineering. Part of freezing language is describing quite precisely what words mean. This is not as easy as it may seem, particularly since it heavily depends on context. If you need to freeze language (in particular when designing information systems or other data-intensive constructs), you need to be aware of the pitfalls. This issue lies at the core of data governance, and though it is not normally called freezing language, you see it whenever people are discussing terminology issues. These debates can become quite heated, because people tend to care about their own language: it is part of their identity and how they do their work. It is a precision tool that they value. They may well resist having to change it, or even to give it up in favor of some "foreign standard". At a time where the world becomes more and more pervaded by data in many forms and guises, I believe this aspect of data management becomes increasingly important.

Any attempts to deal with this through (even advanced) AI or language technology have largely failed because this technology is bad at dealing with context, in particular with many small, highly specific contexts with very nuanced aspects of word meaning that cannot be "mined" because there are no large volumes of explicit data to mine from.

a For more information on a ship's telegraph (also: engine order telegraph), see https://en.wikipedia. org/wiki/Engine_order_telegraph, last checked: 29 July 2019.

Stijn Hoppenbrouwers is professor of Data & Knowledge Engineering at HAN *University of Applied Sciences, Arnhem and assistant professor at Radboud University Nijmegen.*

Several important points can be learned from this sidebar. First, the word *languaging* is a verb and its (playful) use in this context suggests that getting a (shared) understanding of business concepts requires work. Someone has to make the effort to document the meaning of a business concept and verify with stakeholders in a given area that this meaning *works* for them. The wider the context is chosen, the bigger the group of stakeholders that are involved and, as Stijn suggested, the bigger the chance that debates become heated.

Second, some attempts to standardize the meaning of words are easy where others aren't. When it turns out that writing a standardized definition for a business concept is really tough because stakeholders cannot agree on the (shared) meaning, then this is often the result of a context that is too wide. An example is the term *Customer*:

the *Finance* department may claim that "customers are people who have made a purchase of our products within the last six months", whereas the *Marketing* department may claim that "customers are people who have made a purchase in the last two years, or have shown interest in making such a purchase in the months to come". Trying to reconcile these definitions is likely to be hard and the best way forward is to freeze the language differently for each of the two contexts. I will discuss this further in section 28.3.

28.2 DEFINITIONS AND CONCEPTUAL DATA MODELS

Using well-defined terminology (i.e. through business concepts that have good definitions) is a good start for getting a (shared) understanding of data in the context where it is used. This is far from straightforward: language/ terms that work well in one context (e.g. in literature) need not work in another. A term such as "material risk" may have a different meaning in a *finance* setting than in a factory setting. Similarly, a term such as "data steward" may have very different connotations in different organizations – so finding out what works *in the given context* is the key to success. The effect of well-defined terminology can be strengthened by getting a shared understanding of how (the definitions of) different business concepts are related. This is the realm of conceptual data modeling (chapter 11). Sidebar 15 presents an illustration of how a conceptual data model can make all the difference in getting a shared understanding of a domain and, as a result of that shared understanding, getting a project back on track.

Sidebar 15. Interview with Jeroen Cloo (summer 2019)

For my clients, I often see that data modeling is synonymous with the creation of a physical data model. When I start working for a new client, setting up a conceptual data model is often one of the first things I do, purely for myself. This model helps me to understand the context of that company. It helps me to understand their jargon and to interpret the stories from the conversations correctly.

I was hired a few years ago to get a project to implement an Electronic Health Record (EHR) system at a hospital back on track. The project was already halfway through the allotted time and the EHR system was only used in one department. The project leader was unable to get all the specialists on the same wavelength. They did not want to share all their data with specialists from other disciplines. They didn't want to feel controlled by someone from another discipline. A very simple object model that explains the concept that an EHR contains data that:

- All doctors in a hospital must be able to see such things as blood type, use of medication, allergies, the desire not to be resuscitated;
- Is only of interest to your own discipline, such as various measurements, results of research;

- Specifies the diagnosis and treatment plan of a specialist that are of interest to other disciplines.

This simple model, with only three business concepts, reassured the specialists. The result was that the project was completed within the original schedule and budget.

My conviction is that data structures in an organization are far more stable than the systems, processes, and organizational set-up. That is why it is important to understand and model them well. To be a discussion partner with the business, you should not do this by means of technical models. Create a simple logical model and start the conversation. This creates mutual understanding and will reduce misunderstandings.

Jeroen Cloo is partner at Novius Adviesgroep.

The example from this sidebar is exemplary for a broader pattern: seeing is believing. Drawing out the relationships between key business concepts – well-defined with effective definitions – offers a common ground to reason about a business domain. The benefits of such shared insight transcend data management.

As a general rule, I would argue that good *definitions* focus on the "micro level" of a single business concept, whereas conceptual data models focus on the bigger picture. Referring to the discussion about modeling languages in section 11.3: conceptual data models come in different shapes and forms (e.g. ERD, UML class diagrams, or ORM2 diagrams). Informal models can take the simple form of "boxes and arrows" with the sole purpose of visualizing how business concepts are related. Formal models, for example in the ORM2 notation, go a step further and assist in gaining a precise understanding of concepts. Example 59 illustrates this point.

Example 59. Using ORM2 to define business concepts

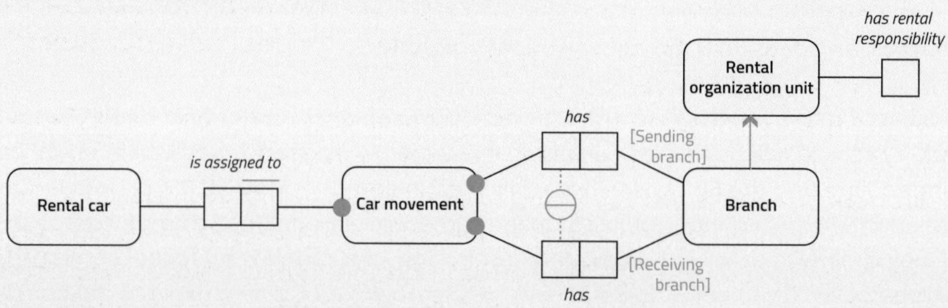

Definitions
- Branch is a Rental organization unit that has rental responsiblity
- Car movement is the planned movement of a Rental car from a Sending branch to a Receiving branch

The above diagram is a partial ORM2 model about car movements in the context of a car rental company. First of all, note the definition of the business concept *Car*

> *movement*, which relates a point of origin (*Sending branch*) to a point of destination (*Receiving branch*). These are represented as named *roles* of a *Branch* in the diagram. Note the definition for *Branch*. In technical terms this is called a *sub type defining rule*, as *Branch* is a sub type of *Rental organization unit*.

The key point this example tries to illustrate is that formal models may *help* in writing precise definitions by considering the relationships between business concepts, yet this comes at a cost: business stakeholders will likely see these diagrams as *technocratic* or even *unreadable*.

28.3 DEFINITIONS IN A CONTEXT

I will now shift gears and discuss writing *effective* definitions. Let's start with defining the word "definition". Bonnie O'Neil writes: "a definition is the meaning of a term" [O'N05]. The simplest rules of a good definition for a business concept that I have come up with over the years is:

> *A good definition of a business concept conveys the meaning of this concept as agreed upon by a group of stakeholders.*

This boils down to the simple pragmatics of *freezing language*: write down definitions that are effective for the stakeholders who work with the business concept. To ensure that stakeholders have a shared understanding of a definition, it helps to clearly document the definition in a *business glossary*. Loosely based on the suggestion by Bonnie O'Neil in [O'N05], I recommend capturing at least the following aspects of a definition:

- **Name** - the name of the business concept. This is usually a noun (e.g. *Employee*).
- **Alias** - other names for the same business concept with the exact same meaning (e.g. *Staff member)*.
- **Homonyms** - the same business concept or term may be reused in another context. Make sure to add links to these homonyms.
- **Broader concept & distinguishing characteristic** - which broader concept does this business concept belong to? This refers to another business concept that is defined (e.g. *employee is-a Person*). In mathematical terms, the population of a business concept is a subset of the population of the broader business concept. In other words: all employees are people but the inverse does not have to hold.
- **Definition** - A clear and concise definition of the business concept. Ideally use the form "a . . . is . . ." to force yourself to write consistent definitions. Avoid definitions that are long and sentences with many clauses. Make sure that

words which refer to another business concept can be recognized as such (for example by underlining them).
- **Governance metadata** - This includes metadata such as ownership, stewardship, date of creation of the definition, etc.

You'll find that this sounds simple, but it can be quite challenging, especially when a large group of stakeholders are involved. A lot of research has been done on collaborative modeling/ definition writing (e.g. [HWR09, IC13]) but my advice is that a simple conversation with a group of motivated stakeholders tends to work best.

This brings me to the topic of context once more. As stated and illustrated previously in this chapter, one business concept may have a different meaning in a different context. For years it has been a common practice to attempt to work towards a single definition for each business concept. While this is a beautiful and lofty idea, it turns out that it is far from practical (as shown in the work on *freezing language*, for example [Hop03] and sidebar 14). It is increasingly common to define business concepts in a *context*, not unlike the approach taken in *domain-driven design* (e.g. [Eva04, Kle17]). Figure 28.1 illustrates the main idea.

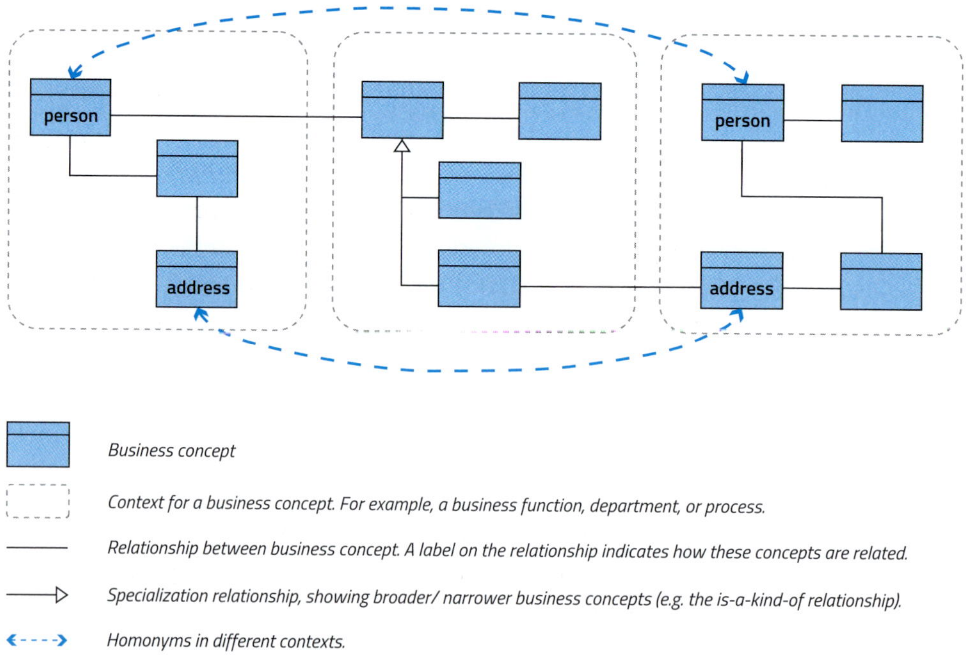

Figure 28.1 Concepts in context

In my view, the way of working should be as follows. The first question that should be answered is: how do we define the contexts for our organization? Ideally these contexts are mutually exclusive (there is no business concept that straddles two contexts) and collectively exhaustive (each business concept is part of a context).

Typically, this is done via the mechanisms that are used to assign data owners and data stewards, as illustrated in figure 25.1: per *subject area, business function*, etc.

The second step is to find a group of stakeholders who understand the context well and are collectively motivated to find the key business concepts for this context as well as document their definitions. A good *working team* will go a long way in striking a balance between *speed* of developing and *quality* of definitions. With this working team you should analyze the selected context. For example, if you have chosen *processes* to define contexts, then you can work with stakeholders to brainstorm the inputs and outputs of these processes. Perhaps there is a group in the organization that already has process models that you can reuse. Similarly, if your contexts are defined on systems, then work with the information management or IT department to analyze which data each system has.

In this step it is crucial to make sure you stay at the *conceptual level* and define *business concepts* in the way that stakeholders use them in the given context. This is a process of *freezing business language* and IT terminology and tech-speak should be avoided. The business concepts that are found can then be documented using the above-mentioned structure. This also includes formal approval of the assigned data owner.

The final step is to *test* your newly documented definitions in practice. This can be done in various ways. Two examples are: (1) pick up old documents (meeting minutes, high-level designs of systems, architecture diagrams) and check for consistency with the new language, and (2) in the next few meetings, ask one team member to monitor for correct language use during the meeting. It is to be expected that there are some deviations from the (new) norm in the beginning but if the definitions are well chosen, there should be gradual improvement in compliance with the new standard.

28.4 RECOMMENDATIONS

Language is a living thing. Professionals tend to prefer their own language and forcing a change is far from easy. I believe in a decentralized approach where business concepts are defined for a given context.

I do recommend that definitions are put under strict governance and are documented in a central repository. In this context, strict governance means that the data owner has signed off on the definition – which means that he is willing to enforce its correct use. The central repository can be something as simple as a wiki page with a list of definitions, or a fancy metadata tool (see chapter 20 for a discussion on tooling).

The final recommendation has to do with human nature. As stated in section 4.7, a successful DM capability is antifragile, meaning that it gets stronger when people use it. Language is the *foundation* for antifragility: you may be able to temporarily *force* people to use language/ definitions that do not fit their needs but eventually this will blow up in your face, meaning that stakeholders will revert to language that *does* suit their needs.

29 Setting up a metadata repository

Synopsis *- Metadata is a key enabler for many data management activities. To be of use, data management professionals – data stewards in particular – should be able to access metadata in an efficient manner: without it they cannot do their job. This is the realm of the metadata repository. In this chapter, I will review basic principles for setting up such a repository. I will link this discussion to governance structures as well as the experimentation mindset.*

29.1 THE IMPORTANCE OF METADATA

In chapter 10, I discussed what metadata is, what kinds of metadata can be distinguished (business metadata, technical metadata, and operational metadata), and why metadata is so important. The short version is that you need to know "things" about the assets you are managing, and for data assets, these "things" are called metadata. Consider sidebar 16 for an illustration on the importance of metadata for (enterprise) architects.

Sidebar 16. Interview with Kiean Bitaraf (summer 2019)

I believe enterprise architecture and metadata management go hand-in-hand and somehow even pursue the same goals. Especially today, we see many organizations drowning in data and experiencing large problems due to overly complex business-IT landscapes. Both disciplines contribute continuously to enabling greater coherency, alignment and integration between business and technology. The combination is vital for resolving data issues at the source of the problem, clarifying relationships between applications and understanding how data is flowing through the organization. By providing business and technical traceability and lineage, metadata management contributes to architects assessing the impact of changes on the IT landscape. At the same time, an architect's holistic view on the business-IT landscape contributes to resolving inconsistencies in stored data sets.

Overall, metadata management and enterprise architecture are two important pillars that help organizations to gain control over processes, technology and data.

Kiean Bitaraf is data management consultant at Deloitte.

In this sidebar, Kiean effectively stresses how data management professionals and architects work side by side to (a) manage the complexity of the interplay between data, processes, and systems, and by doing so, (b) help the organization gain value from its data assets. The DMBOK lists metadata repositories as supporting tools for data modeling and design, data integration and interoperability, data warehousing and business intelligence, governance, and data quality management. Without metadata, it is hard to tell what data you are managing, nor would it be an easy job to understand where the data is used, or how effectively it is used. Metadata is foundational.

It appears that metadata is one of the areas where professionals "refuse to get started" without extensive tool support. Sidebar 17 illustrates the delicate balance between a business perspective and a technical perspective on metadata tooling, as well as the decision to work with extensive tooling from the start.

Sidebar 17. Interview with Tanja Glisin (summer 2019)

Metadata management tools are very appealing to buy when building a data asset inventory itself is the goal. This is often the case from an operational and technical perspective. If metadata repositories are viewed as data governance enablers, then starting with the people and process perspective is more in focus. Frequently this leads to SharePoint experiments which can later be scaled or replaced by tools that are purchased. If the approach is driven by data governance, then it is best to be centralized to start with and slowly pick out more technical areas where the metadata tools and repositories can be leveraged.

Tanja Glisin is an experienced data management professional and frequent collaborator of the author of this book.

29.2 METADATA REPOSITORY ARCHITECTURES

For metadata repositories, the DMBOK refers to the ISO/IEC standard (see [ISO15]) which states that "[data] should be registered, uniquely identified, named, defined, and classified in the repository". The DMBOK then continues to list several sources of metadata [Hen17, section 12.1.3.5]. A short and partial summary is included here for easy reference:

- **Business glossary** - Documents the organization's business concepts/ terminology and definitions.
- **Data dictionaries** - Document the definitions of data elements, as well as the structure and contents of data sets.
- **Data integration tools** - Capture how data flows between systems (the technical term is *lineage*).
- **Database management systems** - Capture the content of databases and describe how data is stored.
- **Data quality tools** - Usually have validation rules and offer the capability to exchange quality scores of data assets.
- **Modeling tools** - Are used to create (conceptual/ logical/ physical) data models which provide insight into the relationships between business concepts and data elements alike.
- **Reference data repositories** - Document the reference data of the organization.

These different sources of metadata are illustrated in figure 29.1. In this case, if you want to know all there is to know about a piece of data (signified by the small orange circle), you'd have to look at each of the listed sources of metadata. The questions that I will discuss in this paragraph are: what should the architecture behind these sources be? Should we build a centralized repository of metadata? Should we keep it decentralized? Or something in between? And most of all, why?

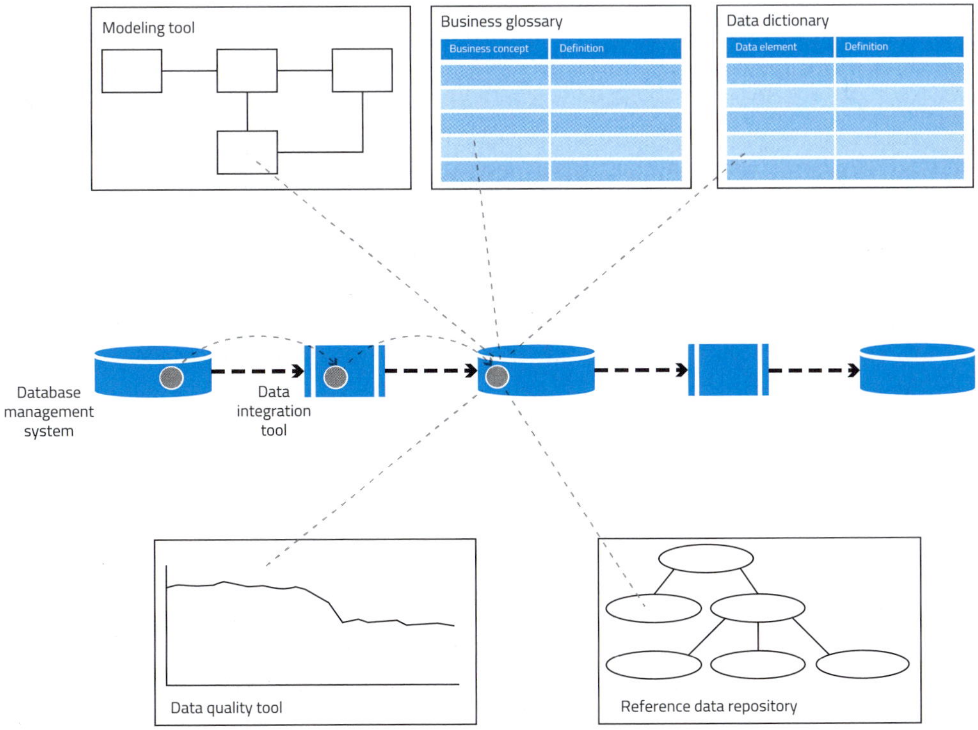

Figure 29.1 Metadata from different sources

The diagram shows, in the middle layer, three databases that are connected through data integration tools. The databases and integration tools all have metadata from these systems. Other metadata can be found in the surrounding tools.

There are different architectures for implementing a metadata repository. The DMBOK lists three:

- **Centralized metadata architecture** - Is an architecture where a single metadata repository holds (copies of) all metadata from various sources. This would mean that metadata from all sources is pulled to a central place where it can be accessed by data management professionals. The advantage of such an approach are twofold. First, it gives a good sense of control, since everything is available in a single place. If a decision is made to collect more/ new metadata then it is immediately obvious where this metadata should go. Another advantage is that everybody knows where to access metadata should they need it for their work. A potential disadvantage is that different units will have to agree on this approach as well as the type of technology used to implement it. Another potential disadvantage lies in the fact that it may be hard to find a single repository that does everything you want it to do for your specific situation.
- **Distributed metadata architecture** - This architecture could entail one of two things: metadata is distributed across the enterprise but *with* or *without* a single central access point. In the former case, metadata is distributed and data management professionals have to hunt it down when they want to find and use it. In the latter setup, the metadata is still distributed but there is now a central "registry" (see also chapter 15 on Master Data Management) that provides easy access to this distributed metadata. The benefit of this approach lies in its implementation: in this setup, there is more local autonomy to work with metadata in a way that fits the local needs. The only thing under central control is the registry. A potential disadvantage lies in the control over metadata structures and approaches, which may diverge between local solutions. Also, cost may be higher because many local solutions are still supported on top of the central portal.
- **Hybrid metadata architecture** - This setup is a mix of both worlds. The idea is that there are multiple repositories that collect metadata (for example: one per business unit) and these can all be accessed via a single, central access point (such as a portal). Through this setup, the organization reaps the benefits of both approaches.

29.3 IMPLEMENTATION STRATEGIES

In my view, there are two sides to an implementation strategy. The first is similar to what has been discussed in part II of this book: following a top-down, big design up-front approach, versus a bottom-up approach where experimentation and learning is key. The other aspect lies in the tension between building your own tools, versus going out on the market and implementing the solution of a vendor. The two aspects are *orthogonal*, meaning that choices for each of these aspects can be made independently. In practice, however, top-down tends to be combined mostly with purchasing an existing package and bottom-up tends to be combined with a grow-your-own approach, sometimes followed by the implementation of an existing system on the market when the organization has learned enough to decide what it really needs to be successful with metadata. In this chapter, I will mostly focus on the former aspect.

29.3.1 Top-down metadata strategy

The essence of a top-down metadata strategy is to start with a set of goals you want to achieve through the use of metadata, to analyze which metadata is required, and to ensure that these requirements are met with an effective system. The line of thinking is not unlike the top-down approach to developing a data management policy, which was discussed in section 27.3.1.

A good example of this scenario is when the (top) management of an organization have decided to implement a data management program as a result of an audit, or new legislation that has been announced. An audit could result in audit points to be addressed, which may lead to specific metadata requirements. Along the same lines, new legislation may demand that certain metadata is available, for example for future inspection by an auditor.

For a successful top-down implementation, the requirements have to be crisp and clear and the overall objective has to be well-known across the organization. Experience shows that it is very hard to motivate people (for developing a metadata solution or otherwise) when they do not understand the purpose of the initiative and when the requirements are unclear.

29.3.2 Bottom-up metadata strategy

The essence of a bottom-up metadata strategy is learning: start with small/ local experiments to identify what you need/ what works for your organization and grow the initiative one step at a time. This line of thinking is similar to the bottom-up approach to developing a data management policy, which was discussed in section 27.3.2.

This approach fits more naturally with settings where local teams have the autonomy to experiment and build local capabilities that could potentially scale to the enterprise level when successful. A good example is the setting where a local team starts to experiment with *business intelligence* work (chapter 18). For such a project, the team would have to find out what data is needed (definitions), where it can be sourced (location, lineage) and what the structure of the data is. Also, a good indication of data quality would be needed to define a good solution. Building a local metadata repository to support the project might attract the attention of other projects, which could seed the further development of the solution.

For a successful bottom-up implementation, several factors are key. First, there should be some room to experiment and build (local) solutions that *might* eventually scale. Second, there should be some level of trust among groups, as well as the will to consider the solutions developed elsewhere in the organization. The "not invented here syndrome" is very real, even among different teams from the same organization. The final factor is time: it may take a while to develop a solution that is ready for wider user than in a single team.

29.3.3 Matching the strategy to the situation

It is not a straightforward task to find a metadata strategy (top-down or bottom-up, centralized or decentralized or hybrid). It warrants a good understanding of the needs of the enterprise, as well as a good understanding of (the importance of) metadata. The latter, in particular, may be difficult to come by, as sidebar 18 illustrates.

Sidebar 18. Interview with Fanny Vuillemin and Céline Lescop (Summer 2019)

Metadata is a topic that is not fully understood and solved in the organization. It is perceived to be blurry and abstract. The data management professionals know that it is really important and are working on a metadata information model that will guide the metadata effort.

People seem to be waiting for a tool or solution before trying anything, which is not helping the initiative. What we want to achieve is a (framework for a) metadata portal that becomes the focal point of all data management activities: to show it has value to business and IT users, which will help to make it grow.

Fanny Vuillemin is senior data manager at AXA *and Céline Lescop is lead data architect at* AXA.

The following list gives some guidance to help decide on an approach. A complete list is not feasible. This guidance is based on my practical experience.

- If there is a push for a big data-driven initiative in the organization, then that is a good clue to go for a top-down approach. This works just as well for a defensive initiative (handling legislation) as an offensive initiative (starting on a big data project).
- If the organization is working mostly with *agile* or *autonomous teams*, then this is a good indicator for a bottom-up approach. In such a culture, teams will likely resist too much interference from outside the team.
- If the organization has a single line of business, or if it has many lines of business but emphasizes standardized solutions and integrated data, then these are clear indicators for a *centralized* solution.
- If the organization has multiple lines of business which are largely independent, then things are harder to analyze. When there is little shared data between these lines of business, then a *decentralized* solution is more likely to work well. When there is shared data (or at least: data with shared definitions), then this suggests a *hybrid* approach.

29.4 RECOMMENDATIONS

I believe that metadata is one of the least understood data management capabilities. I also believe that it is foundational for most other data management capabilities. The conundrum is that learning about metadata requires the organization to work with metadata and gain real benefits from it but building a business case to do so is difficult at best (see also chapter 23).

It is also interesting to note that a lot of metadata *exists*, yet (a) people are not aware of it, or (b) it is scattered across the organization to a degree that using it effectively would take a lot of effort. *Technical* and *operational* metadata already exist in systems and log files[1]. The trick is to find a way to make this data accessible for use by data management professionals.

The same does not hold for business metadata. It is rare to find heaps of business definitions that just happen to be lying around, for example. When someone has taken the trouble to write them, then this is usually a well-known fact, at least in the local context where these definitions apply.

1 A log file is a text file that records events that have taken place on a system, such as transactions that are executed, errors that have occurred, etc.

The best guidance I can offer on building an effective metadata repository is to align it with other initiatives across the enterprise. A metadata repository in and of itself has little value. It only has value when used in other initiatives, so building it should follow the roadmap of those initiatives. Chapter 35 offers further guidance on building an effective data management roadmap.

30 Leveraging enterprise architecture

Synopsis *- Enterprise architecture (EA) and data management (DM) are both supportive functions that help the organization to realize its goals. EA is mostly focused on "the big picture" (more formally: the fundamental properties of the organization and principles guiding design and evolution). Data architecture can be seen as the architecture or the data landscape of the enterprise. The data architecture capability can be seen as a subset of both the EA capability and the DM capability. In my experience, the relationship between the two capabilities tends to be characterized by "drill down". This is too simplistic. In this chapter, I will show that a well-documented EA provides a wealth of information about the data of an organization and is therefore a good source of inspiration for DM professionals. I will use this as the basis for the next section in which I discuss the use of EA models for creating data-related visualizations. This will set the stage for a discussion on the interaction between EA and DM professionals to create sustainable, effective solutions in the organization, for example in relation to data integration challenges.*

30.1 EA AS A SOURCE OF INFORMATION

In chapter 12, I explained that the architecture of a system is (a) the fundamental properties of that system, and (b) the principles guiding design and evolution. Architectures tend to be documented in a mix of architecture principles and models/diagrams. The ArchiMate language is (slowly) becoming the industry standard for architecture models (see example 28). ArchiMate models are intended to provide insight into many aspects of the enterprise that are (also) relevant from a data management perspective. The following list gives some examples of information that is typically captured by an ArchiMate model:

- The relationship between processes and the data that flows along the processes;
- The relationship between systems and the data that flows among systems;

- The functions in systems that store or manipulate data;
- The systems that support business processes.

The list goes on and on. With most EA tools that support the ArchiMate language, the point is to create a comprehensive model that captures all these aspects and to generate or create views based on this model that help to inform stakeholders or help stakeholders to make decisions. Example 60 illustrates this point: insights that are useful from an architecture perspective can also be useful from a data management perspective. When models like this are available, data management professionals should work with the EA team to see if they can leverage these insights. If they are not (yet) available, then it would be a good idea to collaborate and develop these insights together. I will cover this topic later in this chapter.

Example 60. Generated ArchiMate views

This example stems from an assignment that I have recently completed. In this project, I was working with both an architecture team and a data management team, a very productive way to get useful insights. We created a comprehensive model. With one push of a button (plus some time for fixing the layout), we were able to create the following view:

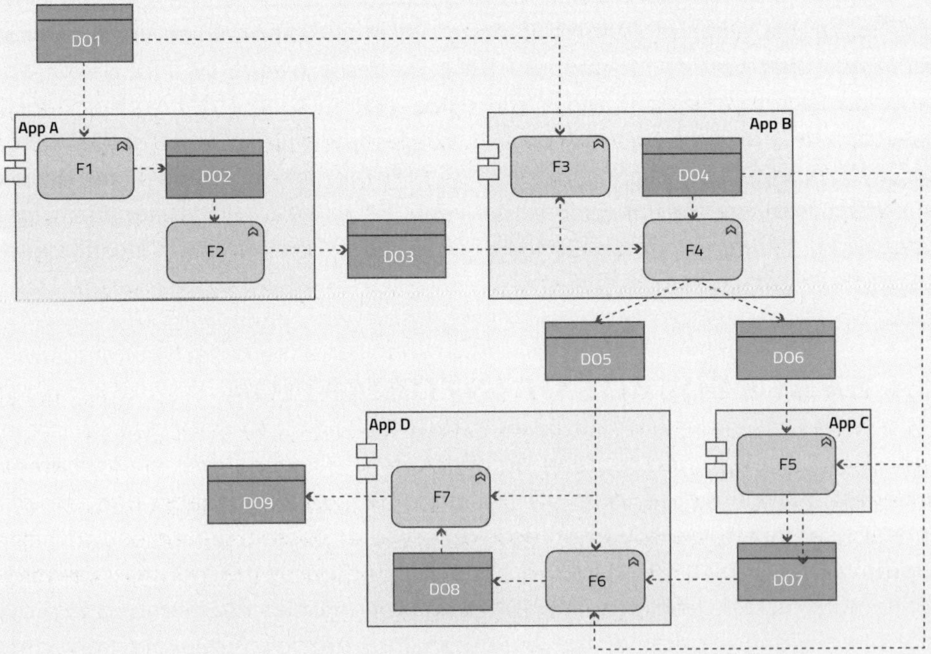

This diagram shows applications (labeled *App*), functions that manipulate data (labeled *F*), and data elements (labeled *DO*, since data elements are called *data objects* in ArchiMate).

We knew that some stakeholders were interested in the diagrams but that others had a big aversion against any type of diagram. Using the same tool, we converted the diagram to the table included below. In this table, the *C* stands for the creating of data, whereas the *R* stands for reading data.

CRUD Table		DO1	DO2	DO3	DO4	DO5	DO6	DO7	DO8	DO9
APP A	F1	R	C							
APP A	F2		R	C						
APP B	F3			R	C					
APP B	F4			R	R	C	C			
APP C	F5				R		R	C		
APP D	F6				R	R		R	C	
APP D	F7					R			R	C

Architecture models are at a high level of abstraction, whereas DM professionals might need more detail. For example, a *logical data model* (section 11.2) will have more detail than what is shown here. This suggests that, from a DM perspective, more information (and more detailed models) may be needed. Still, getting a shared view at the big-picture level can go a long way in collaboration.

30.2 EA MODELS AND VISUALIZATIONS

Many activities related to DM have a communication aspect. DM professionals work with other professionals to help business stakeholders achieve their goals. This requires effective communication – an aspect that is also stressed in [KNPCA19]. Unfortunately, many stakeholders find *data* a complex and abstract subject, which hampers communication. Nuances such as the distinction between the *conceptual*, *logical*, and *physical* levels (section 11.2) are justifiably lost on most business stakeholders.

As DM professionals, we have to be extra careful on *how* we communicate with stakeholders. Experience shows that working with a mix of diagrams and textual (written/ spoken) messages works well, particularly when the visuals are used consistently. Here, the architecture models can help. Much information can be found in good EA repositories and most tools have good visualization capabilities. Example 61 illustrates how ArchiMate models can be extended to help with typical questions that could come up for a given case.

Example 61. Visualizations
The setting for this example is an audit of a system and its data. From a data perspective, typical questions that could come up are: (1) Where does data come from and where does it flow to? (2) Who are data owners and data stewards that are relevant? (chapter 9) and (3) What is the security classification of the data and does

the application have enough controls in place to mitigate key risks? (chapter 17) Some of these questions can be answered directly from the models (see also the previous example in this chapter). For the others, the model could be enriched. The diagram below gives an example.

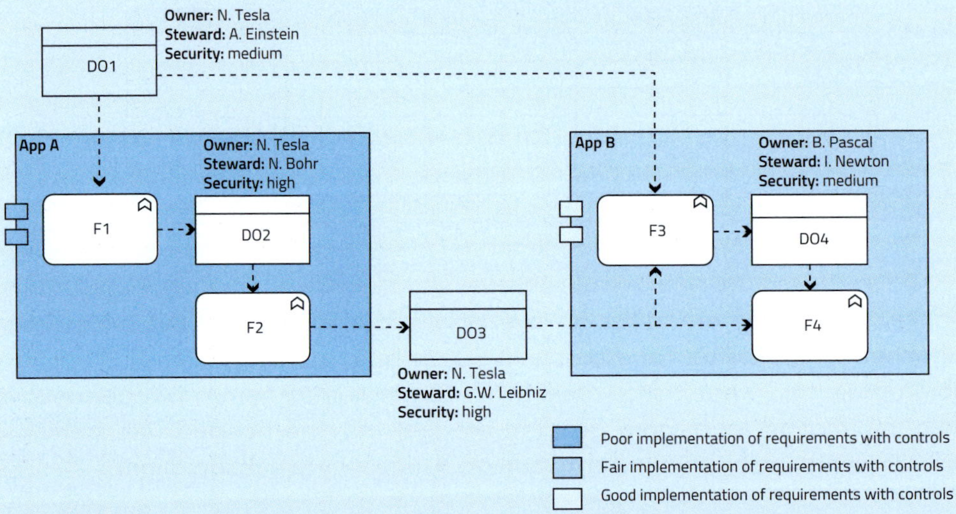

The diagram continues from example 60 and zooms in on *App A*. For each of the data elements, it shows the data owner, data steward, and an indication of the security requirements.

As before, the example serves to illustrate that collaboration is key: when all relevant information (in this case the base model but also ownership, stewardship, security requirements, assessments of the applications) are accessible from one tool, then powerful and valuable analyses can often be performed with a push of the button.

In several chapters of part II, I have discussed the delicate balance between centralized and decentralized solutions, between top-down governance, and bottom-up support. In many cases, there is no single best way to move forward, it always depends on the context of the organization. In my experience, this does not hold for architecture/ architecture models, though: it pays to collect the type of information that was discussed in this chapter in a central (architecture) repository that can be used by professionals in many different roles, including architects and data management professionals. This would optimize the *return on modeling effort* (ROME) – a term introduced first in [OPW+08].

30.3 BUILDING EFFECTIVE SOLUTIONS

In the previous two sections, I have discussed collaboration between EA professionals and DM professionals by building a shared knowledge base that can be used in analyses and communication settings. There is, however, a third area where the two capabilities meet: building effective IT solutions – but with a heavy focus on data. Two settings come to mind.

First is the realm of data integration. As the two examples in this chapter show, architecture models already give a good overview of how data flows through the organization's processes and systems. So far, I haven't discussed *how* that happens, or which *integration techniques* are to be used (chapter 13). This is an area where DM professionals, architects, and IT professionals can collaborate to devise optimal solutions. One of the key reasons to include architects when considering data integration challenges lies in the fact that they have such a good overview of the landscape: they are uniquely positioned to recommend the optimal integration techniques and platforms – by not only considering the local problem but zooming out to consider the bigger picture. This avoids local optimizations which hamper other areas of the enterprise.

Second is the setting where only a big-picture view of who uses which data (and for what) will lead to effective solutions. Certain data is used in many different places across the organization. It frequently happens that the same data is copied and moved to many different parts of the organization. Each of these copies was made for a very good reason. However, keeping them up-to-date and consistent is hard to say the least. Architects are uniquely positioned to spot when this happens and can devise solutions to accommodate, for example, by using *master data management* solutions (chapter 15).

In both these cases, the collaboration between architects and DM professionals is not about data or architecture per se. It is about sharing insights and devising effective solutions to help achieve business goals. Of course, this should not stop at the ideation phase: good ideas will only get you so far. Ideas should lead to project proposals and, ultimately, to solutions that implement the ideas.

This brings me back to the position of business cases (chapter 23). Business cases are notoriously hard to create for enterprise initiatives such as DM. The same holds for the cases that are discussed in this section. Let's say you have a data set about customers. Several teams already receive copies of this data. A new team announces that they would also like a copy. The fast and cheap way to do this is to create a new data flow and give the team what they ask for. Now, suppose an architect is involved. The architect spots that the same data is moved across the organization, causing all kinds of inconsistencies. It is proposed to use a master data management solution.

This will take a while to implement and it is likely to be more costly than quickly adding a new data flow. Making a business case for such a solution is inherently difficult as it requires the organization to (1) learn to take a long-term perspective, and (2) to zoom out and consider the big picture ("enterprise view") rather than the local problem. This, in my opinion, is what EA and DM professionals should really be focused on: helping the organization to take a long-term view and consider the bigger picture when building solutions, one step at a time.

30.4 RECOMMENDATIONS

The title of this chapter is a little bit of a misnomer, since I have discussed the effective relationship between data management and enterprise architecture, rather than only considering how enterprise architecture can be leveraged by data management. It turns out that the relationship between these fields can be truly symbiotic.

The first recommendation in light of the theme of this chapter is to build a good working relationship with the architecture team and work on a joint knowledge base in the form of an architecture repository. It may be tricky to find a good balance in the level of details that is required (data management professionals, as a rule, tend to want more details than architects) but it is well worth the effort. Simply put, architecture models are a great source of information for data management professionals and linking models to e.g. a *business glossary* (chapters 10, 20, and 29) enriches the models in a way that makes them more useful for architects. In my view, more people using this knowledge base means a more sustainable and antifragile solution.

The second recommendation might be a bit broad for the focus of this chapter but this is as good a place as any to make it: data management professionals and enterprise architects are uniquely positioned to help the organization in taking a long-term, enterprise-wide view of data. This may be an up-hill battle initially, as many stakeholders over-emphasize the short-term, local perspective. It may take many compromises along the way but ultimately it will help to attain a better balance between these perspectives. My experience is that it will help in both data management defense (getting to grips with the complexity of the data landscape) and data management offense (getting value from your data assets), mainly due to the fact that process, data, and systems are better aligned (see figure 20.1).

31 Integration architecture

***Synopsis** - In section 12.2, I have discussed the notions of data at rest and data in motion. Data tends to flow through the processes and systems of the organization, which puts the focus on the latter perspective. In chapter 13, I gave an overview of the theory of data integration. In this chapter, I will present good practices for building a good integration architecture to guide data integration efforts in the organization. I will start by stressing that an integration architecture should be built on a few simple principles and will subsequently show how integration patterns can be used to extend the architecture. I will conclude this chapter with practical recommendations.*

31.1 DATA IS EVERYWHERE

Data tends to be distributed across (many systems in) the organization. There are more and more *use cases* where integrated data sets are required. Examples that were mentioned in previous chapters of this book are: reports, dashboards, advanced analytics and building a 360-view of the customer. Data is, regrettably, considered to be an abstract topic by many business stakeholders. This extends to data integration as eyes tend to glaze over when the topic is raised. It is, however, an important topic that should not be left to the architect alone.

In the ideal world, business stakeholders, IT stakeholders, and (integration) architects have a productive conversation where current/ future data integration needs are explored and matched to the desired/ available integration capabilities in the IT landscape. To facilitate that discussion, many architects look for metaphors when discussing data integration. Sidebar 19 gives an example.

Sidebar 19. Interview with Paul Heisen (summer 2019)

De Lage Landen (DLL) has set up a "data apartment building" in Microsoft Azure. This "building" is aimed at housing data, data management solutions, and analytics solutions from experiments through to deployment and sustainable production. The "building" has a shared area that is implemented by a data lake[a]. The real-world equivalent of such an area is the shared infrastructure in a building: piping, water and power supply, elevators, staircases, etc.

Each "apartment" in the building represents a data set from one of DLL's applications. Each apartment is owned by a business owner and can be equipped with "approved" components from the Azure platform. Data for these apartments is obtained via the data lake, which mirrors how water/ power is distributed from central services to apartments in a physical building. In the virtual apartment building, however, apartments may share data with other apartments.

We are now testing/ setting up a virtual logical data model on top of the data lake. At the moment, we have a variety of apartments ranging from DLL's enterprise data warehouse to apartments tailored for machine learning experiments that revolve around credit management and asset management. The value of this "building" is that all data management solutions and analytics solutions share the same technology (cloud) platform but the real value is in the ability to share and combine data with each other.

a A data lake is a centralized repository that allows you to store all your structured and unstructured data at any scale.

Paul Heisen is senior enterprise architect at De Lage Landen (DLL).

This sidebar shows a situation where DLL has built a data integration environment in the cloud and where a metaphor was developed to help discuss even the technical details of this environment with business stakeholders. A productive conversation about what business stakeholders want to achieve with data integration and the technological means to achieve those goals is the key to success.

31.2 START SIMPLE

It is easy to get lost in the technical details of data integration platforms, patterns, and techniques. When setting up a data integration architecture, it is best to start with a few simple principles – perhaps expressed via a good metaphor to improve communication with stakeholders – and keep the architecture as simple as possible. For example, rather than considering each and every connection between systems in your landscape, lift the analysis to a higher abstraction level and build the architecture on the notion that there are *data providing applications* and *data consuming applications*.

Once you are at a certain level of abstraction, make sure you stay at that level – consistency is important. In this case, you could argue that data which flows from a providing application has a data owner – which effectively creates the link to the data governance structure that the organization uses. By modeling the architecture at this (abstract) level, you will end up with an effective, simple, and consistent architecture.

Sidebar 20 gives an overview of the basic principles behind the integration architecture of ABN AMRO called DIAL and is based on an interview with its creator, Piethein Strengholt, as well as a presentation that Piethein gave at the *Enterprise Data World* conference in Boston in March of 2019.

Sidebar 20. Interview with Piethein Strengholt (summer 2019)

The philosophy behind DIAL (Digital Integration & Access Layer) is to accelerate data consumption by different parties in the organization, while at the same time being very much in control by knowing what data is consumed, for what purpose and by whom.

In contrast to the "traditional" data warehouse model (where data from different sources is brought together for integration into a consistent whole), data in the DIAL isn't integrated. Instead each application from every business domain is requested to connect to the integration layer and has to deliver high quality, consumable data as it is used in its own context. Because the data is not transformed when it is moved to DIAL, we are able to see the true/ original data values and quality of the data. This setup also helps us to ensure accountability of data owners and data stewards. By enforcing that all data flows through the same single logical layer, we create maximum transparency, which should speed up the data consumption as well. Last but not least, our integration layer is connected to the tools that support our metadata capability. This will give us the insight and controls that a large enterprise must have to stay on top of the flow of data through the organization.

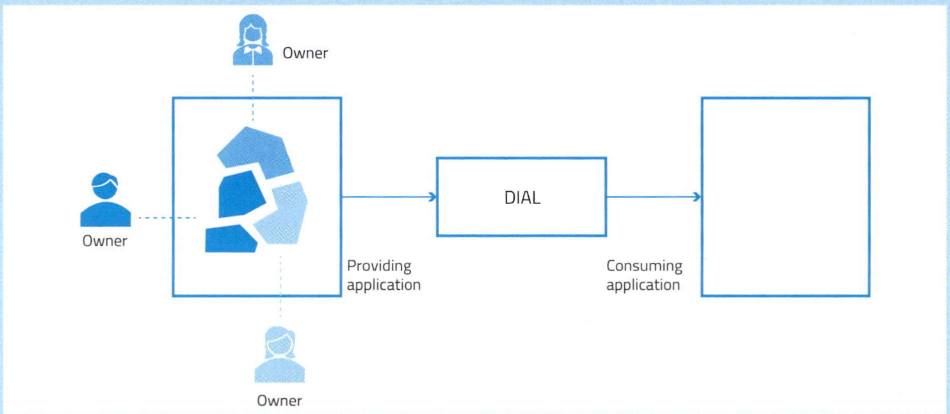

Piethein Strengholt is principle data architect at ABN AMRO.

The simple idea that underpins the architecture from sidebar 20 is that data moves from providing to consuming applications via the digital integration and access layer and that data remains unaltered. This is *one* choice where laying it out concisely will help the organization to tackle integration challenges in a consistent manner. By contrast, the architecture that was described in sidebar 19 is built on the simple idea that (1) DLL's systems retain their own data as much as possible, (2) that existing data flows between systems are untouched, but (3) that a new "data hotel" is created specifically for business intelligence and analytics purposes.

Note that I am not claiming that there is a single best way to setup your data architecture, or that the DIAL setup is the best way forward. The point that I am trying to make is that it pays to have a few simple principles to start with and expand from there. What works well always depends on the situation in the organization. For example, in some cases it *does* help to integrate data when moving it from providing to consuming applications. Or, perhaps the organization uses an integration architecture based on *data virtualization* (section 13.2.5) and avoids moving data around as much as possible to begin with.

31.3 KEEP IT SIMPLE

The previous section recommended starting with a few basic/ simple principles to structure your data integration architecture. This should help to ensure that the foundation/ basic components to support the data integration landscape are built in a consistent manner. The next step is considering the different contexts in which your data integration architecture is going to be used and finding out the different *patterns* to support these *use cases*.

A pattern, in this context, can be defined as a reusable solution for a common problem (see e.g. [GHJV95, Fow97] for a good introduction to the use of patterns). Initially this may seem fairly straight forward. Example of initial use cases and their associated patterns are as follows:

- We have a common use case where we want to move data around in batches. How do we solve this? → We will use the ETL component of our favorite vendor.
- We have a common use case where we want to have real-time access to the data that is stored in another system. How do we solve this? → We will create a shadow-copy of the system[1] and access this data through *service calls*[2]. We use synchronous service calls[3] and accept the time delays this might cause.

1 In technical terms, an operational data store. See section 18.2.
2 In non-technical terms, this means that the system sends a specific request (for data) to another system, which sends a response back.
3 This means that the requesting system has to stop its processing until the supplying system has sent back its reply. The alternative is to use asynchronous service calls, which greatly increases the complexity of the system.

- We have a common use case where we want to analyze fast changing data in real-time, such as the *click stream* of users on our website. How do we solve this? → We will use the stream processing capabilities of our favorite vendor.

This list can be extended further, of course, as more and more use cases are discovered. The basic data integration architecture that you have set up can now be extended to also include these patterns. This means that the rather simple diagram from sidebar 20 will become a little more complicated. I recommend being careful which version of the diagram to show to which stakeholder, so it pays off to maintain both a simple and a more elaborate version. Sidebar 21 illustrates these patterns in the context of ABN AMRO and also raises another challenge that I will discuss shortly.

Sidebar 21. Interview with Piethein Strengholt (summer 2019)

Standardization on integration patterns is extremely important. Integration is very complex and the data integration capability is intertwined with many of the other data management capabilities such as metadata, governance, security, etc. Within ABN AMRO we have decided to standardize on three patterns: batches with ETL, APIs, and streaming data. These integration capabilities are deployed on all platforms, both on-premise and in the public cloud. We again distinguish between "enterprise" data integration (across domains in the bank) and local data integration (within a domain in the bank). The distribution and integration of data between domains always has to use the enterprise data integration capabilities. Within the domains themselves we are more reluctant, because the use case requirements typically have different patterns and needs.

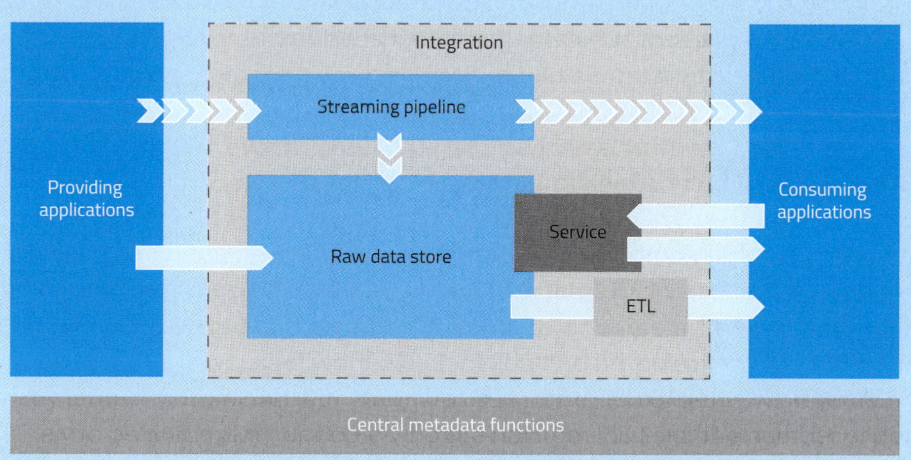

Piethein Strengholt is principle data architect at ABN AMRO.

There is one more step that must be considered for your data integration architecture: how do you deal with data integration challenges across different technical environments? In other words, how do you intend to deal with situations where part of your data is stored in systems that are hosted and managed by the organization itself, whereas another part of the data is hosted in the cloud?

Going into details with respect to this additional challenge would require a technical discussion that goes beyond the scope of this book. I will therefore only highlight some of the considerations involved and recommend that data integration architects discuss this further with cloud-savvy (IT) colleagues when the need arises.

One of the biggest challenges when moving data around, especially between environments (on-premise, in the cloud), is *latency*. This term refers to the delay that occurs when data is processed or transmitted. With modern, high-speed networks it may seem as if data transfer is near-instantaneous but in reality, the little delays that occur add up. Consider the situation where a (local) application needs data that is stored in a cloud environment. The request for data will travel from the local application, via the local firewall, across the internet, via the firewalls at the cloud provider, to the target system. After processing the request, the reply will have to travel the same way but in reverse order. Multiply this by potentially many requests per minute and the delays do start to make a difference with respect to the performance of your systems.

From a technical/ architecture perspective, this means you have to find out whether such delays are acceptable for the users of your data. As an illustration, the DLL "data hotel" is an integration architecture that is mainly used for reporting and analytical use cases in which stakeholders are unlikely to take issue with a delay. For ABN AMRO's DIAL architecture, this may be different so additional (technical) challenges will have to be overcome.

31.4 RECOMMENDATIONS

I predict that data integration will become a key differentiator for organizations in many branches. Having an effective capability to integrate data from many different sources and to be able to deliver high quality data sets to business users when they need them will give organizations a competitive edge in a data-driven economy [Red08, Fis09, CCW16]. The question of how to deal with integration challenges is too important to leave to (only) the integration architect. Ideally, different stakeholders (business, IT, and data management/ data integration) collaborate to develop an effective architecture. Only a productive discussion will ensure a sustainable solution that meets current and future needs of the enterprise.

As a final recommendation, I advocate for an approach to develop a data integration architecture in an incremental manner, with much room for experiments.

Only through real-world pilots can patterns be tested. Short cycles in which hypotheses are formed, a pattern is tested and evaluated before it is added to the architecture is a good way to ensure that it is viable. This, in turn, is required to ensure that business users have or gain access to high quality data.

32 A pragmatic approach to data security

***Synopsis** - Data is a key asset for most organizations and should therefore be carefully stored and protected. In chapter 17, I have discussed the fact that this entails a careful analysis of acceptable risks and implementing security measures to mitigate risks that are not acceptable. I have also explained that the ISO 27000 series provides a good set of standards for vocabulary, lists of risks, controls, etc. In practice, however, there is often a big gap between the high-level discussions in data security policies (principles and blanket statements) and the actual security measures that are implemented (fire walls, antivirus). Therefore, in this chapter, I will present a pragmatic approach (loosely called a security framework) to data security management that connects these two levels. I will start with an approach for specifying security use cases, which describe what happens to data. I will follow-up with an approach to defining security levels in business terms. Last but not least, I will show how these are used to select appropriate security measures.*

32.1 MOTIVATION FOR A SECURITY FRAMEWORK

Follow the news for a while and it is easy to see that hacking frequently happens and hurts both companies and individuals: computers are held hostage, viruses wreak havoc in the networks of companies, information that is supposed to remain confidential is published, credit card information is stolen, fake news from social media influences business decision-making[1], etc. The list is long.

Hackers do what they do for many different reasons, ranging from the thrill of being able to accomplish a technically challenging feat, to financial or political gains. Also, hackers come in many shapes and forms, ranging from novices who use simple tools found on the net "just to see what they do", to professional criminals. Regardless

1 I recently heard a story of an experiment where a 16-year-old used simple photo editing software, social media tools, and a vivid imagination to convince his school for over a week that he was doing an internship at a company whereas, in fact, he was playing on his computer from home. If a 16-year-old can fool everybody, how hard do you think it is for hackers to mislead corporate decision makers?

of these motivations and the proficiency of hackers, organizations are faced with the challenge of protecting their (data) assets against hackers and against misuse. The following sidebar illustrates the need for a security approach and also puts this in a historic perspective.

Sidebar 22. Interview with Raymond Slot (summer 2019)

Information technology (IT) now provides more power than we have ever experienced in our known history. We have many more options at our disposal than ever before. We can use this technological knowledge in a positive way, ensuring that everyone on Earth has a home to live in, clean water and food of sufficient quality, and adequate education. We have more than enough knowledge, skills, technology and money available in the world to solve this. We can also use power in a negative way, toward a "Big Brother" society. This is an approach based on fear. For technological and/ or financial reasons, companies, governments, research and training institutions can't make the right choices regarding the development and application of technology in society[1]. Issues such as critical thinking, personal development, sustainability and ethics must be fully integrated into our training and research programs, and in decisions by governments and companies.

For many years, data security was synonymous with physical security. Before the advent of the internet, the only way to get to data was to physically steal it. Organizations devised extensive procedures to secure the physical data. Even though the internet has been around for many years, it seems that organizations still do not understand very well what it means to secure data that is electronically accessible. The role of an enterprise security architecture is to replace (or extend) the physical security procedures with electronic security procedures. In our educational institutions, we do not train security architects or implement this security architecture function. A key element in moving forward is that IT data security should be seen also as a business topic, while in many cases, it is "left to the IT people". This is a poor idea, since these professionals often do not have a clear understanding of security requirements from a business risk perspective (which parts of the business to protect at what level) as their competence lies in realizing those requirements with technology. Many of today's security incidents are slowly opening the eyes of business management to the fact that information data security is their responsibility and not only IT's responsibility. This understanding is enhanced by new legislation, such as the GDPR[2]. This is the main reason that data security is a hot topic nowadays. However, in many cases, information security decisions by business management are still only incident-based and not structurally incorporated into the procedures and IT of the organization.

1 Here, Raymond refers to the realm of ethics (chapter 21).
2 The GDPR is the General Data Protection Regulation.

Raymond Slot is managing partner at Strategy Alliance. – part of this sidebar is – with permission – based on his public lecture at Utrecht University of Applied Science in May of 2019

This sidebar makes an important point: risk and security management can't be left to the IT department, yet it is perceived to be a technically complex discipline. So, how can business stakeholders be asked to take the lead in this? The ISO standards can certainly help (see section 17.2) but in and of themselves they are insufficient to bridge the gap between the high-level (risk/ policy) discourse among business stakeholders on the one hand, and the detailed/ technical security measures/ controls that are implemented to mitigate risks on the other. In the upcoming sections, I will present a pragmatic approach to bridging that gap.

32.2 SECURITY USE CASES

The first step in connecting high-level policies to concrete security measures is to recognize that there are only so many scenarios/ use cases that you have to consider. Rather than going over each and every situation individually, consider specific security use cases which are defined as:

An (human/ computer) ***actor*** *performing an* ***activity*** *on* ***data****.*

Examples of security use cases are:

- A client visiting the public website of the organization;
- A client inquiring about his account balance;
- Updating an electronic record with client information;
- An HRM clerk entering a new annual salary for an employee;
- The prime minister making a transaction via the web portal.

As these use cases illustrate, you do not have to analyze each situation individually: visiting one page on a public website is pretty much the same as visiting another and it does not really matter whether the online visitor uses a desktop computer or a laptop computer. Finding security use cases is about finding the common *activities* that *actors* perform on your *data* assets. I recommend brainstorming as many as you think are necessary. Any scenario that you can think of now may prevent a potential breach to your data.

A closer analysis will reveal that these use cases can be grouped further which will help to link them to the security policy. By grouping the use cases in logical clusters, you limit the amount of work that has to be done in subsequent analysis steps. Continuing the above list of examples, use cases may be classified as follows:

- *Clients performing low-risk operations* versus *clients performing high-risk operations;*

- *Employees performing low-risk operations* versus *employees performing high-risk operations;*
- *Handling of medical records;*
- VIP *clients performing an operation;*
- *Staff performing critical infrastructure operations.*

Note that these clusters should be meaningful for business stakeholders – especially at the management level, as this is where the key decisions are made with regard to risk appetite and security measures. When a cluster is not clear, it can always be clarified by examining the underlying individual security use cases.

Also, note that these clusters can be visualized using simple diagrams, making it easier to understand what is going on and – in subsequent steps – where risks may manifest/ where measures may be needed. Figure 32.1 provides an example where the cluster VIP *client performing an operation* is visualized.

32.3 SECURITY LEVELS IN BUSINESS TERMS

An effective set of use cases captures as many scenarios as needed to get a sound understanding of a given setting. By clustering them, you end up with a good overview of the *types* of use cases you should consider for further analysis. This next step should be to analyze the security requirements for these clusters in terms of *confidentiality, integrity,* and *availability* (the C-I-A characteristics, discussed in chapter 17). Experience shows that business stakeholders find this a daunting task. An extra layer of abstraction may help, as I will show in this section.

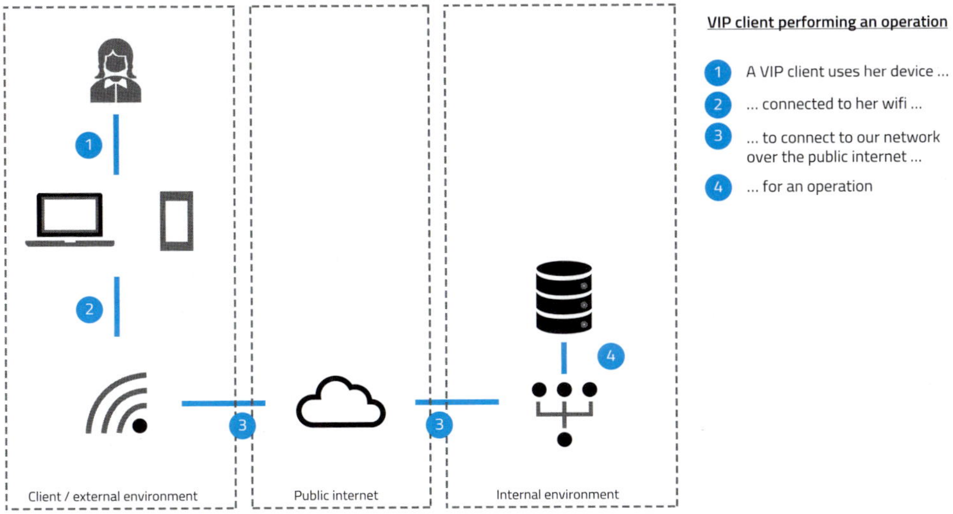

Figure 32.1 (Cluster of) security use case(s)

A security profile has a *name* and specifies what levels of the C-I-A characteristics are associated with that name. For example, a *web profile* could state that the requirements for confidentiality, and availability are "low", whereas the requirements for availability are "medium". This, of course, still requires you to determine what these levels mean, exactly. Ideally you define these levels with your team. The following provides an illustration using low/ medium/ high levels[2]:

	low	medium	high
Confidentiality	Everybody can have access to this data.	Data is only accessible for a limited group of stakeholders.	Data can, when it becomes public, lead to serious monetary/ reputational damage.
Integrity	There is limited risk associated with the data, there are limited negative consequences.	The consequences of a compromise are significant, up to $250,000.	The consequences of a compromise have a major impact on the financial situation of the company and its reputation.
Availability	Processes and systems do not have a time-critical component and can be unavailable for longer periods of time, up to one week.	Processes and systems are often used and should be available during business hours with limited down time, up to one hour down time per month.	Processes and systems are crucial for the continuity with a maximum of one hour down time per year.

Using these definitions of the different levels of security requirements, the task for business stakeholders is simplified: both the clusters of use cases and the levels are specified in terminology that business stakeholders can understand. This allows them to fill in a *business security matrix* as illustrated below:

Cluster	Confidentiality	Integrity	Availability
Clients performing low-risk operations	low	low	low
Clients performing high-risk operations	high	medium	high
Employees performing low-risk operations	low	medium	low
Employees performing high-risk operations	high	high	medium
Medical records are handled	high	high	high
VIP clients performing an operation	high	medium	high
Staff performing critical infrastructure operations	high	medium	high

2 Other ways to achieve levels is to use numbers, for example from 1–5.

32.4 THE LINK TO SECURITY MEASURES AND CONTROLS

The last step in this analysis is to link the different security levels to actual measures. As explained in chapter 17, this tends to be a technical discussion where the merits of measures are weighed. The good news is that if the approach as described in this chapter is followed, then this step can mostly be delegated to (highly trained) security professionals. Armed with a sound understanding of (clusters of) security use cases on the one hand and required security levels (and their implications) on the other, they can determine which measures should be used when. This can be done for each of the C-I-A factors. The table below provides an illustration of *confidentiality* :

Confidentiality				
Group	**Measure**	**low**	**medium**	**high**
Access	Basic authentication	√		
	Two-factor authentication		√	√
Transport	Encryption for external data		√	√
	Encryption for internal data			√
Storage	Data is backed up	√	√	√
	Data is encrypted		√	√
	Data is backed up off-site			√
Logging	Attempts to use data are logged		√	√
	Security team alerted to suspicious access attempt			√

Similar tables/ mappings can be constructed for *integrity* and *availability.* The list of potential security measures is huge. I recommend using a group of security professionals to build these mappings and use outside help (e.g. consultants) to periodically review and check them to ensure that the selected measures add up to an acceptable level of risk, in line with the security policy.

32.5 TYING IT TOGETHER

In this chapter, I have presented a pragmatic approach to linking the high-level language of data security policies to the concrete, technical measures used to mitigate security risks. This approach is based on the notion of *separation of concerns*, which means that:

- Business stakeholders should be in the driver's seat. They deal with defining the acceptable levels of risk (risk appetite) and defining security requirements for specific (groups of) security use cases.
- Security professionals use this as input, to translate requirements *in the context of* these use cases to an acceptable set of measures.

As always, the interplay between stakeholders is key: one can't be effective without involvement of the other. Using the Cynefin terminology (section 4.7), it is sometimes argued that data security is in the *complicated* domain. I believe this is false: it is in the *complex* domain because so much depends on the behavior of human beings which, by its very nature, is complex. In several places in this book, I have advocated using a *visual* approach to improving communication between stakeholders, especially when (technically) complex topics are concerned. This is also true in this case: figure 32.2 illustrates how the outcome of the analyses as suggested in this chapter (define the clusters of use cases, specify the security requirement levels, link them to security measures) can be visualized. By involving all (business/IT/risk/security) professionals in the process and collaboratively developing solutions, the organization should be confident that its data assets are kept secure.

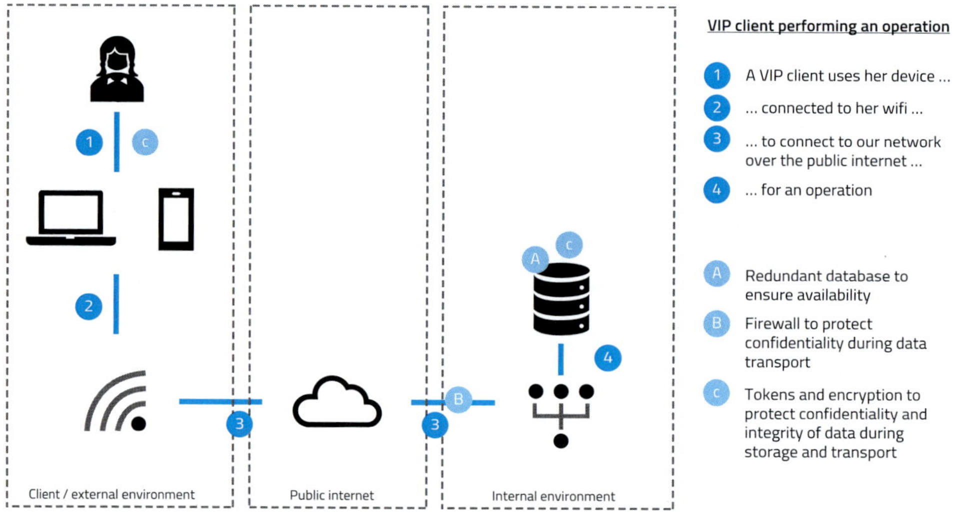

Figure 32.2 Visualizing impact of security measures

33 Roles in data management

Synopsis *- When the topic of "building or improving the data management capability" is raised, the typical response comes in the form of two questions. The first question is defensive in nature: "Are you saying we are not doing our job well?" The second question is more forward looking: "What does that mean for me?" In this chapter, I will discuss the latter question. I will give an overview of typical roles in data management. I will provide a short description of these roles, based on the DMBOK [Hen17]. I will also link these to the Skills Framework for the Information Age (SFIA). I will end this chapter with a short reflection and recommendation on assigning roles to professionals.*

33.1 CHANGE AND RUN

So far, I haven't made a distinction between the "change" and the "run" side of organizations. The discussion has mostly been about how to manage data as an asset in terms of data management defense/ offense (see section 3.2). This largely pertains to the "run" side of the business (executing the normal, day-to-day business activities to deliver value to the customer). There is also a strong relationship between data management and the "change" side of the business (changing the configuration of the organization in terms of processes, departments, data, and systems). The *change* aspect is often overlooked which has a negative impact on the effectiveness of the data management capability in the organization. Sidebar 23 illustrates the impact of data management on change teams in an organization. In the remainder of this chapter, I will discuss roles related to both the change and run side of the business.

Sidebar 23. Interview with Robin Vuyk (summer 2019)

When I asked Robin about his view on the relevance and importance of "data", his response was as follows:

In the past, most changes focused on processes and systems. The fact that data inputs, processing, and outputs were the real essence of the requirements was an afterthought at best. In the same vein, it was often all but ignored that an integral view of data across the process/ systems of the organization is required to ensure that the "machine" runs smoothly. Ignoring this key principle might go well for a little while. However, at some point you will see that implementing changes in an increasingly complex landscape becomes harder, more costly, and takes more and more time. In my view, data is both the oil that makes the "machine" (processes and systems) run smoothly, but also is the fuel for this "machine".

In the next part of the interview, Robin spoke of the implication of increased attention to data management:

Data management is, in my view, a function that covers both "change" and "run". Implementing data management requires a major change in the way of thinking, even in our organization. Making plans and getting enough support for them is a big challenge. We hired a new chief operating officer from outside with experience in data management. This helped in pushing the initiative to the next level but a true implementation will take years still. Within our organization, change teams will focus on the big picture which includes processes, systems, and data. This will also entail data management professionals as an extra stakeholder.

In the last part of the interview, we zoomed in on increased focus on data in change teams, especially from the perspective of change management professionals and teams:

Data is an essential component of most changes in our organization. In my team, I have change consultants. I believe that is essential for them to understand what data means for the company. Not all of them have to be "data gurus"; knowing which colleagues to involve when an expert opinion is required can be an effective strategy. I have a training program for my team to help them learn more about data. We also form virtual teams in which we collaborate closely with people from the "run" part of the organization to ensure that we always involve stakeholders with the right competencies when addressing complex, data-related changes.

Robin Vuyk is head of business architecture and design at PGGM, *a Dutch pension provider.*

33.2 ROLES IN THE DMBOK

The DMBOK is a highly structured document [Hen17]. It has a chapter for each of the functional areas of the DMBOK wheel (see figure 7.1). Each of these chapters starts with an overview that summarizes the functional area, including a definition, goals/ objectives, inputs/ outputs, and the roles involved.

Table 33.1 Data management roles in DMBOK

Architect	**Auditor**	***Business analyst***
Business management	*Chief data officer*	Change managers
Compliance team	DW/ BI specialist	Data governance bodies
Data integrator	Data management professional	Data modeler
Data owner	Data professional	Data quality analyst
Data quality managers	Data security team	*Data steward*
Database administrator	Developer	Executives
IT operations	Metadata specialist	*Process analyst*
Project management	Subject matter expert	*System analyst*

The roles that are indicated italic are discussed in section 33.4

When summarized, this leads to a long list of roles, included in table 33.1. For some, a clear picture immediately emerges. For example, a *metadata specialist* is likely to be someone who knows everything there is to know about metadata and this role is likely to be relevant each time the organization needs to do something with its metadata. Similarly, the role of *database professional* hardly needs further explanation. For other roles it is less obvious what the role entails and which competences are needed to successfully perform this role. In the section 33.4, a selection of these roles is discussed.

33.3 SKILLS IN THE SFIA FRAMEWORK

The *Skills Framework for the Information Age* (SFIA) is a comprehensive framework for professional skills, tailored to the needs of professionals in the information age. For purposes of defining roles and associated competences, this framework goes beyond the e-CF-framework that was used in chapter 26 (see also [fS16]). Figure 33.1 gives an overview of how the SFIA framework is structured.

On the horizontal axis, the diagram shows 102 professional skills, several of which are relevant for the realm of data management. The vertical axis lists the seven levels of responsibility. Each level of responsibility is broken down into more detailed aspects. Each *skill* is defined with a *generic description* as well as a clear definition

102 professional skills →

		Analytics	Animation development	Business analysis	Business modeling	Data management	Data modeling and design	Data visualization	Data administration	Database design	...
Level 7 - Set strategy, inspire, mobilize	Autonomy										
	Influence										
	Complexity										
	Knowledge										
	Business skills										
Level 6 - Initiate, infuence	Autonomy										
	Influence										
	Complexity										
	Knowledge										
	Business skills										
Level 5 - Ensure, advise	Autonomy										
	Influence										
	Complexity										
	Knowledge										
	Business skills										
Level 4 - Enable	Autonomy										
	Influence										
	Complexity										
	Knowledge										
	Business skills										
Level 3 - Apply	Autonomy										
	Influence										
	Complexity										
	Knowledge										
	Business skills										
Level 2 - Assist	Autonomy										
	Influence										
	Complexity										
	Knowledge										
	Business skills										
Level 1 - Follow	Autonomy										
	Influence										
	Complexity										
	Knowledge										
	Business skills										

Figure 33.1 Structure of the SFIA framework

for these *aspects* at each of the *levels of responsibility*. Note that not every skill/ level of responsibility combination is appropriate. As an example, the *data management skill* is defined for levels 2-6 and the *enterprise and business architecture skill* is defined for levels 5-7. This shows that certain skills become more and more relevant when the organization matures. In case of the two skills that are mentioned here, the SFIA framework presumes to state that data management skills (even in a basic form) are more relevant earlier than architecture skills. A selection of relevant skills is included in table 33.2.

Table 33.2 Selected skills from SFIA

Analytics	Business analysis
Business risk management	Continuity management
Data management	Data modeling and design
Data visualization	Database administration
Demand management	Enterprise and business architecture
Information governance	Information security
Information systems coordination	Innovation
Organization design and implementation	Problem management
Quality management	Software design
Strategic planning	Systems development management

33.4 DEFINITION OF ROLES

In this section, I will set out to give an overview of roles that are related to data management. Before diving into this discussion, note that these role definitions are a good practice and suggestion only. Some roles have a very different meaning, depending on the organization (or even depending on the department of an organization). My recommendation is to use these descriptions as a basis and adjust where necessary. In the following sections, I will discuss the roles in alphabetical order. Also note that I speak of *roles*, not *job functions*. It is often the case that a person in a function will perform more than one role depending on the context.

33.4.1 Architect

There are several types of architects. As explained in chapter 12, their primary role is to consider (1) the fundamental organization of a system and (2) the principles that guide its design and evolution. By definition, architects adopt a "big picture view" of the landscape of the organization. Architects tend to connect different perspectives – most notably the process perspective, data perspective, and systems perspective.

In the role of architect, it is key to be able to align with other roles. On the one hand, architects tend to confer with business management and executives about strategy and the grand scheme of things. On the other, architects work with (process/ data/ system) analysts on the nitty gritty details. Being able to navigate these different levels of complexity is one of the key (mental) skills of the architect. With respect to the SFIA, the following skills are most relevant for architects. I have left out "enterprise and business architecture" as it is obvious that this is *the* key skill for this group.

- **Data management** - Architects should have a sound understanding of data management. Through enterprise-wide thinking (rather than focusing on a single, local challenge), architects can help create an environment that will enable the organization to take the data management initiative to the next level.
- **Strategic planning** - Architects are uniquely positioned to understand how all the pieces of the puzzle fit together, which is key in strategic planning of the future course of the organization. With respect to data/ data management, this means that architects should always consider/ include the data aspect in their strategic analyses.
- **Business analysis, system design** - If architects worry about the *big picture*, then others – often analysts – are concerned about the details. Architects should collaborate closely with analysts, and should promote that these analysts also include the data perspective in their work. As mentioned in several places in this book, success largely depends on balancing between these perspectives.
- **Security** - Security is often seen as a complex and technical discipline (chapter 17 gives an overview of the discipline and chapter 32 introduces a pragmatic approach) that potentially touches all aspects of the organization. In my view, architects should closely collaborate with security professionals to ensure that security measures are effective, keeping data assets safe while giving stakeholders access to the right data with the right quality at the right time.

33.4.2 Business management

This section pertains to the broad category of business managers. This can be either at the department level, unit level, or even the team level. Organizations use different structures. The key task of business management, usually, is to manage part of the business, be it an organizational unit, a value stream, or a process. The distinction between business and IT is fading rapidly but for the sake of discussion, I will discuss the business aspect separately here. The key skills from SFIA are:

- **Data management** - Business managers should be aware of the fact that data is a key asset for the organization that can be used (data management offense) to create value when managed properly (data management defense). Business managers are usually also good candidates for the role of business owner. Business managers may not play a leading role in data management per se, but should be able to articulate their needs, concerns, and challenges with respect to data. Also, they should know enough of the topic to collaborate effectively with data management professionals.
- **Quality management** - Business managers tend to be accountable and responsible for running part of the business. Data is a key asset to make that happen. Data quality management can be seen as part of the *quality management* skill. Business managers are able to influence (*level 6)* the level of quality management.

- **Organization design and implementation** - One of the roles of business managers is to assign roles and responsibilities for their teams/ direct reports. This organization design should take data roles and responsibilities into account (which is one of the reasons why business managers should have data management skills, at least at a basic level).
- **Innovation** - In some cases, innovation – especially data-driven innovation – is assigned to a separate group/ team. Increasingly, this task is assigned to business managers themselves. Data-driven innovation is a good example of *data management offense*. Business managers should have a sound understanding of the role of data/ data management for successful innovation.

33.4.3 Data owner, data steward

I have chosen to discuss the *data owner* and *data steward* roles together (see also chapter 9). The reason for this is simple: these roles are very similar in nature. Data owners tend to be *accountable* for a dataset (e.g. *product data* or *customer data*). They are accountable for ensuring that people in the organization have access to fit-for-purpose data. Typically, this is a role played by business managers. Data stewards, by contrast, tend to be more hands-on. They tend to be *responsible* for the tasks of which the data owner is accountable. Data stewards (sometimes called "data custodians") can have a business background, IT background, or mixed background. These two roles are specific data management roles.

- **Data management** - For both roles, data management is a key skill. For data owners, the emphasis is more on policy development and (strategic/ tactical) decision-making, whereas for data stewards the emphasis is on the more operational aspects of the field. As an illustration, data owners would be more involved in developing a strategic roadmap for data management, or a policy for data quality management (and would, of course, incorporate key inputs from their data stewards), whereas data stewards are more involved in the hands-on work of collecting data quality requirements and measuring/ correcting data quality issues.
- **Information governance** - This skill is close to the *data governance* functional area in the DMBOK (see chapter 9). Both roles are typical governance roles. Therefore, information governance is a key skill for both data owners and data stewards alike.

33.4.4 Project management

The relationship between data management and project management may not be immediately obvious, yet I believe it to be vital. Project managers (or their counterparts from the agile world) play an important role in staffing and shaping change projects. It is crucial that they at least *think* about the data subject when doing so. Relevant skills are:

- **Demand management** - For project managers, one of the key tasks is to get a firm understanding of what it is that the organization wants to achieve. This should, of course, include data. See also sidebar 23.

33.4.5 Chief data officer

I am a little torn about the role of Chief Data Officer (CDO). The role has become more and more popular in the last few years (see e.g. [AG13]) to ensure that data gets enough attention at the management table. In the ideal world, this wouldn't be necessary since other executives should recognize data as a key asset and act accordingly. Regrettably this is far from reality just yet. A CDO can play an important motivational role and, at the same time, can act as the ultimate *decision-making unit* for all things related to data. Key skills are:

- **Data management** - The CDO should be the catalyst for many data-related initiatives in the organization. The CDO need not have (much) hands-on experience but should have sound experience with/ knowledge of data management. This includes both the defensive and the offensive aspects.
- **Information governance** - In a way, the CDO is ultimately accountable and responsible for every- thing that happens with data. Most of this is delegated (e.g. to data owners and data stewards, and perhaps also to other governance bodies).
- **Organization design and implementation** - As an executive, the CDO has a big say about what the organizational design behind the implementation of the data management capability should be, at least at the big picture level.

33.4.6 Business analyst, process analyst, and system analyst

Organizations tend to employ many different kinds of analysts. The names vary as much as roles and responsibilities do. In my view, analysts have a role to play in both *change* and *run* activities. In the realm of change, analysts pick up the analysis where architects tend to stop, worrying about the details rather than the big picture. Business/ process analysts focus on business aspects (which should also include data), whereas system analysts focus on IT aspects (which also includes data). Key skills are:

- **Data management** - These analyst roles should have basic data management skills. That is, they should be aware that data is a key consideration in their work. Presumably, (data) modeling (chapter 11) is one of the key data management skills that is most relevant for this group.
- **Quality management** - Analysts are uniquely positioned to both (1) find out what key data quality requirements should be, and (2) what efficient/ effective solutions would be to ensure that these requirements are met. Ideally this is done in close collaboration with data stewards (sometimes analysts also have the role of stewards) and architects.

- **Business analysis, software design -** Analysis and design are the essential tasks for this group of professionals, so these skills are key. From a data management perspective, it is essential that data gets enough attention in these tasks.

33.5 REFLECTION AND RECOMMENDATION

I have heard several sponsors during projects make statements such as, "Isn't . . . part of their normal job? Why don't they just *do* it?!" (where, of course, ". . ." stands for a task related to data management). This is a tough topic. Roles and responsibilities are assigned in many different ways by organizations. One option to get an answer to this type of question is to look at formal job specifications, but before doing so, you have to consider if that is the best way forward. Why take the formal route?

In my experience, *making* people perform a certain task (to state it more explicitly: *forcing* people to do something) is far from effective. When data is recognized to be an important asset for the organization *by these professionals*, then they tend to be more motivated to pick up certain tasks. The motivation is then more intrinsic, which results in more efficiency and faster adoption. This is not an easy route, but it does tend to be worth it.

In short, my recommendation is to attempt to apply both the "stick" and the "carrot" at the same time by trying to find those stakeholders who already have a vested interest in data, or who are motivated intrinsically to work with data already. These can be the *ambassadors* for building and improving the data management capability one step at a time. Roles can be formalized further when the data management capability matures and more and more people get involved.

34 Working with big data

***Synopsis** - A topic that can't be ignored is big data, as it seems to be the embodiment of effective data management offense at the moment. It appears that the hype is slowly fading, though, and organizations are starting to find out how to successfully leverage big data for business success. I believe that big data and its associated technologies should be treated as any tool that enables innovation. I will therefore begin this chapter with some general observations about starting with big data and follow-up with good practices around fostering an innovation culture. I will end the chapter with a discussion on linking data management offense/ the use of big data, to data management defense, setting the stage for the next chapter which discusses how to build a roadmap for data management.*

34.1 OBSERVATIONS ABOUT BIG DATA ADOPTION

This chapter picks up where chapter 19 left off. Ever since the term "big data" made it into management literature, managers have been pushing for big data in their own organization. The promise is simple: literature suggests that big data may offer the next big competitive advantage – so why should you not experiment with it? Why not start with adopting new technologies and try to reap these promised benefits? It appears that numerous initiatives are started with a technology focus, rather than a business or data focus. In sidebar 24, Ronald Damhof shares his thoughts on the technology aspect.

Sidebar 24. Interview with Ronald Damhof (summer 2019)

When technology comes into play, I am always reminded of an interview with the brilliant Gerald Weinberg. He was asked the question "In your experience, what is the most notable 'constant' in the world of software?" His answer:

> *The infatuation with the latest fad which is supposed to "increase productivity" by some arbitrary amount, with no clue as to how that "productivity" is measured. For the most part, these fads are usually a new set of names for old practices. Yet at the same time a segment of the developer population goes ga-ga over the fad, a much larger segment doesn't even attempt to learn what is good about the fad. The majority of developers are working the same primitive way their predecessors did 50 years ago, just using more machine power to do it.*

These are wise words and should be considered whenever we 'buy' or are infatuated with the newest fad, aka newest technology. In the data world this seems to be particularly true and big data is a good example.

In all the hype and buzz, the technology aspect is portrayed as a huge differentiator in competitive advantage. When, in fact, the technology is highly irrelevant in terms of attaining a competitive advantage (it is, however, a prerequisite!). Some companies might have an edge for some time, purely based on some innovative use of it but it will not last. It will be copied extremely fast over and over again by others.

Technology is by far the easiest aspect and therefor the most tempting one to start off with, you can buy it and live in a fantasy world where you think your problems will be solved. You cannot buy your way out of the data misery you are in.

Ronald Damhof, "just a data-guy", self-employed, often in the role of enterprise (data) architect in large (mostly public) organizations.

The sidebar confirms that technology is an important enabler but that *data* and *business needs* should be front and center of big data initiatives. I will revisit this later and will now focus on the approaches to starting with big data that I often see in practice.

The first pattern that I have come across, is to build a business case first, build a test environment next, and only then start doing experiments with big data and associated technologies. An advantage of this approach lies in the fact that the approach gives many stakeholders and departments the opportunity to join in on the initiative, and to create synergies between initiatives that would otherwise have been tackled separately. A disadvantage is that, without clear use cases and expected benefits, a business case will be hard to build: how are you going to quantify the benefits of a big data initiative if you don't know which use cases you will be implementing? In my experience, finding the right use cases is one of the hardest things for big data initiatives – which is also confirmed by sidebar 25.

Sidebar 25. Interview with Daan Riepma (summer 2019)

The first step in getting started with big data (or, more precisely, analysis of data), always is to determine a topic of interest and a scope. The latter is important because (a) technology makes it possible to endlessly explore data and run experiments, without really getting anywhere, and (b) because it is likely that you end up loading data that only obscures the real results you are after.

With a clear view of what you want to achieve, the second step is to research the data sets that you want to use. In the case of big data, this could easily include regular structured data that the organization already has as well as streaming data, perhaps even from a third party. Data warehouses, data marts, and even spreadsheets are also common sources of data.

The third step is to try to answer the research question with available tools. In my experience, Python, R, and PowerBI are quite common. It is also my experience that in approximately 70% of the cases, you will not get any good results from your analysis because the right data is missing.

Completing the analysis does not end the process: if you do get good results, then it is important to share them with the organization and to validate whether they make enough sense to lead to decisions and action. Also, if the analysis is such that it will be equally useful in the future, then the solution should be handed over to regular IT teams to ensure they can go into production following the organization's standards.

Daan Riepma is a smart data consultant at Axians.

The second pattern is the complete opposite and consists of running small, local experiments first, and expanding step by step. The advantage of this approach is that local experiments can be run without big investments and give the organization a chance to figure out what type of use cases work well for them. The disadvantage of this approach is that several departments may be running their own experiments without one party knowing of the initiatives of the other, which is likely to lead to less learning and less synergies. An even bigger challenge may be to ensure that the organization at large will adopt the results of your analysis and that big data solutions are brought into production as a result.

Both approaches have their advantages and disadvantages. They may work well but often a mixed approach makes more sense: start with small experiments and make sure that the results of those experiments add up to a business case for a more top-down implementation. An enterprise-wide initiative is likely to be adopted more easily when it is preceded by results of small experiments. After all, success sells. These findings are also confirmed by the interview in sidebar 25. Figure 34.1 visualizes this synthesis.

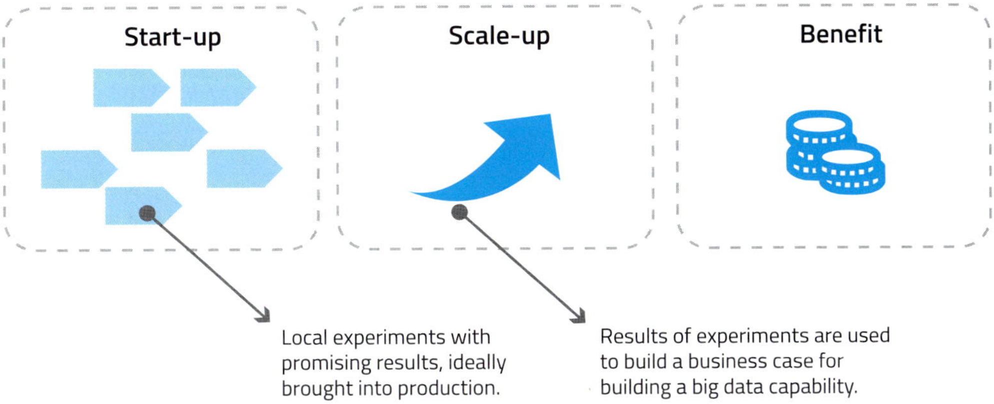

Figure 34.1 Start-up, scale-up, benefits

34.2 BUILDING A CULTURE OF INNOVATION

It is not my intention to equate big data and innovation but, as I will argue in this section, I do believe that a culture of innovation helps to get started with big data initiatives. A culture of innovation is characterized as follows:

- There is no such thing as failure in a culture of innovation: the point is to experiment and learn from these experiments. If an experiment has positive results, scale-up. If it doesn't, learn and move on.
- There is a strict process that governs innovation/ experimentation. In this process, the ideas worth exploring are selected (building an "innovation funnel") and experiments are rigorously evaluated.
- People are empowered to bring all of themselves to the table: all their passion, skills and ideas are valuable when trying to achieve the innovation goals.

It is rare to find organizations who pull this off well. The first point is hard to swallow for many mangers bent on getting as many successes as possible. In that mindset, it is difficult to accept that the outcome of an experiment, by its very nature, is unsure. This is also true in a big data setting. As the previous section – see sidebar 24 – shows, this journey is not about technology but about finding ways to use technology and data characterized by high volume, high velocity, and high variability, to achieve desirable business outcomes.

Building the proper mindset takes time and willingness by a few strong sponsors, sufficiently high up the management food chain, to get the organization going. Building this mindset opens the door for experiments, which will ultimately lead to an effective big data capability.

34.3 LINKING TO DATA MANAGEMENT DEFENSE

Data management *offense* can only be successful when paired with effective data management *defense*. This requires that the culture of innovation is paired with formal processes and procedures that ensure that the right data with the right quality is available for stakeholders when they need them. This, in turn, requires that the groups of professionals working on the offensive side and the defensive side of data management not only understand what the other is trying to achieve but also align in terms of goals, deliverables, approach, and roadmap – a topic that will be discussed in the next chapter.

Note that I am (deliberately) staying away from proposing solutions of an organizational nature. There are many options in this respect, including (1) bringing teams under unified leadership, (2) working with a competence center, and (3) working with virtual teams, etc. The organizational structure is highly dependent on the context of the organization. To be successful it is more important to consider the way data is *produced* and *used*. The *data quadrant model*, developed by Ronald Damhof, provides a useful analysis framework to clarify this point and is outlined in sidebar 26.

Sidebar 26. Interview Ronald Damhof (summer 2019)

What you should be doing is discussing the actual (data) concerns in your organizational context, be extremely vigilant in separating these concerns, stay away from hollow wording and technology and have a holistic perspective on data. How? Start with a dialogue where all stakeholders can participate. Be it senior executives, engineers or domain experts. A sensemaking framework that might work is the Data Quadrant Model, illustrated below.

This model assists in balancing data concerns. The vertical axis distinguishes between systematic and more opportunistic development of (technology that works on) data. The former has a more natural fit with formal governance processes and procedures of data management defense. The latter is closer to the innovation mindset that is required for handling big data and other offensive/ exploration projects. Along the same line of reasoning, the horizontal axis deals with activities that work with data sources (data supply), versus activities that focus on the use of data (demand).

The trick is that data stemming from the top left quadrant can be from both the top-right or bottom-right quadrant: data that was created while under data management/ governance can be used anywhere. This type of data is equally useful in regular situations as in innovation settings. The inverse is not true: data that was created under an optimistic regime should not be allowed to be used in a regular, systematic setting.

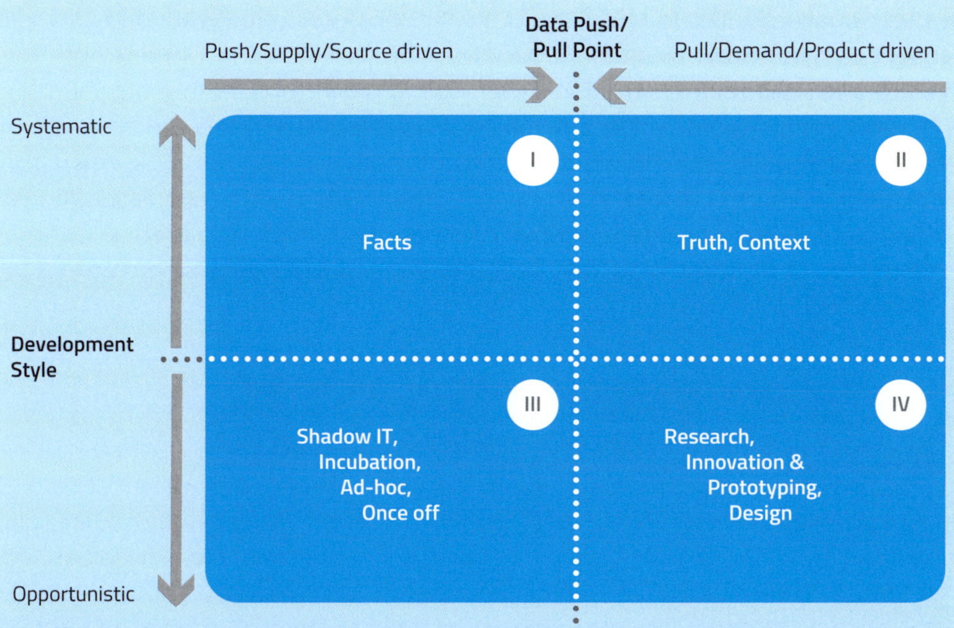

Ronald Damhof, "just a data-guy", self-employed, often in the role of enterprise (data) architect in large (mostly public) organizations.

To me, the data quadrant model captures the heart of how organizations can successfully start a big data program. This entails (1) fostering a culture of innovation in selected parts of the organization and ensuring that professionals work well together during innovation projects, and (2) ensuring that there is a well-defined link from the realm of innovation to the realm of more regular/ systematic development of IT and data following the lines of the quadrant model.

34.4 THE FUTURE OF BIG DATA

Niels Bohr famously said: "prediction is difficult, especially about the future". I think this definitely applies to the world of big data. Big data technologies are maturing: even though it appears that new tools and platforms pop up every few weeks or so, it seems the core is increasingly stable. More specifically, I expect that the current technologies that are used for handling big data challenges will be obsolete in just a few years' time and will be replaced by new ones with capabilities that we can't even fathom at present.

The main challenge lies in using big data technologies effectively and ethically to solve business problems. Business practices around fostering big data are also maturing and I expect this maturity to continue to grow. I expect that organizations will increasingly find ways to leverage their data assets and will learn that the majority of valuable data will come from outside the company. Last but not least, when (top) management becomes more "data savvy", organizations will be better positioned to balance data management offense and defense, which also means that they will be able to brainstorm, plan, and execute successful big data initiatives.

35 Building a data management roadmap

***Synopsis** - The chapters in part II have all focused on a single aspect of building a data management capability. In this chapter, I will take a broader perspective and discuss an approach to building an integral roadmap that ties these topics together. To this end, I will rely heavily on existing (architecture) approaches – especially TOGAF [The11, GD14] – and related techniques. I will first discuss the necessity of building a roadmap. Then, I will give a high-level overview of the steps to building a roadmap, discussing each step in turn. I will end this chapter with recommendations.*

35.1 TO ROADMAP OR NOT TO ROADMAP

I can't count the number of times that I have been asked questions along the lines of: How do we start with data management? What are the "no-regret actions" that we have to do anyway? What are the logical steps to take when building a data management capability? Can you please help us with a good roadmap to build our data management capability one step at a time?

It seems there is a fundamental belief that a single best process exists that, when followed, will always lead to a sound data management capability. The bad news is, there isn't. The good news is, there are approaches to help you build your own roadmap. Before embarking on such a journey, though, ask yourself the question: what do I expect from such a roadmap and do I really need it? In many cases, the word "roadmap" has the connotation of a detailed overview of goals, objectives, milestones, deliverables, and deadlines, showing how the portfolio of projects and initiatives will ultimately lead to the desired end state. In other cases, the word "roadmap" is used more loosely to indicate a rough idea of the desired end state and a slightly more detailed idea of the first step to be taken to get there.

Creating a shared definition (see also chapter 28) of the term "roadmap" is the first thing to be done. My experience is that building a data management capability is – in Cynefin terms (see section 4.7) – a complex task and planning ahead in great detail is not very useful. This is also the premise for the following sections. My working definition of a roadmap is: a rough idea of the steps to be taken to achieve an end goal, often with more detail for early steps rather than later steps.

35.2 THE STEPS TOWARDS AN EFFECTIVE ROADMAP

If a roadmap is about a rough idea of the steps to be taken to achieve an end goal, then what do you need to develop this roadmap? In other words, what are the inputs for the activity "make a roadmap"? In my view, a roadmap should be based on the identification of *gaps* between what is already in place and what you will need to achieve desired outcomes. This, in turn, should be based on a clear identification of these outcomes which can be captured in a vision statement or business blueprint[1].

If you put these steps in a logical order, you will end up with something that is remarkably close to TOGAF's *Architecture Development Method* (ADM), which is shown in figure 35.1[2]. Simplifying the working of the ADM slightly, this process can be used to build a data management capability as follows:

- **Vision:** The first step is to build a shared vision for the future and capture this in a business blueprint. This maps to phase A of the ADM.
- **Analysis:** The second step is to perform a capability gap analysis, which identifies the gaps between what is already in place and what is needed to achieve the vision. This maps to phases B, C, and D of the ADM.
- **Portfolio:** These results are used to build a portfolio of change initiatives and decide which of these initiatives should lead to projects that can be started immediately. This maps to phases E and F of the ADM.
- **Execute:** Finally, these first projects should be executed. This also includes evaluation of the new "as is" situation, as well as identifying the next series of change initiatives that can be started through new projects. This maps to phases G and H of the ADM.

Example 62 illustrates this process.

1 I will use the term *business blueprint* loosely here, to indicate a diagram that visualizes a (future) situation for the organization in terms of processes, data, and systems.

2 A full discussion of the ADM is beyond the scope of this book. All details of the standard can be found online, at https://pubs.opengroup.org/architecture/togaf9-doc/arch/, last checked: 24 August 2019.

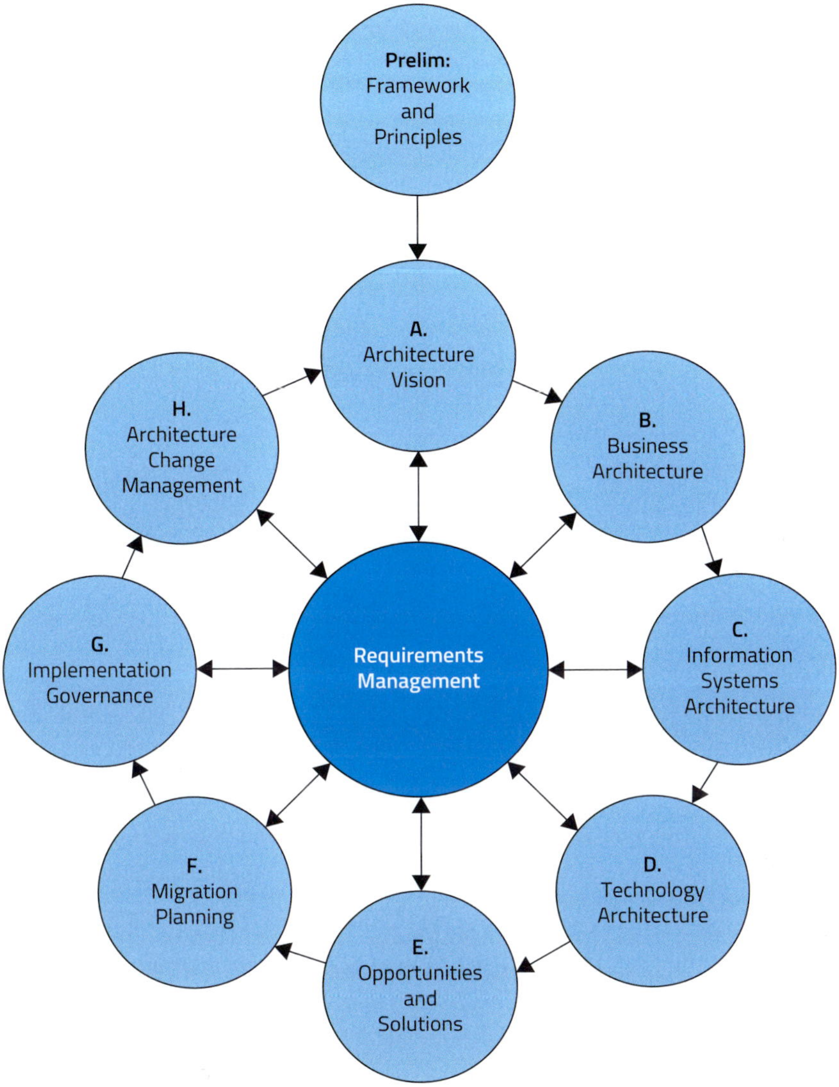

Figure 35.1 TOGAF's Architecture Development Method (taken from [The11])

Example 62. Roadmap
This example is based on a real-world case. The organization from the financial services industry requested to remain anonymous. The results below are close to the original project deliverables.

Vision
This company started on their data management journey with the idea of improving their data quality after a series of incidents. They recognized the need for a governance structure and after much debate it was decided to make each of the three business units accountable and responsible for their own data as much as possible. Local

initiatives were supported by a data management office, and a data governance board was institutionalized for strategic/ tactical decision-making. The resulting blueprint was as follows:

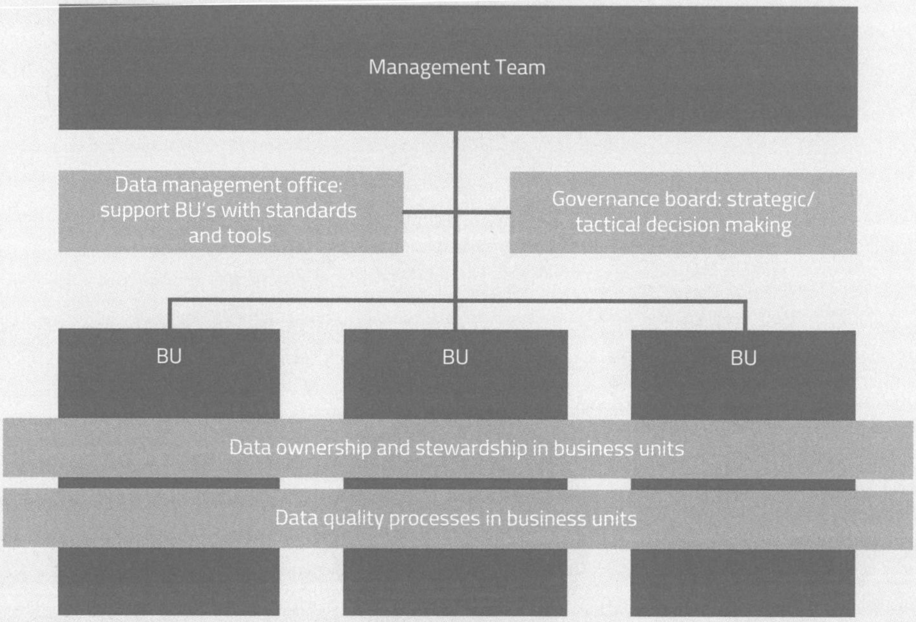

Analysis
With the vision in hand, an extensive analysis was conducted. The main point of this analysis was to find out which existing capabilities the organization could leverage to make a head start. A full discussion of the gap analysis is beyond the scope of this example. Suffice to say that the units already had good incident management processes and IT decision-making structures in place, but they were mostly lacking in terms of data management.

Portfolio
Overall the gap was big. The idea was to build little pieces of capabilities that would add value immediately, one step at a time. A partial list of projects in the portfolio were: (1) build an incident management process including dashboards to show status quo; (2) link the incident management process to the portfolio management process to ensure that issues that are found can be resolved by funding "data quality projects"; (3) build a capability for managing data flows through data agreements to get more grip on the flow of data in the organization; and (4) build a data profiling capability to proactively see if data matches the data quality requirements. Each of these projects had a training element in it. The idea was also that the governance capability would be built one step at a time as people learned more about their role. This was difficult to plan in detail.

Execute
The portfolio was well structured and consisted of about a dozen projects in total. The good thing about the execution phase was that there was no rush: the company

took the time to complete each step before moving on to the next. This caused some friction between people eager to make more progress in a hurry, and those who were more conservative, but overall it worked out well. One of the harder parts was letting the data management office do their work. Despite the best efforts of this team, the business units experienced a strong case of "not invented here syndrome" and felt that "outsiders" were interfering. It took several projects and long months of debating before there was enough trust such that this central team could perform their role effectively.

35.3 TECHNIQUES

In this section, I will present some techniques to use with the above-mentioned approach. My recommendation is to experiment and try different techniques. The general rule is: try it out and keep using it if it works!

35.3.1 Vision phase

The objective of this phase is to build a shared understanding of what the organization is trying to achieve through data management. In my experience, if you flat-out ask for goals and objectives, you end up with blanket statements such as "we want to become a data-driven organization", or "we want to deliver information-rich products and services to our customers". These statements are too broad to be useful directly, but they do provide a good starting point for further analysis. I have become a big fan of *benefits realization management* [Bra16]. The (slightly adapted) version that I use is illustrated in figure 35.2.

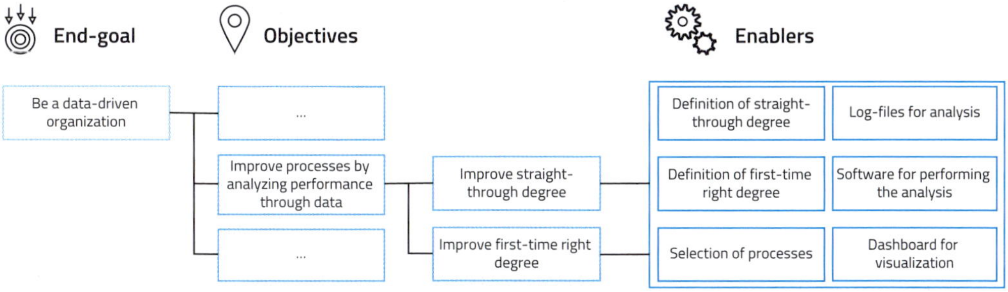

Figure 35.2 Benefit realization diagram

First, brainstorm a few end goals. Ideally these are high-level goals that have management support. With everything you do, keep these in mind. The idea is to keep asking a simple question: does my current activity contribute to achieving this goal or should I adjust my course of action? End goals tend to be vague and are translated into more concrete objectives and, if necessary, sub objectives. These, in turn, can be translated to a set of enablers: the "things you need" in order to realize the defined objectives.

One of the interesting aspects of this approach, is that a relatively simple analysis gives enough detail to actually get started. In the example of figure 35.2, you know enough to start working on the selected objective of improving processes. However, if you do this at scale – that is, for the whole organization and for a longer time-scope – it also provides input for a business blueprint that represents the desired end state. A partial diagram is included in figure 35.3.

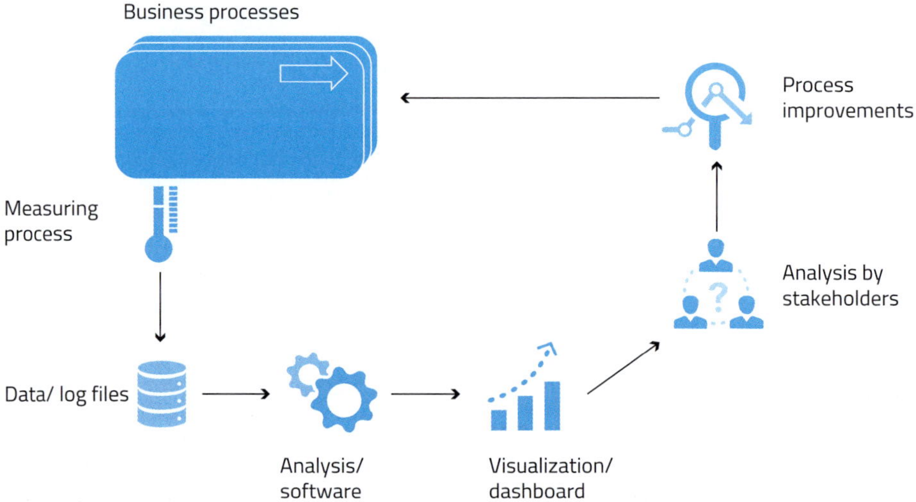

Figure 35.3 Business blueprint

35.3.2 Analysis phase

The objective of this phase is to understand, in light of the defined objectives in the previous phase, what the capability gap is. There are numerous publications on capability-based planning and associated techniques (see e.g. [Dav02, The16b, Gui17]). I use a simplified version where each capability is assessed *in light of the objectives* for fit on five dimensions. This is illustrated in figure 35.4.

The figure shows two things. The left shows a *spider web diagram* with the analysis of one capability, say, data governance. The inner line shows the current level of capability. The outer line shows the desired level of capability. There have been many attempts to come up with an objective method to quantify these levels. In my experience a subjective analysis by a focused group of professionals works best. Together they should be able to consider a capability in light of a set of objectives to conclude "we feel that we want to move from x to y and we believe that the gap means we have to fix z". These gaps should be cross-checked against the enablers of the previous phase, making sure you haven't forgotten anything. The right side of the diagram shows a matrix that can be used to consolidate the analyses of each of the individual capabilities. I tend to use the DMBOK functional areas as capabilities. Each cell in the matrix lists the from/ to levels and I have used a color-coding to indicate how big the gap is. The matrix in the example at least suggests, among other things, that some big steps are to be taken on the people and organization side and that technology is to remain relatively stable.

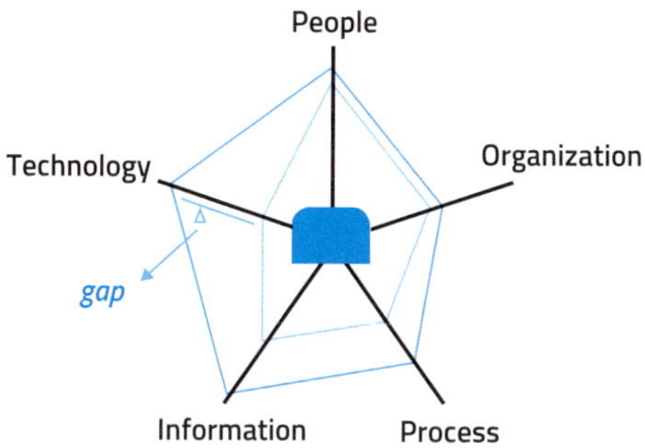

	Governance	Metadata	Architecture	Master data	Data quality	Data integration	Security	...
People	1-3	1-2	2-3	1-1	2-4	2-3	1-4	..
Organization	2-4	1-2	1-3	1-1	1-4	2-3	3-3	..
Process	2-4	1-3	2-3	1-1	2-3	2-2	2-3	..
Information	1-2	1-3	2-3	1-2	2-3	2-3	2-3	..
Technology	1-1	1-3	2-2	1-1	1-3	3-3	1-3	..

Figure 35.4 Capability analysis

35.3.3 Portfolio phase

When you have quantified all the gaps in the previous phase then you are all set to define your portfolio. The idea is to group these gaps into initiatives, that may eventually become projects to achieve a certain outcome. Gaps can be clustered using different criteria. For example, you could group all the gaps pertaining to the *organization* dimension and turn these into projects, or group gaps from different capabilities and dimensions in order to form a set of projects that will help you to kick-start your data quality program.

As before, my recommendation is to perform this analysis with a group. Decide on a grouping criterion and create the clusters. You can then visualize your portfolio with initiatives using a bubble-chart. An example is shown in figure 35.5, where initiatives are classified on estimated budget size, the probability of success, and the size of the rewards. The same rules apply as before: choose a style of visualization that suits your needs.

35.3.4 Execution phase

The last phase is about the execution of your plans. If you have followed the process so far, then you will have a clear view of goals and objectives, how they translate into a vision for the future, what this entails in terms of capabilities, and how the capability gaps are grouped into potential change initiatives. Now it is a matter of selecting initiatives, forming a team, and executing the plans using your normal change management/ project management approach.

This is not the end, though. In the course of the execution of the selected initiatives – more precisely, towards the end – it is important to revisit the analysis that you have performed. Confirm once more that the goals and objectives are still valid. Verify if the blueprint still captures what you want to achieve. Verify the capability gap analysis once more and check for properties. This will put you in a good position to start the second round of projects when the time is right.

35.4 RECOMMENDATIONS

From the realm of program management, it is a well-known fact that building an effective roadmap and keeping it up-to-date as organizational priorities shift over time, is probably one of the hardest things to do. I believe two key factors complicate things: first, the tension between a top-down/ command-and-control approach to change, versus the more bottom-up/ agile approach to change that has been discussed in several chapters in this book, and second, in many organizations there is a tendency to prioritize short-term, local objectives over long-term objectives that are more enterprise-wide. This often leads to counter-productive behavior, which hampers the progress of enterprise-wide initiatives.

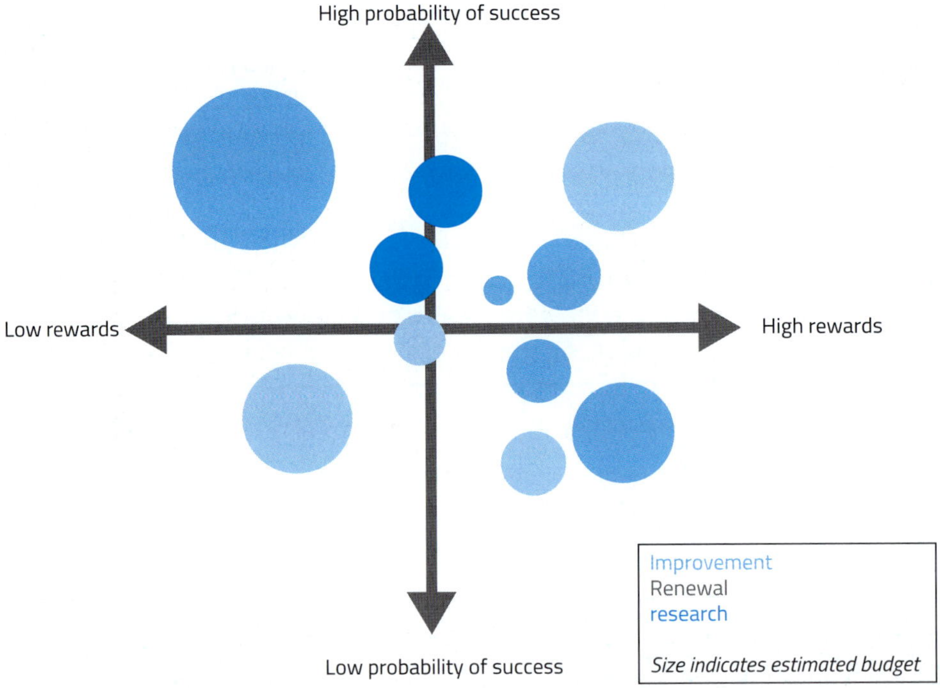

Figure 35.5 Portfolio analysis

Rather than being frustrated over this fact, it seems best to accept that this is reality and turn this potential pitfall into a strength. By going through the recommended process with a group of stakeholders who represent both long-term/ enterprise needs and short-term/ local needs, you will end up with a good portfolio and roadmap with the added benefit of support from stakeholders across the organization.

PART III

Closing remarks

36 Synthesis of the recommendations

Synopsis *- In part I, I have given an overview of the theory behind data management. In part II, I have discussed several use cases for building an effective data management capability in practice. The purpose of this chapter is to present a synthesis of my ideas. I will first discuss the link between theory and practice, and between data management offense and defense. I will then consider the good practices from part II regarding the complex task of building an antifragile data management capability.*

36.1 DATA MANAGEMENT

I started this book with the analogy "if processes are the value creation engine of the organization then data is its fuel". The point of the analogy was to show that data is a key asset of the organization and should be managed as such. This is the realm of data management.

I have explained that the purpose of data management is twofold. On the one hand, it concerns getting a grip on the data landscape (data management defense). On the other hand, it concerns value creation with data (data management offense). Considering this from the perspective of the DMBOK, the former is related to topics such as governance, data architecture, metadata management, and data quality management. It is concerned with understanding what data the organization has, where it can be found, and what the quality of data is. The latter perspective refers to getting value from data, through data-enriched value propositions and using data for strategic/ tactical/ operational decision-making.

Organizations have to decide how to balance between offense and defense. This is not an either-or decision: only "doing defense" will lead to a situation where the organization has access to high quality data - but has chosen not to do anything with that data. Only "doing offense" will lead to a situation where oodles of data are used but the results will be lacking due to the fact that data is probably of low quality.

In my view, offense and defense are two sides of the same coin. Balancing between the two perspectives is *pivotal* in supporting the organization to be effective: it helps to ensure an effective configuration of aligning processes, data, and systems. This is illustrated in figure 36.1 which shows the fundamental balancing act between offense and defense, as well as between theory and practice. This balancing act has been the key driver for writing this book and is also the leading principle for designing its structure.

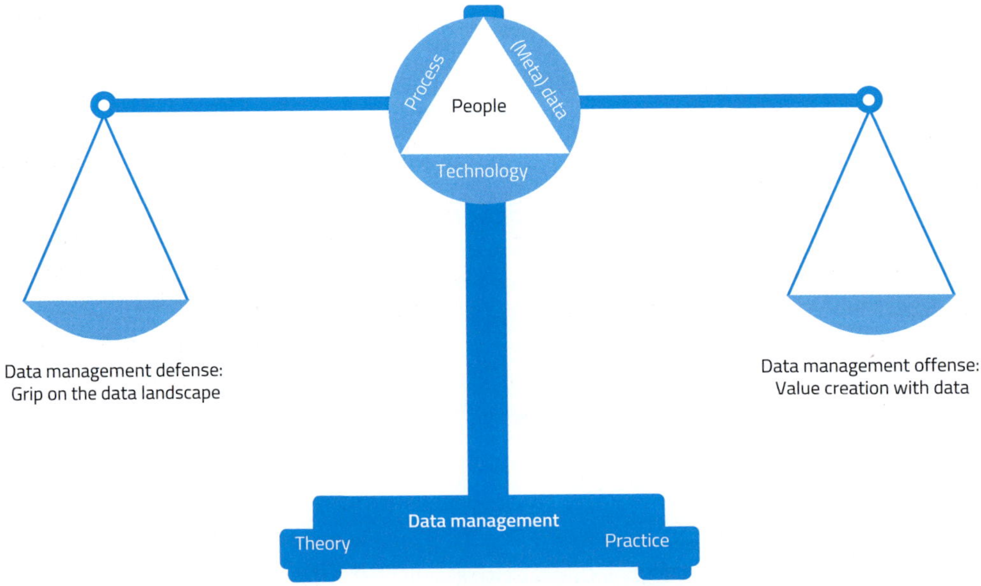

Figure 36.1 Balancing data management offense and defense, theory and practice

36.2 ANTIFRAGILITY AND COMPLEXITY

The work of Prof. Taleb on *antifragility* was introduced in section 4.7. As a brief recap: antifragile systems are characterized by the fact that they perform better when they are under more stress. Our brains are considered to be antifragile (training them only makes them work better), whereas bridges are not (they will collapse when strained too much).

I have proposed that the data management capability of an organization should have antifragile characteristics. It is my firm belief that in an increasingly digital world, organizations should put their people first. I believe that putting people first is the key to building antifragile systems. The way of thinking should be: if (a) our professionals know their *role* in the grand scheme of things, (b) are *trained / skilled* at their job, and (c) are given the freedom and trust to solve challenges that come their way (while taking the overall goals of the organization into consideration), then the organization as a whole will adapt and learn regardless of what the future might bring[1]. I will use a slightly adapted version of the *dynamic framework for social change* (taken from [CH18] and illustrated in figure 36.2) to clarify this further. The diagram shows that four spheres of influence should be considered in light of change:

- **Institutional -** Deals with regulations, governance structures, policies etc.
- **Individual -** Deals with the individual beliefs, aspirations, skills, knowledge, attitudes, etc. of stakeholders involved with your organization.
- **Social -** Deals with social networks, group dynamics, and interactions between individuals.
- **Material -** Deals with availability of materials, infrastructure, services, assets, etc.

The diagram shows that there are overlaps between all these spheres of influence. Important factors with respect to building/ improving the data management capability – which is a major change initiative – can be positioned in (the intersection of) these spheres of influence. For example, the factor of "being allowed to use time, money, and other resources by individuals in order to improve the capability" would fall in the intersection of *material* (time, money, resources), *governance* (being allowed, balancing concerns around scarce resources) and *individual* (the professionals doing the work).

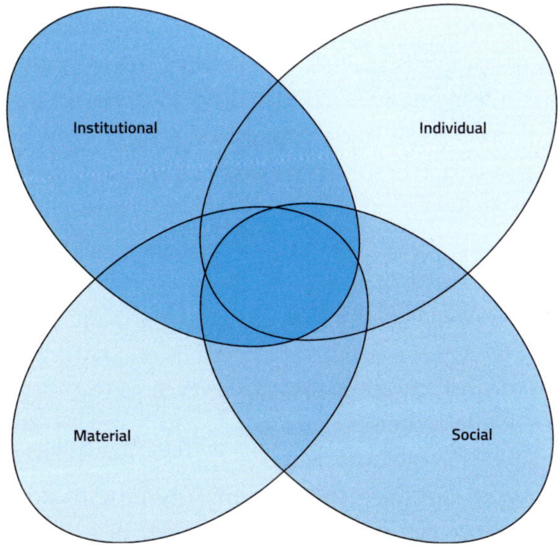

Figure 36.2 Dynamic framework for social change

Based on [CH18]

1 This idea is also illustrated by the work of Marquet. See the YouTube recording on "turn the ship around", or [Mar13].

The dynamic framework for social change can be used for reasoning about an antifragile data management capability. When the data management capability is designed without involving key stakeholders across the organization (*individual* sphere) then it is likely that these stakeholders will push back: they will feel unappreciated, that their skills and expertise are not valued, and that the way they do their work is not under their own control (intersection between *institutional* and *individual* spheres). It is also likely that people will talk among themselves, venting their concerns and grievances. This will result in a negative atmosphere – especially towards data management – in the organization, which is counter to what you want to achieve. Not giving people the time to learn, to figure out *how* to achieve certain outcomes is, in my experiences, the fastest route to disaster. Note also, that "complete freedom" also is unlikely to work: the need to include governance in the considerations is part of the institutional sphere.

When building/ improving a data management capability, the number of variables and their interplay that must be considered are enormous. Think of all the processes, people, teams, systems, reports, etc. that are interlinked. Using the terminology of the Cynefin framework, this puts the effort of building a data management capability in the complex domain (see [SB07] and section 4.7). The way of working in the complex domain is: *probe* (try an intervention), *sense* (evaluate if the intervention has the desired effect), and then *respond* (by dampening or reinforcing the intervention).

Combining the "people first" aspect of building an antifragile data management capability with the probe-sense-respond way of working is the heart of the recommendations that I have given in part II of this book. In each of the chapters, I have tried to give recommendations in line with these principles: balance top-down with bottom-up initiatives, focus on training, involve key stakeholders, focus on communication, and use visuals to get the point across. They are all examples that fit with this overall approach. The summary and *synthesis* of these recommendations are visualized in figure 36.3.

36.3 EXPECTED BENEFITS

In my opinion, many organizations already have a data management capability in place, sometimes without even knowing it. Many organizations tend to have people working on data/ data management, but the overall framework for aligning these might be missing, or needs improvement. This is the main theme for this book. Throughout the book, part II in particular, I have set out to share my experiences and "good practices" to help you with this. I deliberately chose this term over "best practices" because it stresses the fact that there is no single best solution to building/ improving the data management capability at your organization.

People-first
Everything you do to build the data management capability is done in a collaboration between key stakeholders across the enterprise. Balance the concerns of stakeholders in business and IT roles, as well as the concerns of (top) management and operations. Make sure there is time for learning new skills.

Iterative and incremental
Accept the inherent complexity of building/ improving the data management capability. A pure engineering approach is doomed to fail. Keep the end goal in mind. Develop a high-level roadmap. Use short cycles (iterative, incremental) and an experimentation mindset to achieve each plateau in the roadmap, one step at a time.

Adopt a long term, enterprise perspective
The local and short-term concerns of stakeholders are often top of mind for professionals. These concerns determine the what and how of day-to-day work. When building a data management capability, these concerns must be balanced with a long-term and enterprise perspective to avoid local optimizations, and to make sure that high quality data is available for all professionals across the organization.

Do not reinvent the wheel
Data management is an increasingly important capability for many organizations. There is a large and ever-growing body of knowledge that can be used to support initiatives of organizations. Don't reinvent the wheel but use what is already there. Learn from reference visits, conference visits, and literature. More importantly: contribute to this body of knowledge by sharing your experiences.

Figure 36.3 Synthesis of recommendations in part II

The question that remains is: what is the effect of following these practices? This is a tough question and I will attempt to answer it with some cases from recent data management assignments. Most of these have been covered in this book already in some shape or form.

The first case pertains to example 43. In this case, I worked with a small team of consultants to resolve an issue that turned out to be the effect of changing a business rule in one system, and not harmonizing those rules across the entire data value chain. The interesting aspect of this case was that initially teams were very reluctant to work with us. Everybody understood that there was a problem, but everybody was also convinced that someone else must have made a mistake. In other words, there was a culture where all teams worried about their own turf without seeing the big picture.

Our approach was to work with the teams as much as possible, training and empowering them to find out on their own what was going on. People on the work-floor found this very liberating, as did top management – mostly because they saw the positive effects of the approach. We did experience quite a bit of push-back from middle-management during this project. I believe this was because their job was designed to maximize *local* benefits as much as possible, even at the expense of the way the system as a whole works. This is not something that is easily overcome yet I believe our project contributed to a better and more efficient working environment.

A second case comes from a big data initiative in which I was involved. One of the challenges that this organization experienced was bringing data innovations into production. There were several times where they were very good at quickly developing innovative solutions in a lab setting, but bringing them to production was a frustrating process for everyone involved. Management wanted to bring innovations into production as soon as possible and so did the innovation team. Several other teams had serious objections. Chief among them were: are the IT standards followed? Is the solution tested and secure? Are there enough controls in place when innovations entail the handling of privacy sensitive data?

Getting a solution into production was much like a "battle" each time. My main contribution in this case was, again, a simple one: (1) involve all disciplines (data management, security, privacy, architecture, IT) as early as possible to get a good understanding of what is happening and (2) create a separate IT environment where innovative solutions are taken into production, giving IT teams the chance to adjust them to match corporate standards at their own speed. This solution turned out to be a good way to balance the *offense* side of data management (i.e. quickly developing data-driven innovations) with the *defense* side of data management (i.e. ensuring that they match standards, quality criteria, etc.).

As a final example, I have helped several organizations to build and improve their data management capability. In most cases, I have experienced resistance from teams initially. The most cited reason is related to professional pride. When talking about building/ improving the data management capability, teams asked "but are you saying we are not doing our jobs well?".

In many cases, the answer to such a question is twofold. First, teams tend to try to do the right thing. In essence, these teams are working very hard to keep the business running smoothly, but simply have little or no formal processes, procedures, and tools in place to support them from a data perspective. Second, they are not (yet) doing a good job because there is a lot to learn. Raising this topic will almost always lead to discussions about costs versus benefits/ added value and teams being reluctant to change their way of working.

Early on during these engagements, there are two things that I tend to focus on. First, I try to initially stay as close as possible to the "normal" way of working and add data management practices one at a time. The initial increments are chosen to add as much value as possible each time. Second, I make sure the teams have time and room to explore and learn. I also make sure they get the credit for good results. Third, I spend a lot of time and effort on training. Mixing theory and practice in training gives teams the tools they need to not only make a step now, but also to keep the ball moving. To me, this is a good step in building an *antifragile* data management capability. At the management level, I sometimes experience push-back since spending so much time on training and experimentation *appears* to cost time, but I am convinced that it pays off in the long run.

The effect of this approach is twofold. First, the initial reluctance quickly fades when trust increases and teams start to make progress. As knowledge and experience grows, teams are more than willing to think and plan ahead, considering the big picture, and even to formalize processes, procedures, and accountability when needed. When that happens, it doesn't take long to pick up steam and get the much desired results. This, again, shows that people are the key to successful data management.

37 Conclusion

***Synopsis** - This book is based on the premise that data is an important business asset and deserves to be managed as such. This book is intended for "students with an interest in data" and "busy professionals who are actively involved with managing data". It intends to give an overview of the field of data management from both a theoretical and practical perspective. In this chapter, I will provide a brief review of this book with respect to its goals and the audience. I will then present my views on the (near) future of data management. I will end this chapter with a call to action.*

37.1 REVIEW

In the opening chapters of this book, I used the analogy of the engine (processes) and fuel (data) to stress the importance of data. This, in turn, lead to the conclusion that data should be managed as such. In my experience, many professionals/organizations struggle with what it means to manage data as an asset. It is a big topic that entails many disciplines, including governance, data quality management, and others. It is not always easy to see how the pieces of the data management puzzle fit together. Even more, it is hard to see how data management fits into the overall design of the organization, let alone how to design an effective data management function for an organization.

The goal of this book is to demystify the field of *data management* and to show that *data management* is an exciting and valuable business discipline that is worth the time and effort. To achieve this goal, I have adopted a strategy of discussing data management from a theoretical perspective (part I) and from a practical perspective (part II).

The book is aimed at two groups of people:

- **Busy professionals -** This group is diverse and includes many different roles. In section 1.2, I mentioned the data governance office/ council, data owners, data stewards, professionals involved with data governance, (enterprise/ data) architects, process managers, and (business/ IT) analysts. For this audience, the practical part may be most valuable as it provides guidance on solving specific data management problems and challenges. The theory part provides a sound basis and terminology that helps to gain a better understanding of the problem area itself, as well as the approach to solve it.
- **(Bachelor's/ Master's) students -** There is a large group of students with an (academic and/ or practical) interest in data and data management. Typical programs are information management, business economics, business administration, computer science, and data science. For this group, the theory part lays a sound foundation for understanding core concepts and fundamental challenges in the field. The interviews with other professionals and academics, together with the practical guidance helps to prepare for tackling data management challenges in the real world.

The short chapters offer focus and make it easier for readers to study the specific topics that they find most interesting. Citations show that this book is firmly rooted in the body of knowledge about data management. Examples and interviews with professionals and academics align with the day-to-day practice "where the rubber hits the road".

37.2 OUTLOOK

I have used the famous quote by Niels Bohr before in this book but it seems fitting to repeat it here. He famously said that "predictions are difficult, especially when they concern the future". This is also true for the realm of data management. We live in a fast-paced world, and developments – especially where technology is concerned – are high-paced. Technologies that are modern today are considered to be legacies in a few months' time. Some ideas, however, are timeless and I do feel that parts of the path ahead are clear. My ideas for the (near) future are as follows:

- **Process and data -** In the 1990s and early 2000s there was a big movement around understanding, redesigning, and optimizing business processes – with less attention to data. Today, it seems that this is reversed: there is increasing attention paid to data and data management, but it appears that the attention for processes and process management has faded a little. In several places in this book I have argued that there should be a balanced approach that considers the interplay between process, data, and systems. In my opinion, an increasing number of universities and business schools have also adopted this "holy trinity" and use it as a foundation for the curriculum. Many organizations are learning how to balance these perspectives better. I predict that they will continue to converge and that organizations will seek better ways to balance these concerns. With younger professionals who have this broad mindset joining the work force, this may go faster than we think possible at present.

- **People first -** It is my firm belief that in an increasingly digital world, you have to put the people first. Over the last few decades, I have observed in my consultancy assignments as well as in the conferences that I have attended, that there is increased focus on adopting a people-first approach to building capabilities. Organizations that fail to do so will miss the boat and are likely to lose their relevance in the marketplace. People (employees) want to be valued and do meaningful work. Being passionate about work, developing new skills and solving (complex) tasks and puzzles that will help the organization in achieving its aspirations is increasingly important. I predict that this will continue to be the case in the near future. There will be more and more attention to building the data management capability, to raising awareness for data management, and to training staff to perform their role well and effectively.
- **Ethics, regulations, and trust -** Under the influence of new possibilities that arise from the use of artificial intelligence and big data, it appears that more and more people – academics and professionals – are involved in the ethical debate around data. People have a (strong) opinion about what is right/ wrong in the use of data and how they feel about the distribution of costs and benefits between companies and consumers/ the general public. For example: is it ok that big companies make a fortune at the expense of losing our privacy online? People are vocal about their opinion and regulations/ legislation are trying to provide legal guardrails. Given that the internet is a global (and perhaps soon interstellar?) phenomenon and that data (especially in the cloud) is literally everywhere, it stands to reason that law makers will always be at least a step behind recent developments. I believe that this is not a productive way forward.

  We saw a similar development around concepts such as *sustainability* which has ultimately lead to the development of sustainability principles that have been adopted by many organizations (a "coalition of the willing") as well as the general public. My prediction is that there will be a similar "movement" around data (handling) ethics. I expect that principles about the ethical use of data will be adopted by a coalition of the willing and that a large number of people will demand that suppliers/ companies adopt these principles.
- **Technology -** I don't know of any area where developments are as fast as in the realm of IT. I don't see any reason why this will slow down in the years to come. I think the trend to move toward the cloud will continue, but perhaps with a twist. As sustainable IT as well as ethical principles become more commonplace, I expect that cloud providers can gain a big competitive advantage by following these principles.

I also believe that data will be increasingly distributed. Organizations will use data that is scattered across the internet and mix that with their own data. As a result, I think that the data integration capabilities of organizations will continue to gain in importance.

- **Non-invasive, antifragile data management** - This may sound like a heading with a lot of buzzwords glued together. This is mainly because I have not yet been able to come up with a better name that captures the idea that data management will become second nature in most organizations. When people are trained in this important discipline, it will not be seen as a burden, but as a normal part of day-to-day work. Even more, when professionals collaborate effectively and are open to learning (from each other – both internally and across organizations – as well as from the evaluation of how effective the data management capability operates in their organization), this will ensure that the capability *improves* when it is used more.

37.3 CALL TO ACTION

This brings me to the last topic to be addressed: a call to action. My data management journey started during my studies at Tilburg University many years ago. Since then, I have followed courses, studied books and articles, attended conferences, taught classes, and undertaken many assignments in/ related to data management. Time and again, I have seen that sharing ideas and stories about this exciting topic is the best way to move our field forward. Good practices developed in one organization may be of great help in another organization as well – even across industries. Sharing failures may prevent others from making similar mistakes. Publishing stories – in papers, books, and at conferences – offers scholars the opportunity to study them, and to develop new theories which may further the field even more.

The logical conclusion from this observation is that the most effective way to move forward is to build a strong community and share ideas and experiences: think "ecosystem" rather than "egosystem"[1]. By building, joining, and sharing our ideas and experience we can move towards the ideal of an antifragile data management capability. Therefore, I will end with the following call to action:

Build an effective data management capability for your organization. Join the data management community.
Share your ideas and experiences with the data management community.

1 I'm using the term *egosystem* to indicate situations where organizations focus on isolation, protecting their own ideas and interests at all cost, as opposed to the *ecosystem* perspective where the focus is on collaboration across organizational boundaries.

Bibliography

[AB13] P. Aiken and J. Billings. Monetizing data management: Finding the value in your orga- nization's most important asset. Technics Publications, 2013.

[Acc16] Accenture. Building digital trust: The role of data ethics in the digital age. https://www.accenture.com/_acnmedia/PDF-22/Accenture-Data-Ethics-POV-WEB.pdf, last checked: 24 July 2019, 2016.

[ACL18] T. Akidau, S. Chernyak, and R. Lax. Streaming systems: The what, where, when, and how of large-scale data processing. O'Reilly Media, Inc., 2018.

[AG13] P. Aiken and M. Gorman. The case for the chief data officer: Recasting the C-suite to leverage your most valuable asset. Newnes, 2013.

[Agr19] V. Agrawal. Big data in a nutshell - big data is everywhere, but how can we use it? https://jaxenter.com/big-data-nutshell-159112.html, last checked: 11 July 2019, 2019.

[App86] D. S. Appleton. Information asset management. Datamation, 32(3):71–76, 1986.

[Bal14] J. Ball. How safe is air travel really? The Guardian, July 2014.

[BDPR11] A. Berson, L. Dubov, B. Plagman, and P. Raskas. Master data management and data governance. McGraw-Hill, 2011.

[BKW14] W. Baker, D. Kiewel, and G. Winkler. Using big data to make better pricing decisions. McKinsey & Company Insights, June 2014.

[Bra16] G. Bradley. Benefits realization management. A practical guide to achieving benefits through change. Routledge, second edition, 2016.

[BRS19] K. Bergener, M. Räckers, and A. Stein, editors. The art of structuring - Bridging the gap between information systems research and practice. Springer, 2019.

[Car16] P. Carpenter. Using the predict, prevent, detect, respond framework to communicate your security program strategy. Technical report, Gartner, April 2016.

[CCW16] J. M. Cavanillas, E. Curry, and W. Wahlster. New horizons for a data-driven economy: A roadmap for usage and exploitation of big data in Europe. Springer, 2016.

[CH18] *B. Cislaghi and L. Heise. Using social norms theory for health promotion in low-income countries. Health Promotion International, 2018.*

[Che76] *P. Chen. The entity-relationship model: Toward a unified view of data. ACM Transactions on Database Systems (TODS), 1(1):9–36, 1976.*

[CMG14] *K. Crawford, K. Miltner, and M. L. Gray. Critiquing big data: Politics, ethics, epistemol- ogy. International Journal of Communication, 8:1663–1672, 2014.*

[Cod70] *E. F. Codd. A relational model of data for large shared data banks. Communications of the ACM, 13(6):377–387, 1970.*

[Cod79] *E. F. Codd. Extending the database relational model to capture more meaning. ACM Transactions on Database Systems (TODS), 4(4):397–434, 1979.*

[CS09] *L. Corr and J. Stagnitto. Agile data warehouse design - Collaborative dimensional modeling from whiteboard to star schema. DecIsion Press, 2009.*

[Dat04] *C. J. Date. An introduction to database systems. Addison Wesley, eighth edition, 2004.* **[Dat12]** *C. J. Date. Database design and relational theory: normal forms and all that jazz. O'Reilly, 2012.*

[Dav89] *F. D. Davis. Perceived usefulness, perceived ease of use, and user acceptance of informa- tion technology. MIS Quarterly, pages 319–340, 1989.*

[Dav02] *P. K. Davis. Analytic architecture for capabilities-based planning, mission-system analysis, and transformation. RAND, 2002.*

[DD17] *L. DalleMule and T.H. Davenport. What's your data strategy? The key is to balance offense and defense. Harvard Business Review, pages 112–121, May-June 2017.*

[DH11] *I. Dobson and J. Hietala. Risk management - the open group guide. Van Haren, 2011.* **[DHM+09]** *A. Dreibelbis, E. Hechler, I. Milman, M. Oberhofer, D. Wolfson, and P. van Run. Enterprise master data management - An SOA approach to managing core Information. IBM Press, 2009.*

[Die06] *J. Dietz. Enterprise ontology. Enterprise Engineering Series. Springer, 2006.*

[Dis13] *G. Disterer. ISO/IEC 27000, 27001 and 27002 for information security management. Journal of Information Security, 4:92–100, 2013.*

[DMGG16] *A. De Mauro, M. Greco, and M. Grimaldi. A formal definition of big data based on its essential features. Library Review, 65(3):122–135, 2016.*

[EG15] *S. Etlinger and J. Groopman. The trust imperative: A framework for ethical data use. Altimeter, https://bigdata.fpf.org/wp-content/uploads/2015/11/ Etlinger-The-Trust-Imperative.pdf, last checked: 24 July 2019, 2015.*

[Eva04] *E. Evans. Domain-driven design: Tackling complexity in the heart of software. Addison- Wesley Professional, 2004.*

[FHL+98] *E. D. Falkenberg, W. Hesse, P. Lindgreen, B. E. Nilsson, J. L. H. Oei, C. Rolland, R. K. Stamper, F. J. M. Van Assche, A. A. Verrijn-Stuart, and A. Voss. A framework of information systems concepts. IFIP WG 8.1 Task Group FRISCO, IFIP, Laxenburg, Austria, EU, 1998.*

[Fis09] *T. Fisher. The data asset - How smart companies govern their data for business success. Wiley and Sons Business Series. Wiley, 2009.*

[Fow97] *M. Fowler. Analysis patterns - Reusable object models. Object Technology Series. Addison- Wesley, 1997.*

[fS16] *European Committee for Standardization. e-competence framework (e-CF) - a common European framework for ICT professionals in all industry sectors - part 1: Framework, 2016.*

[GD14] *B. van Gils and S. van Dijk. The practice of enterprise architecture - Experiences, tech- niques, and best practices. BiZZdesign, 2014.*

[GD15] *B. van Gils and S. van Dijk. ArchiMate: From theory to practice. BiZZdesign, 2015.*

[GHJV95] *E. Gamma, R. Helm, R. Johnson, and J. Vlissides. Design patterns - Elements of reusable object-oriented software. Addison-Wesley Professional Computing Series. Addison-Wesley, 1995.*

[Gil06] *B. van Gils. Aptness on the web. PhD thesis, University of Nijmegen, 2006.*

[Gon17] *C. Gonzalez. Dynamic systems for everyone: Understanding how our world works. Springer, 2017.*

[Gue12] *M. Guenther. Intersection: How enterprise design bridges the gap between business, technology, and people. Newnes, 2012.*

[Gui17] *Business Architecture Guild. A guide to the business architecture body of knowledge (bizbok guide) - edition 5.5, 2017.*

[Hal07] *T. Halpin. Fact-oriented modeling: Past, present and future. In Conceptual modelling in information systems engineering, pages 19–38. Springer, 2007.*

[Hay11] *D. C. Hay. UML & data modeling. Technics Publications, 2011.*

[Hay13] *D. C. Hay. Data model patterns: Conventions of thought. Pearson Education, 2013.*
[Hen17] *D. Henderson, editor. DAMA DMBOK - Data Management Body of Knowledge. Technics Publications, 2017.*

[HHSB15] *J. Hintzbergen, K. Hintzbergen, A. Smulders, and H. Baars. Foundations of information security - Based on ISO270001 and ISO270002. Best practice. Van Haren, third edition, 2015.*

[HM10] *T. Halpin and T. Morgan. Information modeling and relational databases. Morgan Kauf- mann, 2010.*

[Hop03] *S. Hoppenbrouwers. Freezing language, Conceptualisation processes across ICT-supported organizations. PhD thesis, Radboud Universiteit Nijmegen, December 2003.*

[Hsu09] *C. W. Hsu. Frame misalignment: Interpreting the implementation of information sys- tems security certification in an organization. European Journal of Information Systems, 18(2):140–150, 2009.*

[Hub14] *D. W. Hubbard. How to measure anything. Finding the value of "intangibles" in business. Wiley, third edition, 2014.*

[HV93] *C. Henderson and N. Venkatraman. Strategic alignment: Leveraging information tech- nology for transforming organizations. IBM Systems Journal, 32(1):472–484, 1993.*

[HW04] *G. Hohpe and B. Woolf. Enterprise integration patterns - Designing, building, and depoy- ing messaging solutions. Addison-Wesley Signature Series. Addison-Wesley, 2004.*

[HWR09] *S. Hoppenbrouwers, H. Weigand, and E. Rouwette. Setting rules of play for collaborative modeling. International Journal of e-Collaboration (IJeC), 5(4):37–52, 2009.*

[IC13] *J. L. C. Izquierdo and J. Cabot. Enabling the collaborative definition of dsmls. In Inter- national Conference on Advanced Information Systems Engineering (CAiSE 2013), pages 272–287. Springer, 2013.*

[ISA12] *ISACA. COBIT 5: A business framework for the governance and management of enterprise IT. Isaca, 2012.*

[ISO07] *ISO. Standard 19440:2007(en) enterprise integration - Constructs for enterprise modeling, 2007.*

[ISO11] *ISO/IEC/IEEE. Systems and software engineering - Architecture description (42010:2011), 2011.*

[ISO12] *ISO/IEC/IEEE. Standard 31320-2:2012(en) information technology - Modeling languages - part 2: syntax and semantics for idef1x97, 2012.*

[ISO13a] *ISO/IEC. ISO/IEC 27001:2013, information technology - Security techniques - Information security management systems - requirements, 2013.*

[ISO13b] *ISO/IEC. ISO/IEC 27002:2013, information technology - Security techniques - Code of practice for information security controls, 2013.*

[ISO15] *ISO/IEC. Standard 11179-1:2015(en) information technology - Metadata registries (mdr) - part 1: Framework, 2015.*

[ISO18] *ISO/IEC. Standard ISO/IEC 27000:2018, information technology - Security techni- ques - Information security management systems - Overview and vocabulary, 2018.*

[Kir09] *M. Kirchmer. High performance through process excellence. From strategy to execution with Business Process Management. Springer, 2009.*

[Kle17] *M. Kleppmann. Designing data-intensive applications: The big ideas behind reliable, scalable, and maintainable systems. O'Reilly Media, Inc., 2017.*

[Kle19] *A. Klein. Credit denial in the age of AI. Report, https://www.brookings.edu/rese arch/credit-denial-in-the-age-of-ai/, (last checked: 24 July 2019), April 2019.*

[KM16] *R. Kitchin and G. McArdle. What makes big data, big data? exploring the ontological characteristics of 26 datasets. Big Data & Society, 3(1), 2016.*

[Kni15] *D. Knifton. Enterprise data architecture - How to navigate its landscape. Data Architec- ture Fundamentals. Paragon, third edition, 2015.*

[KNPCA19] *G. C. Kane, A. Nguyen Phillips, J. R. Copulsky, and G. R. Andrus. The technology fallacy - How people are the real key to digital transformation. Management on the cutting edge series. MIT Press, 2019.*

[Lad12] *J. Ladley. Data governance: How to design, deploy, and sustain an effective data gover- nance program. Newnes, 2012.*

[Lan12] *R. van der Lans. Data virtualization for business intelligence systems: Revolutionizing data integration for data warehouses. Elsevier, 2012.*

[Lan17] *M. M. Lankhorst, editor. Enterprise architecture at work - Modelling, communication and analysis. Springer, fourth edition, 2017.*

[LO15] *D. Linstedt and M. Olschimke. Building a scalable data warehouse with data vault 2.0. Morgan Kaufmann, 2015.*

[Los10] *D. Loshin. The practitioner's guide to data quality improvement. Elsevier, 2010.*

[Los12] *D. Loshin. A data quality primer: Using data quality tools and techniques to improve business value. Melissa Data Corporation, 2012.*

[Los13] *D. Loshin. Business Intelligence: The savvy manager's guide. Morgan Kaufmann, second edition, 2013.*

[Mar89] *J. Martin. Information engineering, Book 1 - Introduction. Prentice Hall, 1989.*

[Mar90a] *J. Martin. Information engineering, Book 2 - Planning & analysis. Prentice Hall, 1990.*

[Mar90b] *J. Martin. Information engineering, Book 3 - Design & construction. Prentice Hall, 1990.*

[Mar13] *D. Marquet Turn the ship around!: A true story of turning followers into leaders. Penguin, 2013.*

[Mar18] *B. Marr. Here's why data is not the new oil. Forbes - https://www.forbes.com/sites/bernardmarr/2018/03/05/heres-why-data-is-not-the-new-oil/, (Last checked: 16 March 2019), March 2018.*

[Mas97] *J. R. Mashey. Big data and the next wave of infrastress. In Computer Science Division Seminar, University of California, Berkeley, 1997.*

[MBEH09] *M. Mosley, M. Brackett, S. Earley, and D. Henderson, editors. The DAMA guide to the Data Management Body of Knowledge. Technics Publications, 2009.*

[McG83] *C. McGinn. The subjective view: Secondary qualities and indexical thoughts. Oxford University Press, 1983.*

[MGR97] *G. Morgan, F. Gregory, and C. Roach. Images of organization. SAGE Publications, 1997.*

[MSC13] *V. Mayer-Schönberger and K. Cukier. Big data: A revolution that will transform how we live, work, and think. Houghton Mifflin Harcourt, 2013.*

[Mur09] *A. P. Murray. The library: An illustrated history. Skyhorse, 2009.*

[New15] *S. Newman. Building microservices: Designing fine-grained systems. O'Reilly Media, Inc., 2015.*

[OJ15] *B. O'Kane and S. Judah. Critical capabilities for master data management of customer data solutions. Technical Report G00273560, Gartner, 2015.*

[O'N05] *B. O'Neil. Business metadata: How to write definitions. http://www.b-eye-network.com/view/734, 2005. [Online; accessed 30-July-2019].*

[OPW+08] *M. Op 't Land, H. A. Proper, M. Waage, J. Cloo, and C. Steghuis. Enterprise architecture - Creating value by informed governance. The enterprise engineering series. Springer, 2008.*

[Pai99] *H. Paijmans. Explorations in the document vector model of information retrieval. PhD thesis, Tilburg University, September 1999.*

[Par17] *D. Parkins. The world's most valuable resource is no longer oil, but data. The Economist, 2017.*

[PB89] *M. M. Parker and R. J. Benson. Enterprisewide information management: State-of-the-art strategic planning. Journal of Information Systems Management, 6(3):14–23, 1989.*

[Per16] *J. Persse. The ITIL process manual. Van Haren, 2016.*

[Pol13] *A. Polsky. Data stewardship on the ground, notes from the field. Presentation at the Data Governance conference in London, 2013.*

[Pom15] *J. Pomerantz. Metadata. The MIT Press Essential Knowledge series. MIT Press, 2015.*

[RBD+18] *C. Rodriguez, A. Barrow, S. Dangore, U. Pathak, and J. Talledo. Applying data analytics to big data obtained from wearable devices. In Proceedings of Student-Faculty Research Day, CSIS. Pace University, May 2018.*

[RBM19] *J. Ross, C. M. Beath, and M. Mocker. Designed for digital: How to architect your business for sustained success. Management on the Cutting Edge. MIT Press, 2019.*

[RD99] *V. Reijswoud and J. Dietz. DEMO modeling handbook - Volume 1. Delft University of Technology, 1999.*

[Red98] *T. C. Redman. The impact of poor data quality on the typical enterprise. Communications of the ACM, 41(2):79–82, 1998.*

[Red08] *T. C. Redman. Data driven: Profiting from your most important business asset. Harvard Business Review Press, 2008.*

[RJB04] *J. Rumbaugh, I. Jacobson, and G. Booch. Unified modeling language reference manual, the. Pearson Higher Education, 2004.*

[RR13] *M. A. Rob and A. Roy. The value of IT certification: Perspectives from students and IT personnel. Issues in Information Systems, 14:153–161, 2013.*

[Rub12] *K. S. Rubin. Essential Scrum: A practical guide to the most popular agile process.*

Addison-Wesley, 2012.

[RW12] *E. Redmond and J. R. Wilson. Seven databases in seven weeks. The Pragmatic Bookshelf, 2012.*

[RWR06] *J. W. Ross, P. Weill, and D. C. Robertson. Enterprise architecture as strategy - Creating a foundation for business execution. Harvard Business School Press, 2006.*

[Sar15] *P. Sarkar. Data as a service: A framework for providing reusable enterprise data services. Wiley-IEEE Computer Society Press, 2015.*

[SB07] *D. J. Snowden and M. E. Boone. A leader's framework for decision making. Harvard Business Review, 11:68–76, 2007.*

[SC12] *L. Sebastian-Coleman. Measuring data quality for ongoing improvement: A data quality assessment framework. Newnes, 2012.*

[Sco18] *Rodney Scott. Group model building: Using systems dynamics to achieve enduring agree- ment. Springer, 2018.*

[SFI19] *SFIA Foundation. SFIA framework, version 7. https://www.sfia-online.org/en/framework/sfia-7, last checked: 11 October 2019, 2019.*

[Sha48] *C. E. Shannon. A mathematical theory of communication. Bell System Technical Journal, 27(3):379–423, 1948.*

[Soa11] *S. Soares. Selling information governance to the business: Best practices by industry and job function. MC Press Ketchum, 2011.*

[SqE08] *SqEME foundation. Proces management based on SqEME. Van Haren, 2008.*

[Tal12] *N. N. Taleb. Antifragile: How to live in a world we don't understand, volume 3. Allen Lane, 2012.*

[The11] *The Open Group. TOGAF Version 9.1. Van Haren, 2011.* **[The16a]** *The Open Group. ArchiMate 3 specification. Van Haren, 2016.*

[The16b] *The Open Group Architecture Forum. Open group guide - business capabilities. Technical Report G161, The Open Group, 2016.*

[Wes07] *M. Weske. Business process management - Concepts, languages, architectures. Springer, 2007.*

[Wie14] *G. Wierda. Mastering ArchiMate - A serious introduction to the ArchiMate(R) enterprise architecture modeling language. P&A, second edition, 2014.*

[WP11] *S. Wahe and G. Petersen. Open Enterprise Security Architecture (O-ESA): A framework and template for policy-driven security. Van Haren, 2011.*

[WSE19] *G. Westerman, D. L. Soule, and A. Eswaran. Building digital-ready culture in traditional organizations. MIT Sloan Management Review, 60(4):59–68, 2019.*

[You89] *E. Yourdon. Modern structured analysis. Prentice Hall, 1989.*

[Zac87] *J. A. Zachman. A framework for information systems architecture. IBM Systems Journal, 26(3), 1987.*

[ZEDR+11] *P. Zikopoulos, C. Eaton, D. De Roos, T. Deutsch, and G. Lapis. Understanding big data: Analytics for enterprise class hadoop and streaming data. McGraw-Hill Osborne Media, 2011.*

Index

About the author

The topic of "data" has been a big part of my career, ever since I started my studies at Tilburg University where I obtained my MSc in *information management and technology* in 2002. Key topics in this program were strategic alignment, modeling, and the design of effective information systems. After obtaining my MSc, I continued my studies at Nijmegen University where I worked on *information retrieval on the Web* under the supervision of Prof. Proper and Prof. van der Weide. I successfully defended my dissertation with the title *Aptness on the Web* in 2006 and obtained my PhD in Computer Science.

Since then I have fulfilled various roles in many different organizations. I have worked for the Dutch police, where I helped to design and implement information systems, as well as introducing architecture discipline to the organization. I have also worked as a consultant in strategy and leadership for Strategy Works/Strategy Academy. When I rediscovered my passion for (enterprise) architecture and data management, I started working as a consultant, trainer, and researcher for BiZZdesign. In that capacity, I have undertaken numerous projects in different industries and different countries.

Throughout my career, I have always been actively involved in teaching and research. I have had the pleasure of teaching courses and delivering guest lectures at several universities (Tilburg University, Nijmegen University, Utrecht University of Applied Science, Open University) here in the Netherlands, and continue to do so. My research has resulted in several articles (academic and professional) as well as the publication of a number of books. I have also been a speaker at various conferences and have supervised dozens of students in their Master's thesis projects.

In 2016, I decided to start my own company – Strategy Alliance – together with my partner, Raymond Slot. Our company offers consultancy, training, and coaching services in the realm of digital transformation. We believe that *data* and *data management* are key to digital transformation and we made this an integral part of our company. This also applies to enterprise architecture, strategic management, and security management. We strongly believe in using/contributing to open standards such as TOGAF, ArchiMate, and the DMBOK. With respect to data, we felt that something was missing: a good and practical book that provides an overview of the field, balancing theory and practice. Having worked as an academic and practitioner in this field since 2002, I felt that I should be the one to write this book.

Over the last few years, I have worked with many driven professionals on exciting projects. My ambition is to continue to do so. I believe that *in a fast changing, increasingly digital world, we need a human-centric approach to transformation,* and that *balancing academic rigor with practical relevance* is an effective strategy with which to move forward. I am looking forward to many more challenging projects and collaborations in the field of digital transformation in general and data management in particular.